Of the People
Essays on Indian Popular Culture

Of the People
Essays on Indian Popular Culture

Biswarup Sen

CHRONICLE BOOKS
An Imprint of DC Publishers
New Delhi
2006

© Biswarup Sen 2006

Chronicle Books is an imprint of DC Publishers

Distributed by
Orient Longman Limited

Bangalore   Bhopal   Bhubaneshwar   Chandigarh
Chennai   Ernakulam   Guwahati   Hyderabad   Jaipur
Kolkata   Lucknow   Mumbai   New Delhi   Patna

ISBN 81-8028-027-6

Typeset in Giovanni Book
by Eleven Arts, New Delhi
Printed in India by Paul Press, New Delhi
Published by DC Publishers
S-7&8, Green Park Main Market, New Delhi 110 016

To the memory of my father

Acknowledgments

This book began as a series of newspaper articles concerning particular aspects of Indian popular culture. It is situated within the field of cultural studies, a discipline that has in the past decade experienced phenomenal growth in this country. Colleagues based in initiatives like Sarai, New Delhi; the Centre for the Study of Culture and Society, Bangalore; the Centre for Cultural Studies, CIEFL Hyderabad; the Department of Film and Media Studies, Jadavpur University; as well as in many other locations both in India and elsewhere have generated an exciting body of work that has transformed the project of understanding the relationship between popular culture and Indian society. In writing this book I have relied heavily on the work of these scholars, as well as those of journalists and commentators on contemporary culture. I am immensely grateful to these various authors for inspiring and instructing me. Needless to add, any errors in exposition or interpretation of their material is entirely mine. In writing this manuscript, I have not attempted a comprehensive review of literature or any systematic archival research. To the extent that I have offered theoretical speculations, it has been in the spirit of adding to ongoing dialogues rather than trying to provide a definitive account of the subject matter. This work is therefore best described as a collection of essays written from the vantage of a passionate fan of Indian popular culture. However, my diasporic location has limited the topics I could properly investigate. Thus, missing from this account are analyses of many crucial sites like television, advertising, malls, multiplexes, food and fashion. My insistence on the "horizontal" relations that constitute the Indian popular likewise derives from this perspective.

I owe a very special debt to my friend Rudrangshu Mukherjee, editorial chief at *The Telegraph*, for the intellectual support and encouragement he gave me and for providing me with a public forum for my ideas. Aditi Nath Sarkar insisted, much against my misgivings, that these scattered writings could be developed into a book-length project. Aditi's suggestions gave crucial shape to my manuscript and it is no exaggeration to say that without his direction this book would neither have been conceived nor completed.

I am especially grateful to Lee Becker, James Carey, Cliff Christians, Larry Grossberg, Robert Jones, Howard Mclay, Ellen Wartella and Chuck Whitney. These exemplary teachers and scholars were a source of inspiration and guidance. I hope they recognize their influence in the pages of this book.

I would like to thank Professor Brian Stoddart, of the University of New England, New South Wales, for his personal communication on the topic of cricket in the West Indies. Ritwik Mitra was kind enough to provide me with an acute commentary on the state of Indian hockey and football. I must also thank my nephew, Anirudh Chari, for unearthing arcane bits of cricketing lore.

Over the years, many friends have contributed to my understanding of culture, politics and society. In particular, I must thank Shera Ahmad, Catherine Barnes, Jack Bratich, Linda Belau, Kalyan Chatterjee, John Consigli, Jon Crane, Peter D'Souza, Ivy Glennon, Dana Heller, Mohan Mahapatra, Ramdas Menon, Imke Meyer,

Manisha Mirchandani, Sanjay Misra, Sujata Moorti, Vivek Murthy, S. Nagarjuna, Jon Nerone, Nick Newman, Deepak Sanan, Heidi Schlipphacke, S.Shivkumar, Mrinalini Sinha, E. Sridharan, S. Sriram, Chandrasekhar Tibrewal and Galina Tsoy.

My publisher, Aloke Roy Chowdhury, has been a constant source of goodwill and encouragement. I have profited greatly from his comments and suggestions, and working with him has been a most pleasant experience. I must also thank Arundhati Nath, Joyati Sen and Malini Menon of Chronicle Books for their help in seeing this work to press.

My parents provided me with an upbringing that stressed the importance of the life of the mind. My mother Jayanti Sen, herself a poet, introduced me to the pleasures of reading and writing. My brother Debal and I discovered the joys of rock and roll together, my love and appreciation of that music is closely bound to his. My father-in-law, Ganesh Gopal Iyer and my brother-in-law Shankar constantly instructed me on matters pertaining to Indian sports. My sister-in-law Tammany Kramer shared with me her enthusiasm for all things popular. I have also benefited immensely from countless *addas* with many members of my family, most notably the Sens of Ballygunge—Debdatta, Panchali, Sudipta, Lyn and Sujaya and the folks at Rawdon—Kumkum, Sridhar, Sharmila, Mumshi, Ishan, Bubul, Mimi, Pradip and Pritha. I thank them all for their unfailing love and constant support. I find it hard to adequately convey the debt I owe to my wife, Sangita Gopal. As intellectual companions and collaborators, our thoughts are so comingled that this work must be considered as much hers as it is mine.

I dedicate this book to the memory of my father, Dilip Kumar Sen. It is my utmost regret that he did not live to see its publication.

Contents

Introduction

The Study of Culture

India is often associated with a familiar set of texts, motifs and figures: Vedic rituals and Hindu gods, the *Ramayana* and the *Panchatantra*, the ragas and *Natyashastra*, Mughal architecture and Urdu verse, mandirs and mosques, sadhus and pirs, and the *kisan* with his bullock cart. However, not even the most ardent fundamentalist will claim that this string of symbols exhausts the meaning of the times. Our daily lives may still bear the vestiges of ancient tradition, but they are far more marked by the practices that comprise modernity: cricket matches, Bollywood movies, television serials, talk shows, Hindi film music (*filmigeet*), MTV, shopping malls, multiplexes, food courts, internet cafés and the World Wide Web. These new formations are everywhere, all of the time, providing the sights, the sounds and the flavors that comprise the world we inhabit. To think of India in its current incarnation then, is to contemplate its popular culture.

This book is based on a theoretical approach—often referred to as "cultural studies"—which distinguishes itself from the more traditional disciplines in the humanities and social sciences by insisting that popular cultural practices like cricket or Bollywood films are objects of study as legitimate as, say, the reign of Akbar, landholding patterns in rural Tamil Nadu, caste politics in Uttar Pradesh or the poetry of Rabindranath Tagore. This perspective grows out of the fact that the logic of capitalist development after World War II has led to a "cultural turn" that dramatically increased the role played by the arts, the entertainment industries and the media in the functioning of society. Thus, the shift from manufacturing to service industries that has taken place in the last five decades or so has radically changed the nature of economic practices. The enormous emphasis placed on quality control, total management systems, and customer satisfaction, and the exponential growth in marketing, advertising and public relations has meant that economic activity is now crucially determined by notions of communication and interactivity. When call-center representatives take on Anglicized names and modify their accents to cater to western customers, their behavior is governed by the culture of globalization. Also, the rise of information technology means that material goods have cultural practices embedded in them. The major inventions of the modern era—the personal computer or the cell phone—are far more than gadgets of convenience; they contribute to the making of culture in significant ways. This is not to suggest that memorable icons from the past like the Janata stove, the Godrej steel almirah and the Ambassador car were without any meaning. The Janata stove, with its connotations of mobility and modern technology, symbolized the nuclear couple which had liberated itself from the *chullah* as well as the joint family; the Godrej almirah embodied middle-class anxieties regarding savings and security; while the Ambassador car was the symbol par excellence of the nationalist program of industrialization and self-reliance initiated after Independence. But none of these commodities were *productive* of culture in the way PCs or cell phones, using features like e-mail, chat rooms, web pages, ring tones and instant messaging, happen to be. This development implies that the economy, once thought of as a sovereign level that dictated the form of society as a whole, must now be reconceptualized as a domain that is intimately connected to cultural norms and practices and is both determined by and generative of the semantic milieu we live in.

What is true of the economy holds true in equal measure for other areas of the social formation. Politics in modern democracies is so reliant on mass media, especially television, and on communicative strategies borrowed from the corporate world that it often seems indistinguishable from entertainment and advertising. And even traditionally autonomous domains like education and religion have begun to internalize the modes of functioning—from relentless profit making to MTV style marketing—that characterize life outside their cloistered walls. The importance of culture, then, increases as areas of life previously thought to be independent of it begin to fall under its influence. This "culturalization" of the totality is accelerated by the processes of late capitalism which replace manufacture with service, material objects with representations, and citizens with consumers. At the same time, television, movies and other forums of popular culture have begun to replace traditional authority figures like parents, schoolteachers and religious leaders as sources of information, advice and values. Consequently, the mass media now play an increasingly important role in shaping the beliefs and attitudes of younger people as well as offering them behavioral role models. All these changes imply the following: popular culture is by far the most important instrument we have for thinking about ourselves, about others and about the entire world.

How does one analyze texts and practices whose most visible function is to generate the thrills that are the core of modern life? To begin with, we need to go beyond the judgment that a popular film or television show is just "entertainment". A hit film like *Dilwale Dulhaniya Le Jayenge* (1995) should not be regarded as merely a fix for an "escapist" urge; we need to recognize that it performs a crucial role in redefining notions of pleasure and consumption. We must also resist the temptation to see popular culture as just a conduit for "dominant ideology". To read *Dilwale Dulhaniya Le Jayenge* as, say, an unreflective celebration of economic liberalization would be to miss its full import. As practitioners of cultural studies have convincingly demonstrated, culture performs the complex and ambiguous task of negotiating between competing meanings and visions regarding our social being. *Dilwale*, for example, may be an advertisement for consumerism, but it simultaneously promotes a model of the family quite incongruent with the logic of late capitalism. It focuses in great detail on traditional customs and values, but by featuring a Non-Resident-Indian (NRI) as its protagonist it also acknowledges the irrevocably global nature of Indian modernity. Thus, a fruitful study of culture must begin by recognizing that the popular is a complex domain in which the inner essence of a particular social formation is brought out in relief. Such a study also takes for granted the commodity nature of popular art—the fact that it is typically mass produced by large organizations with a view to making profit. However, to focus exclusively on the manipulative aspect of this process is to run the risk of elaborating on the obvious. A more productive way to interrogate the texts of popular culture is to analyze them through the category of *pleasure*. Whatever else the popular is, it is that which elicits intense positive affect. As Richard Dyer and Ginette Vincendeau put it in the introduction to their book on popular European cinema "There is a sense in which 'the popular' is what it is most popularly assumed to be: what people like."[1] The series of likes and dislikes that make up the fortunes of the popular also provide us with a perspective into its meaning. It is this methodological stance that informs much of the writing in this book. Thus, the intensity of passion surrounding cricket in contemporary India, rather than its aesthetic beauty or its sociological function, provides us with a clue about its actual meaning. Again, the enormous satisfaction that audiences derive from song and dance routines in Hindi films demand that they be treated as serious artistic devices that contain a central truth about Bollywood cinema. My emphasis here should not be taken to mean that I am in any way supportive of the tendency—prevalent in some quarters dominant within cultural studies for a while— to celebrate pleasure as the site of empowerment and resistance. In fact, as will be evident shortly, my take on cricket suggests the exact opposite. Nevertheless, any student of the popular who ignores the aspect of pleasure does so at risk to his own analysis. Only through an examination of the intricacies of the effect that culture produces can we come to an understanding of its latent meanings and its role in the constitution of subjectivity and society.

The importance I am granting to the analytical value of pleasure explains why, in this book, I have continued to use "popular" as a prefix before "culture" in spite of some recent pleas that we need to abandon the term. Thus, Arjun Appadurai and Carol Breckenridge have proposed *public* as an alternative to *popular* on the grounds that "it appears to be less embedded in such highly specific western dichotomies and debates as high versus low culture."[2] Christopher Pinney echoes this view when he writes that "conventional notions of 'popular culture' have little analytical use in the context of a global modernity, and in the context of South Asia's position within that modernity."[3] While I would concur with the claim that the "popular" in India bears little resemblance to that in the West, I would also argue that adopting "public" in its place leads to very little gain. The term "public" has strong associations with the nation-state and with national boundaries; this connection is made explicit in Appadurai and Breckenridge's definition of "public culture" as the "space between domestic life and the projects of the *nation state* where different social groups [...] constitute their identities by their experience of mass-mediated forms in relation to the practices of everyday life"[4] (italics mine). Such a formulation seems to suggest that our contemporary culture is located and contained within the space of the nation. Yet, as the subsequent chapters in this book hope to demonstrate, modern Indian culture has always been transnational both in its content and in its appeal. Even as it helps to construct the nation, it incessantly transgresses its boundaries—film music has turned to African and Latin music for inspiration and has been hummed in the Caribbean and in Russia; Bollywood movies travel to Egypt and Japan and feature characters living in London or New York; the Indian diaspora takes old art forms like bhangra and makes them utterly contemporary. Indian culture *exceeds* the nation and is thoroughly global, and is therefore far better described by a term like "popular" which captures both its immense reach as well as the passionate following it enjoys.

The Meaning of Indian Popular Culture

Popular culture is a phenomenon of the modern age. We may legitimately identify certain aspects of culture in past eras as "popular", but the popular, in its truest sense, can be said to exist only within the context of contemporary industrial society. This link between modernity and the popular derives from the vast economic, social and technological transformations that took place in the hundred years between the mid-nineteenth and the mid-twentieth centuries. These changes first originated in the West, but soon spread elsewhere as a consequence of a colonial world order. Of the many developments that would alter the nature of societies, three were of special significance in terms of the making of popular culture. Firstly, the spread of suffrage and of democratic principles meant that popular will and popular taste acquired a value it had lacked before. Where once culture belonged exclusively to the upper classes, now whatever appealed to the masses could also be a claimant to the status of art. Secondly, a series of technological inventions and innovations that included the photograph, the moving pictures, the phonograph, the radio and television, made possible the creation of cultural products that were easily reproduced and transmitted. Insofar as all new artistic production was mass mediated, all "culture" was necessarily inserted into the domain of the popular. Finally, the consolidation of capitalism into its classic form facilitated the crystallization of art and entertainment into exchangeable commodities. Consequently, art could circulate alongside other commodities as part of the vast circuit of consumption that characterizes modern life.

India's status as a British colony meant that the social and technological changes described above reached the country soon after their emergence in the West. The process of creating a modern popular culture, therefore, got under way very early on: the first cricket club was started in 1868, the first Indian movie was made in 1913, and the first radio broadcast took place in 1926. From the very beginning, Indian popular culture would function in ways that differed substantially from its counterpart in the West. The latter's task, broadly defined, was to create a nationwide space where entertainment, meaning-formation and the needs of advertisers could be negotiated. In other words, popular culture functioned as a mediating term between individual desire and dispositions on the one hand, and the state and civil society, particularly the economy and the polity, on the other. In traditional western scholarship, the popular has been thought of as a site that expresses the will of the oppressed and the marginal. The politics of the popular, analyzed through the categories of class, race or gender, is therefore conceived of as one of opposition and resistance to the dominant order. To take an example which I treat in some detail in Chapter 3, rock and roll has typically been seen as a sort of permanent revolution against the established order. Or again, a film like *Thelma and Louise* (1991) is interpreted as expressing the accumulated rage of women suffering under patriarchy. While these instances may indeed embody some sort of oppositional politics, it is doubtful whether popular culture as a whole is as "progressive" as some practitioners of cultural studies want it to be. Thus, one would be hard put to demonstrate how hit shows like *CSI, Desperate Housewives* or *Seinfeld* are to be construed as challenges to the socio-economic order.

In a colonial formation like India, popular culture had to fulfil a far more complex and acrobatic role. The fact of Empire implied that not only did it have to perform the tasks I have just described; it simultaneously had to imagine a nation and a society that did not yet exist. That being so, the "politics from below" model is even less applicable in the case of India. As I have indicated above, indigenous artistic production in the colonial period was, by dint of its location in a worldwide imperial system, necessarily implicated in the politics of empire. Entrusted with the charge of speaking for the Indian nation, popular culture tried to approximate *swadeshi* culture. Many popular forms—the "mythological" in early cinema for example—consciously sought to build a consensus around the set of values that distinguished Indian culture as a whole. This i .pulse would be intensified in the post-Independence era when, except for some stray leftist deviations, all popular art joined hands with the statist program of building a strong and self-reliant nation. The process of imagining the nation by means of culture would acquire greater momentum after the coming of Independence: witness the incredible popularity of *Mother India* (1957), the promotion of hockey as the "national sport" and the efforts to introduce an overarching musical culture through the agency of All India Radio. What these instances exemplified was the shared assumption, on the part of producers and consumers of culture alike, that popular culture would provide the "glue" necessary to keep a disparate nation together. Only with the coming of liberalization would this nationalist urge become diminished and be eventually sidelined. The following remark, by the diplomat-novelist Shashi Tharoor, is representative of the widespread belief in popular culture's unifying mission:

> Indian films, with all their limitations and outright idiocies, represent part of the hope for India's future. In a country that is still 50% illiterate, films represent the prime vehicle for the transmission of popular culture and values.[5]

It is debatable as to what extent Indian popular culture has managed to fulfil the charge of providing a set of beliefs and values that apply to the entire nation. It could be argued, for example, that the recent spate of NRI movies—many featuring Shah Rukh Khan—that have come to define Bollywood have little to do with the culture and values that concern rural India. This example sheds doubt on claims of inclusiveness, but at the same time it foregrounds what may be popular culture's most important role—that of representing and articulating modernity. The relation between the modern and the popular is not one of simple cause and effect but rather that of a reciprocal determination. The conditions of modernity, as I have shown above, provide a ground for popular culture; at the same time the popular is the most important means by which the modern comes to be. This is especially true in the case of postcolonial societies like India, whose defining feature is thought to be one of "incomplete" modernization. Every such society which constructs its present by synthesizing the layers of social practice which constitute tradition with the "modern" is a composite structure consisting of a set of values that reflect the impulses of the moment as well as a combative stance towards the weight of the past. One of the main functions of popular culture is to produce repeated "solutions" to the dilemma concerning past and present that is constitutive of modernity. The resolutions it offers vary according to the character of the times they are part of—the city flicks of Raj Kapoor approach poverty and social injustice quite differently from the "revenge" films starring Amitabh Bachchan. Though the parameters of modernity that come into play within the frame of the popular are typically derived from the West, the compromise made between modernity and tradition within the space of the popular is startlingly original. The creation of Hindi film music as a distinct musical genre, during the decades of the 1930s and 40s, is a case in point. In this attempt to define Indian modernity, popular art habitually went beyond the boundaries of the nation. There were precedents to this expansiveness; one could argue that the Bengal Renaissance, the first great exercise in modernization in Indian history, was similarly global in inspiration. And just as the wave of westernization induced by that intellectual movement was to facilitate the birth of the nationalist movement, the hybrid nature of popular culture would also not detract from the mission of positing the "unity that is India". What the global dimensions of popular culture do imply, however, is that any facile equation between popular and national is likely to be erroneous; the popular, in every instance, is constructed out of materials which bear the mark of the global in crucial ways. Even as it participates in the construction of a national culture, the popular exceeds the scope of its mission and becomes inextricably implicated in the dynamics of the larger world.

The Politics of Sport

It is one of the main arguments of this book that Indian popular culture is more than Indian and that the meaning of our cultural forms needs to be analyzed not just in terms of the indigenous but by taking into account the extended implications of each cultural form. Each of the five chapters that make up this book tries to decipher the meaning of culture in contemporary India by looking at the specific ways in which the popular has dealt with the problem of defining and expressing modernity within the framework of globalization. The first chapter looks at cricket, a sport whose phenomenal popularity raises two puzzling questions. Firstly, how and why did cricket eclipse hockey and football to become the only team sport of consequence in post-Independent India? Secondly, given the country's new profile as an emerging global power, why have Indians fixated on cricket, a game played by a handful of relatively unimportant nations, and not, say, on soccer, undoubtedly the world's most dominant international sport? Theories of Indian cricket, influenced by more general accounts of postcolonial society, tend to accommodate the history of cricket within nationalist narratives of self-expression and empowerment. To take two well-known formulations, Ashis Nandy holds that "cricket is an Indian game accidentally discovered by the English" while Arjun Appadurai, the eminent theorist of globalization, has contended that cricket is a "means of modernity" utilized by the nation state as it constituted itself after Independence. My own analysis focuses less on these positive features and foregrounds instead the profound lack in our collective psyche that the game signifies. The almost pathological obsession that Indians of every background display towards it makes implausible the suggestion that cricket belongs to us, or that it is a primary device for nation building. Instead, as I argue in Chapter 1, cricket represents the anxiety that Indians feel about their place in the world order; it is not so much an assertion of modernity as a fear that we may not be modern enough. The reason why cricket became the foremost bearer of this neurosis surrounding "catching up" has a lot to do with the history of the game. As I point out in the first section of the chapter, from the very moment cricket was transformed from a rural sport played by commoners into a pursuit of the English upper classes, it also became an instrument for signification. At every stage in its subsequent history cricket would represent something more than mere sport—the style of Empire, the pomp and circumstance of the princely states, the passions of community politics before Partition, the fervor of Independence and, finally, the anxieties surrounding identity and nationhood in the globalized age. In the second section of the chapter, I argue that the structure and practice of cricket today—in terms of its organization, rule-making, umpiring as well as player and crowd behavior—reflects and is mediated by the racialized world order we inhabit. The phenomenal growth in the game's popularity in the post-Independence period has much to do with this political characteristic. It needs to be realized that the entire trajectory of postcolonial history had been structured around the notion of development, a term which, in the last analysis, signified the imperative to catch up with the West. With the onset of liberalization, the urgency behind this desire has reached unprecedented heights. The explosive growth in centers of consumption—shopping malls, multiplex cinemas, boutique stores, "multicuisine" restaurants, and coffee shops—attests to the pervasive desire to be part of a circuit of commodities that now characterize the entire globe. The adoption of cricket—a game that has always connoted the privileged position of the West—as the one and only team sport is therefore analyzable in terms of the lack that structures the drive to modernity. Indians obsess about cricket because the game's inherent features allow it to be symptomatic of a deeper social condition.

The remarkable success enjoyed by *Lagaan* (2002) is no doubt due to its skilful depiction of the way cricket and race has always meshed together, but the film also provides us with another perspective on the game's popularity. Since I have not explored this alternative reading in the chapter we are discussing, I would like to briefly indicate the direction in which such an insight could be developed. I had pointed out earlier that while cricket's popularity is a mystery that needs solving, it is equally puzzling as to why a sport with such limited international appeal should become our national pastime. Football, it seems, would be a far better candidate for legitimizing a country's arrival at the world stage. In fact, most of the emerging powers in the last fifty years— Japan, Korea and more recently China—have focused on developing first-rate soccer programs. India is the odd man out in this respect—the national team is ranked 125th in the world, and the nation's sporting public shows no signs of shifting its attention from cricket to football. *Lagaan* helps us understand this fixation by inscribing cricket into a nationalist narrative that portrays the game as a crucial element in our history. By choosing cricket as the domain where a hastily organized group of Indian villagers manage to vanquish the might of the British, it grants the game a special ontological status. What *Lagaan* then does is to place cricket as a necessary part of our history, as one of the crucial ways in which we have come to be. One could speculate then, that the national hysteria around cricket is really a historiography that constructs a unique national identity by means of this peculiar institution. It then becomes irrelevant that cricket is a minor sport at the international level, for it is as central to our modern culture as baseball is to the American way of life.

Such an assertion cannot unfortunately be made about either hockey or football. In Chapter 2, I look at why these sports which, at the time of Independence, were almost at par with cricket, have since declined precipitously in terms of popularity and patronage. Cricket, as we just saw, gets its charge through its status as a signifier of postcolonial lack, as well as by providing the means to imagine a unique history of the nation. Both hockey and football, I suggest, have failed as competitive sports because they were never really national in their scope. In the case of hockey, the great international success enjoyed by Indian teams between the 1920s and the 1960s obscured the fact that the game was mainly supported and played by a succession of minority groups—Anglo-Indians, Muslims and Sikhs and, most recently, "tribals." Never really accepted by the mainstream, hockey lacked the glamour that cricket always seemed to possess. It could remain fairly prestigious and robust during the first twenty-five years after Independence because it was propped up by a Nehruvian state that deemed it necessary to oversee most aspects of leisure and entertainment. It could also be argued that the bitter rivalry between India and Pakistan after Partition helped to keep some interest in the sport. By the 1970s however, two developments would contribute to hockey's decline as a major sport. Firstly, the developed countries of the West began to nurture strong hockey programs that soon matched sub-continental standards. At the same time, the introduction of astroturf and changes in the rules of the game encouraged a physical style of play at which First World players were more adept. Soon after these developments both India and Pakistan were dethroned as world champions; this in turn diminished the significance of their rivalry and caused the public's interest in the sport to fall very rapidly. Even more importantly, once the country opened up to the forces of globalization, market forces began to impinge on the game's fortunes. Hockey was incapable of attracting the audience—and hence the advertisement revenue and sponsorship rupees—required for a sport to flourish in the age of mass media. Consequently, as early as the 1980s, hockey had become a second-class sport that continued to exist primarily because a structure for organizing the sport was already in place. The public at large seems to care very little about this survival—a typical match in the once-prestigious Beighton Cup tournament can only draw a crowd of 50 or 60! Hockey, once branded as the "national game," has proved to be the most minor of sports.

The tragedy of Indian hockey is linked to a fact about cultural politics—the fundamental inability of Indian society to properly accommodate its minorities. The recent history of the nation is replete with evidence of this shortcoming: the flight of the Anglo-Indian community soon after Independence; the movement for Khalistan; the tortured history of Hindu-Muslim relations from the Partition to Godhra; and the profound lack of adjustment on the part of the state vis-à-vis tribals from both the hills and the plains. The failure of hockey, then, is not just a matter of sports alone, it reflects the failure, at a very deep level, of the Indian state. A game played *by* minorities ended up, in the era of global capitalism, being marginalized as a game meant only *for* them.

As I show in the second section of Chapter 2, football too would suffer a similar fate. The game went through a brief nationalist moment in the wake of Mohun Bagan's celebrated 1911 IFA Shield victory; it then acquired a communal tinge during Mohammedan Sporting's reign as champions of Calcutta football in the 1930s. As in the case of hockey, government patronage in the immediate post-Independence period produced the illusion that football was a major sport, and like hockey it too collapsed at the national level once the forces of globalization set in. The sudden disappearance of famed teams like Andhra Pradesh Police, Punjab Police, Integral Coach Factory or HAL provides a graphic proof of this deflationary process. Football, unlike hockey, would not lose its entire constituency. Whereas hockey was condemned to survive on the support of dispersed and economically underprivileged social groups, football could bank on the fanatic following it enjoyed in two regions—Bengal and Goa. Its true history is therefore reducible to the local histories of these states. In Bengal, football was initially a vehicle for nationalist aspirations; by the 1930s however it had become the means by which two culturally distinct groups of Bengalis—*ghotis* and *bangals*—could negotiate their commonalities and contradictions. In Goa, football was introduced under Portuguese rule and was further popularized through the efforts of local churches and educational institutions. After the liberation of the state, football remained very popular because for Goans it was a marker of ethnic identity. Insofar as football was grounded in the cultures of Bengal and Goa it could better withstand the onset of globalization. Though the game is certainly not as popular and widespread as it was in the 1950s and 1960s—it has almost completely disappeared from the south and from the Punjab—it continues to have a strong appeal in the eastern and western parts of the country. But even in these regions, the popularity of domestic football has declined relative to the globalized game. In Kolkata, for example, the aura that surrounded the classic Mohun Bagan-East Bengal encounter has faded considerably, as fans have increasingly shifted their attention to matches involving international franchises like Manchester United or Inter-Milan. The main argument of my second chapter can be summed up as follows: the meaning of popular sport is determined by its role in a rapidly globalizing India. The entire country is fanatical about cricket because that sport functions as a competitive endeavor that reflects our current standing in the league of nations. Serving no such grand purpose, both hockey and football are forced to struggle for respect and for survival.

Beyond the National

The next two chapters of the book focus on Bollywood—the only other modern cultural form that rivals cricket in terms of popularity and impact. Beginning in 1913 with the release of *Raja Harishchandra* the film industry has grown into a gigantic enterprise which produces the highest number of films in the world and whose total audience surpasses that of Hollywood. In spite of this success, Bollywood has had more than its share of detractors. Perhaps no aspect of Bollywood has come in for more criticism than the song and dance sequences that are an inevitable component of every Hindi film. In the next two chapters of this book I argue that Hindi *filmigeet* (film song sequences)—whether in their musical or "picturized" forms—are not only a part of the greatest artistic achievements of twentieth century Indian culture, they are also of the utmost theoretical importance in understanding the nature of the popular. That is so because film music *is* popular music, insofar as the movies are the only available forum for the dissemination of modern song. It is the history of this music that I look at in Chapter 3, beginning with the early years of the studio era and tracing its development right up to the sounds of the new millennium. In the 1930s and 1940s, the music directors at Bombay Talkies, Prabhat Studios and at New Theatres faced the daunting task of having to literally invent a musical sound which would adequately express the conditions of life shaped both by the freedom struggle as well as by the forces of modernization. Though Bombay Talkies and Prabhat had supremely talented artistes on their roster, most of them were too entrenched within their classical training and could not quite envision the rhythms and beats that any form of modern music needed to be based on. On the other hand, Calcutta's long history as the capital of British India had led to the creation of a polyglot and cosmopolitan culture which encouraged experimentation and innovation. Operating in this milieu, the music directors at New Theatres—R.C. Boral, Anil Biswas, Pankaj Mullick and several others—were not shy of stepping out of traditional formats in search of a new sound. These directors would be the first Indian composers to introduce large orchestras that included guitars and saxophones, melodic lines based on the principles of western musicology, and the uniquely Indian practice of playback singing. This is not to suggest that Bengal was the only source of artistic creativity and innovation. The Pakistani author Ashraf Aziz[6] has argued that though the Bengal school played its part in the creation of *filmigeet*, it was the Punjabi composer Ghulam Haider who was responsible for devising the beats and rhythms that would come to characterize modern film music. Ali's contention is debatable, but in any case it does not detract from the more general point I am making here. Bengal's singular role was not restricted to the seminal productions at New Theatres; it also contributed to a second wave of modernity that reconstituted Hindi film music. After an initial period of experimentation *filmigeet* entered what is commonly described as its "golden era." Encompassing the decades of the forties and the fifties this period saw the flowering and maturation of such outstanding singers as Geeta Dutt, Lata Mangeshkar, Mukesh and Mohammed Rafi, as well as legendary composers like Naushad, Madan Mohan, Sachin Dev Burman and Shanker-Jaikishen. Though the music created by these artists was enchanting and sublime, there came a time when it was out of joint with the world outside. By the mid-sixties India was far more urban and industrialized. This new reality could no longer be adequately captured by the gentle and languorous tones of golden era music. A far grittier, faster and upbeat sound was called for, and just such a style would be created by two unschooled and maverick musicians who were not afraid to challenge the assumptions of the musical establishment. Neither Rahul Dev Burman nor Kishore Kumar had received much formal training, and as Bengalis they were less burdened by the conventions and dictates of North Indian classical culture. Consequently they were able to "import" rhythms and beats from sources all over the globe and create music— exemplified by such classics as "Roop Tera Mastana" and "Mere Samne Wali Khirki Mein"—that would become the definitive sound of modern India. I end my survey of *filmigeet* by looking briefly at the careers of perhaps the two most important figures in the recent history of Indian music. Both Biddu and A.R. Rahman embody the spirit of hybridity and eclecticism characteristic of RD and

Kishore, and their compositions define contemporary music by incorporating a variety of global sounds—disco, rock, reggae, and rap—into a totally indigenous mix. In its constant search for new sources of musical inspiration and in its refusal to stay within any set of prescribed boundaries their work is at one with the earliest efforts of the pioneers at New Theatres. The history of *filmigeet* is one of constant reinvention and synthesis. Consisting of an ever-changing mix of native and foreign traditions, the evolution of the form illustrates the truth that the modern can only be represented by means of the impure, the ad hoc and the hybrid. In other words, Hindi film song becomes popular by incorporating the entire globe within itself.

The globalization of Indian popular culture has no better instance than the current craze surrounding "Bollywood": Hindi films are now released simultaneously in Mumbai and London; the typical blockbuster now earns about 35 per cent of its revenues abroad; Aishwariya Rai appears on David Letterman and Oprah Winfrey and becomes a L'Oreal model; Amitabh Bachchan gets voted as the greatest actor in the world; *Lagaan* and *Devdas* (2002) compete for the Oscars; and desi films like *Monsoon Wedding* (2001) and *Bend it Like Beckham* (2002) become box-office hits. While Bollywood may have only recently become a buzzword in the West, it has had a vast presence in other parts of the globe—in Africa, in West and South-East Asia, in Eastern Europe and the former Soviet Union and even in Latin America—for a very long time. Indeed, it is estimated that Bollywood now has a larger worldwide audience than Hollywood, and is a rare instance of popular art from the global South competing successfully against western cultural products. In spite of this success—or perhaps, because of it—Hindi films have traditionally been dismissed as "commercial" and "escapist." It is only in the very recent past that our intelligentsia has deemed Bollywood to be a worthy object of study, and the last decade or so has seen a spate of publications that cover almost every aspect of its products. Even these writings, however, have paid little or no attention to the ubiquitous "song-

and-dance" sequences that have been an essential part of every Hindi film from *Alam Ara* (1931), the first Indian talkie, to *Bunty Aur Babli* (2005). One cannot escape the conclusion that even defenders of Bollywood find song-dance to be an embarrassing artistic device whose meaning and purpose are either unclear or trivial.

Chapter four of this book addresses the problematic issue of song and dance. My inquiry is based on the supposition that a practice which has survived for almost eighty years and which is so loved by the public at large cannot be purely ornamental or accidental. On the contrary, I argue, song-dance is a crucial and necessary part of the Hindi film because it performs a set of functions that the "story" is unable to do. Firstly, song-dance is not contained by the film text. As I have discussed in Chapter 3, song-dance is the source of all popular music in India. It also impacts television in powerful ways through shows like *Chitrahaar* and *Antakshari*; provides the basis for remixed tracks that play in discos and clubs; and is directly responsible for the boom in the cassette and CD industries. It thus extends well beyond cinema to permeate the entire field of Indian popular culture. Song-dance may be even more significant for the work it does inside the film itself. Because of its status as an extra-diegetic entity—it has very little to do with the plot or with character development—it is granted the license to function as an instrument of imagination and fantasy. It performs this role with astonishing versatility and style: song-dance is at once a private setting for romantic love, a site of hyper-sociality that uses hundreds of extras, a tourist brochure for faraway places, a shop window for fancy products, a ramp show for the latest fashions, a sexualized space for the display of the body, a documentary for the affairs of the nation, and of course a site where the tunes of modernity find their visual representation. Song-dance, then, is anything but escapist, for it portrays that which is real but which consistently escapes the grasp of narrative. Hindi film narrative, has, until recently, been far too concerned with playing out the endless battle between modernity and tradition—most often depicted as a conflict between the passions of romantic love (based on bourgeois individualism) and the expectations of a familial order (based on feudal patriarchy). This opposition itself was typically enacted within a statist and traditionalist framework that was committed both to the ideology of national improvement represented by selfless doctors, incorruptible police officers, idealistic scions of wealthy families, as well as to eternal human values embodied in stereotypical figures like sadhus, peasant folk, family retainers, and womenfolk. The highly formulaic resolutions characteristic of most Hindi cinema is a function of this highly artificial frame. More importantly, the limits imposed by the triangulation I have just described allowed little room for the expression of pleasure and desire within the narrative itself. There was a need, therefore, for a supplemental device within the body of the Hindi film which could act as a conduit for the flow of pleasure. The song-dance sequence, then, can be thought of in mechanistic terms as a machine or engine that enables the text, its characters and the spectator to take off on what the French philosopher Giles Deleuze has called a "line of flight." Its unique function is to imagine and posit the *new*, a construct born out of the velocity of longing and the joy of becoming. This newness cannot be grasped by realism; it needs an act of imagination that can boldly visit the realm of the unknown. In the ascetic and teleological climate of nationalist and post-Independence socialist India, song-dance was the only site that allowed the presence of a productive fantasy whose purpose was neither escape nor negation, but the enactment of modes of being that were not available elsewhere. The resilience of the song-dance as an artistic form is due to this innovative role it performs for film and culture. It may be, though, that this era is about to draw to a close. Now that in the wake of liberalization life itself approximates to one big consumerist song and dance, the need for a formal instrument that enunciates novelty and pleasure may well disappear. The phenomenon of the "urban" film—a genre that increasingly disavows the use of song-dance sequences—is probably a pointer to a future where film and song will part ways.

Nowhere is the arrival of the new illustrated with more force than in the case of the cultural forms that emerged within the context of the Indian diaspora. In the fifth and final chapter of this book, I trace the rise of this global desi culture as it has taken shape in the last two decades or so. The origins of this new expression of "Indianness" lay in the two major waves of immigration out of India that took place over the course of the last hundred and fifty years. The first such movement occurred in the last decades of the nineteenth century and consisted mainly of unskilled labor recruited to work in various British colonies all over the globe. As a result of this flow, sizeable Indian communities were established in places like Malaysia, South Africa, in the Pacific Islands and in the Caribbean. Transplanted onto alien soil, these populations struggled not only to survive at the material level, but also to hold on to their sense of cultural identity. This latter endeavor would lead to the emergence of new and exciting cultural forms that combined traditional Indian artistic practices with influences derived from their new homelands. In Trinidad, for example, descendants of the coolies who worked in the sugar plantations combined Hindi lyrics and instrumentation with Caribbean calypso beats to create the hugely popular genre known as chutney. These Indo-Trinidadians—operating many thousand miles away, in conditions radically different from Calcutta *bhadralok* society of the 1930s—replicated the moves made by the directors at New Theatres in fusing different traditions into modern art. Around the same time, the British-born generation belonging to the Punjabi diaspora would "invent" a modernized version of bhangra which has since become the most popular pan-Indian musical style at the global level. The story of bhangra or chutney then is also the history of diaspora and the struggle for identity by means of popular culture. As I point out, "desi", a word which used to connote cultural backwardness, now signifies global chic. The astonishing success enjoyed by Indian migrants, especially in the wake of the IT revolution, has given Indian culture abroad a vitality and confidence that is in keeping with the country's emergence as an economic power. What desi ultimately means is the coming-to-be of the Indian diaspora; desi culture is Indian popular culture which has been globalized. Yet it is not just an export item. As the recent spate of "NRI films" demonstrates, local cultural production has now begun to be flavored according to international taste. What the phenomenon of desi establishes is the fact that from now on Indian popular culture cannot be anything but global. Indeed this whole book can be seen as an extended inquiry into the relationship between popular culture and globalization.

If the book has a central thesis, it is something like this: in a postcolonial society like India, the meaning of popular culture is intricately bound up with the crucial role popular texts play in mediating national aspirations and global realities. Thus cricket, the national obsession, is an index of the nation's anxiety surrounding its status in the world. And hockey and football have failed to take hold as national sports partly because they have little meaning in the international arena. Again, *filmigeet* is an outstanding example of how the popular transcends the local and the indigenous in order to create the polyglot sound of Indian modernity. Bollywood film is not only the nation's most successful art form, it also commands a worldwide audience negotiating issues of modernity with an "appropriate technology" consisting of melodrama as well as song and dance. And, as I just argued, desi is the outcome of processing the indigenous through a global filter. Though many areas of contemporary Indian culture have not been covered in the pages of this book—television, advertising, fashion, dining, nightlife and entertainment, to name a few—it would not be injudicious to suggest that they too are equally influenced and shaped by global forces. The "popular", a term which seems to connote that which is exclusively possessed by a certain body of people, turns out, in the last analysis, to exceed both the nation and its inhabitants, grasping modernity and the entire world in an universal embrace.

1

A Whole Nation Padded Up

The Roots of Cricket Mania in Contemporary India

Why is the mere mention of the word, cricket, enough to send multitudes of Indians into a kind of frenzy that may, to the rest of the world, seem like mass psychosis? The Kolkata rickshaw puller who will not eat for two days in order to save up enough to buy himself a gallery seat at the Eden Gardens, the Mumbai taxi driver who can talk about the game with tact and ease ... the innocuous looking Chennai housewife who shows cricketing knowledge that clearly goes beyond the confines of her smoke filled kitchen, the 'techie' from Bangalore who can hold forth on the fortunes of a cricket match with the same felicity with which he can define the worth of software, the tens of millions of others who sleep and wake up perfectly in sync with the time zone within which falls the venue of an India match in some foreign land ... what is it about the Indian heart that longs to see a cricket match almost as passionately as a mother waiting to see her long lost son?[1]

Cricket in India is much more than a sport; it is, along with Bollywood and television, one of the fundamental constituents of Indian popular culture. It far outstrips other sports like football or hockey in terms of publicity or fan following; its appeal cuts through differences of class, caste, religion and even gender; it provides the substance of conversation in a variety of social contexts; and it is the object of obsessive coverage in the national media. It is the burden of this chapter to analyze why a sport once linked only with an imperial ruling class has come to play such a crucial role in the nation's collective psyche. I begin by looking at the evolution of the game from its rural origins to high imperial sport. As one of the emblems of Empire, cricket was an object of desire for the Indian elite whose patronage led to the establishment of two varieties of "native" cricket. Both forms—princely and communal— would make unique contributions to the development of the game and help give it the shape it would assume after Independence. In the second section of this chapter I attempt to understand the obsession about cricket in contemporary India by looking at it as a global practice that came into being after the dissolution of Empire. An examination of the cricketing world shows that it is highly racialized, a fact explored with great creativity in the blockbuster *Lagaan*. While most contemporary accounts of cricket have analyzed it through the category of the nation, I propose that its cultural meaning can only be understood if we see it as an instrument that negotiates between domestic and international culture. In other words, the obsession about cricket is directly linked with the frenetic globalization that Indian society is undergoing. The enormous popularity of cricket, then, is an index of India's emergence as a global nation.

A Brief History of Cricket

While every history is potentially infinite, four strands in the story of cricket are especially important in terms of their influence on the contemporary Indian game: cricket's evolution from a rural game into a modern nineteenth century sport; the trajectory and nature of its export through the agency of Empire; the patronage it received from the rulers of the princely states; and the communalization of domestic cricket in pre-Independence India. Cricket was codified into its present form by the middle of the nineteenth century. The formal aspects of the game had gained shape earlier—the first county match, between Kent and Surrey, took place in 1709, and the first known issue of the *Laws of Cricket* came out in 1744. By the end of the eighteenth century, cricket, along with racing and boxing, was the sport of the masses and it had acquired many of its familiar features: upright wickets consisting of three stumps, the leg-before-wicket rule, the taking of the new ball at the start of an innings, short runs, as well as the practice of rolling, watering, mowing, and covering the wicket. Most interestingly, the first collection of scores and batting averages had also appeared by this time—Samuel Butcher's *List of all the Principal Matches of Cricket that have been Played in the Year* first came out in 1791.[2] By Victorian times, therefore, cricket already had its rules, its organizational structure, its fans, its vocabulary and its discourse. What the Victorians added to this entity was a layer of ideological meaning. As Keith Sandiford points out "Far from being a simple physical activity, cricket became a powerful symbolic and representational force for the Victorians who believed that it embodied all that was noble in the Anglo-Saxon character. In a fiercely nationalistic era Englishmen regarded cricket, an exclusively English creation unsullied by outside influence, as proof of their cultural supremacy."[3] In other words, cricket, in the Victorian era, acquired a set of meanings which had little to do with sport. While the celebrated "village green" was the symbol par excellence of cricket's sanctification, cricket's rise to prominence was due to the fact that the aristocracy, the landed gentry as well as the rising bourgeoisie were all convinced of its social value. The ruling classes in Victorian England backed cricket in order to transform it into a ruling idea.

Cricket had, in previous centuries, been part of a popular domain that stood outside of the law and was often in adversarial relation with it. When Parliament legalized cricket in 1845, an intimate connection developed between the state and the sport.

Thus, many members of the MCC—the game's ruling body—happened to be titled peers or members of Parliament, often holding important posts in the Cabinet. Martin Bladen, better known as Lord Hawke, is a perfect example. Educated at Eton and Oxford, he captained both Yorkshire and England, led a team to India in 1892–93, and became president of the MCC as well as a member of the House of Lords. Hawke's biography is doubly instructive, for it exemplifies the strong ties between cricket and the educational system that arose from the belief that playing the sport would build manliness, discipline and character. By 1860 cricket was an integral feature of the public school curriculum, and public schools (as well as Oxford and Cambridge) became primary purveyors of the game. Schools employed cricket professionals as coaches, hired teachers who were cricket enthusiasts, and produced graduates who spread the game by founding cricket clubs. This process was aided by the Church of England whose commitment to the doctrine of "muscular Christianity" not only encouraged churchmen to play the game, but also to make strenuous efforts on its behalf. Backed by elites, the government, schools, and the clergy, cricket came to acquire immense symbolic value. This patina could perhaps be best appreciated by an imperial subject: *The Jubilee Book of Cricket*, authored by the Indian prince and cricketing genius Ranjitsinghji, extolled the game for producing self-control, a balanced approach to life, and a sense of social responsibility. Ranji's testimony underscores the fact that by the latter half of the nineteenth century, cricket had become much more than a game, it was revered by the Victorians "as an institution because they believed, that like the Church and the Crown, it had a key role to play in English life."[4]

The development of cricket in the latter half of the nineteenth century followed a trajectory very different from other sports in terms of the rules of the game, its organizational structure, and the social context in which it was played. First, we must take note of the exceptionally long duration of matches. Unlike football (consigned to Saturday afternoons, since the Sabbath had to be observed) and leisure pursuits like darts (played in social spaces like pubs at the end of the workday), a cricket match lasted three whole days. In retrospect, it is quite astonishing that cricket did not start out as one-day cricket. If the demands of capital tended to eat into people's private time (reduction of holidays, increase in the length of the workday) in most areas of life, why were cricket matches allowed to be so long? This irrational duration becomes comprehensible only if one acknowledges that cricket's "purpose" was quite different from that of other sports. Simply put, cricket was not designed to cater to the industrial proletariat.

Secondly, the game's mode of organization pushed it in a direction away from the popular. When the sport was in its rural phase, every small town and village had its cricket team, but the passage to urbanization did not lead to a structure like that of Association football, in which teams represented industrial populations in cities like Manchester, Liverpool or Leeds. Instead, the forums in which the game came to be played were responsible for its constitution as a sport that belonged exclusively to the elites. Before the establishment of county cricket, the game was played at the public schools and the elite universities. Public school boys often ended up playing for touring amateur clubs, the most famous of which was I Zingari. These clubs—the Quidnuncs, Harlequins, Free Forresters, and Incogniti being some among others—were a throwback to the seminal Hambledon team (located in a small Hampshire village, founded by pupils of Westminster school and supported by wealthy London patrons) which dominated the English cricketing scene in the late eighteenth century. The touring clubs often played in that odd and extinct forum known as county-house cricket. County houses, which were houses of the wealthy, played friendly matches between clubs, local players, professionals on the loose, and other assorted amateurs. For a period of twenty odd years county-house cricket provided an alternative model of playing cricket. Tony Mason makes the interesting observation that in the middle of the nineteenth century it looked as though cricket was going to be in the hands of touring elevens of professionals playing each other or local clubs. But unlike football, cricket was not to go the professional route for "the formation of the county club and the coming of touring teams from overseas put an end to that prospect."[5] Given cricket's elitist tendencies it is perhaps not surprising that its ultimate mode of organization would be county cricket. The counties were administrative districts, and therefore quite different from the locales of football clubs. That first-class cricket was to be played at the county level indicates that cricket's elitism entailed an expansionism, the desire to locate its identity over a large and amorphous territory. Since, the county was a space which principally united great landowners, a county cricket club was therefore the recreational face of county government; it was a forum for local elites to congregate and play.

By going beyond the unit of clubs and immediate place, cricket became more than sport—it acquired shades of administration, governance and nation-building. Cricket's elitism would also be reflected in the caste system that divided players into amateurs and professionals. Football too had been initially organized by "gentlemen," but it embraced professionalism in 1885 and the English football team had a professional captaining it as early as 1900. The cricketing establishment was less ready to abolish class distinctions. Amateurs continued to be privileged and pampered, while those who played for pay were treated with little respect. Gentlemen, like Indian princes, preferred only to bat and left the toil of bowling to professionals. The latter also served as service staff who tended the grounds, cleaned kit, and served drinks. The segregation rivaled that of the American South—professionals entered the ground by a separate entrance, changed in different rooms, and had a different system of nomenclature for the purposes of the score card. Lord Hawke's wish "Pray God, that a professional should never captain England," held true till as late as 1936, when Leonard Hutton was chosen to become the first professional to lead the English team.

At a certain point in its history then, cricket became the vehicle for the articulation of a set of intertwined social forces and ideologies: the landed aristocracy, public schools and Oxbridge, the Church of England, Parliament and county government. If football was the sport most appropriate for modern industrial society—by the end of the nineteenth century more people were watching football on Saturday afternoons than a day's play in a Test match—cricket was unique in that it seemed to eschew both modernity and the dictates of industry. There was, however, one version of cricket whose character approximated that of the more proletarian sports. Northern league cricket, of which the Lancashire League was the most famous, was played by teams almost entirely composed of professionals and was patronized mainly by the working classes. It was also far more progressive than elitist southern cricket, allowing colored players like Learie Constantine long before county teams would break the race barrier. However, the northern league has, to this day, remained a minor format, a kind of poorer cousin to Test and county cricket. The essence of cricket lay within those formats which utilized cricket's special semiotic property of signifying a world beyond sport. This made cricket attractive to even those who could not fully participate in the sport. Thus, cricket was very popular with working class boys even though they were often unable to afford the game. As an observer of working class youth in the industrial city of Birmingham noticed, despite "the comparatively small extent to which boys play the game, they nearly all take a great interest in County Cricket."[6]

It was quite natural that a sport which signified wealth and privilege in the domestic context would be appropriated for the purposes of Empire. Nineteenth century ideologues saw sports as a crucial contributor to the imperial project. Thus J.E.C. Weldon, headmaster of Harrow from 1881 to 1885 explained the superiority of the British over competing European powers by arguing that "The pluck, the energy, the perseverance, the good temper, the self-control, the co-operation, the *esprit de corps*, which merit success in cricket or football, are the very qualities which win the day in peace and war."[7] Public schools were of course fundamental to the process of "manufacturing" future colonialists, and the universities and the colonial services were the next stops on this assembly line. The civil services favored sportsmen (overwhelmingly from Oxford or Cambridge) over academics. So many sportsmen ended up in the Sudan civil service that the country became known as the "the land of Blacks ruled by the Blues."[8] The connection between sport and the imperial project found exquisite expression in a poem titled "Vitai Lampada" by Sir Henry Newbolt (1898):

> There's a breathless hush in the Close tonight
> Ten to make and the match to win—
> A bumping pitch and a blinding light,
> An hour to play and the last man in.
> And it's not for the sake of a ribboned coat,
> Or the selfish hope of a season's fame,
> But his Captain's hand on his shoulder smote—
> Play up! Play up! And play the game!
>
> The sand of the desert is sodden red—
> Red with the wreck of a square that broke;
> The Gatling's jammed and the Colonel dead,
> And the regiment blind with dust and smoke;
> The river of death has brimmed its banks,
> And England's far, and Honour a name;
> But the voice of a schoolboy rallies the ranks:
> Play up! play up! and play the game!

As I have stated above, given cricket's ideological value within British society, made it a natural candidate for export. Richard Cashman has spelled out why cricket rather than football was the preferred sport in the colonies. He points out that a majority of colonialists were products of public schools, and thus had a prejudice against Association football. Cricket was seen as a middle class sport, unlike soccer which had strong links with the working class and "hence cricket received greater encouragement than soccer from colonial rulers. Other sports like football or hockey, also introduced by the British, had to fend for themselves without the kind of patronage bestowed upon cricket."[9]

Cricket was initially played exclusively by the colonizer. The Calcutta Cricket Club came into being in 1792, but as Ramchandra Guha has pointed out, the British had no intention of teaching the natives how to play cricket. It would be several decades before cricket would be part of the "civilizing mission". One could formulate the history of colonial cricket in India as consisting of two stages. In the first stage—a period of "self-conscious exclusivity" to use Guha's felicitous phrase—cricket was one of the markers of difference between the colonizer and the colonized. Aside from the menial tasks—grounds keeping, serving drinks, helping at the nets—that he performed, the native's place in this paradigm was quite literally "beyond the boundary." It was only belatedly—when the need for a class of loyal native subjects was deeply felt—that Macaulay's model of colonial imitation was brought into the realm of sports. The 565 odd princes who ruled two fifths of the subcontinent's territory were an obvious target for such a project. Lord Curzon, Viceroy of India between 1898 and 1905, outlined a pedagogy for princes which amounted to an exact paraphrase of the Macaulian doctrine: the young prince had "to learn the English language, and become sufficiently familiar with English customs, literature, science, modes of thought, standards of truth and honour, and ... with manly English sports and games."[10] The princes took to cricket for two reasons. Firstly, their very existence depended on British goodwill, and it thus suited them to cultivate British manners. Thus, to their traditional sports like *shikar*, archery, pig-sticking, fencing, and wrestling, the princes added such westernized sports as snooker, polo and cricket. Secondly, the grand spectacle that cricket afforded fitted in well with the culture of pomp and excess characteristic of all the princely states. When Lord Irwin, Viceroy of India, visited the kingdom of Kolhapur in 1929, he was met at the railway station by a squad of the maharaja's camel corps and a collection of animals including "elaborately painted elephants, camels, greyhounds and ten cheetahs with silken bandages over their eyes."[11] Bhupinder Singh of Patiala, one of the greatest figures in the history of Indian sports, was known to eat 25 quails at one meal and is reputed to have eaten a 10-egg omelet on the day of his death. He also constructed a cricket field which was larger than Lord's and had facilities which rivaled any clubhouse in England. What must have further amazed visiting cricketers was the fact that his palace also housed three hundred concubines and a scented swimming pool. The previous Maharajah of Patiala—Bhupinder's father Rajinder—built one of the most successful polo teams in the country and proceeded to create a Patiala XI which included Ranjitsinghji, professionals from Surrey and Middlesex, and some of the leading Indian cricketers of the day. His son would continue this tradition: amongst those who played for subsequent Patiala teams were famous names like Rhodes, Hirst, Larwood and Frank Tarrant. In 1911, he sponsored a tour to England, and though the team was not particularly successful, winning only two of fourteen matches, it exposed Indian players to foreign conditions and cricketing practices.[12]

There remains to discuss the most famous cricketing prince of all—Kumar Sri Ranjitsinghji of Nawanagar. Ranjitsinghji, or Ranji as the British called him, was the distant heir to a small state in the Kathiawar region. Educated at Rajkumar College—an Indian public school based on the English model—he went to England to study at Trinity College going on to play for Sussex and then for England. So astounding were his batting performances and so unique was his cricketing genius that Neville Cardus once wrote of him "Cricketers will never see the like of Ranjitsinghji; he was entirely original, and there is nothing in the history of batsmanship with which we can compare him."[13] Glorious though his cricketing life was, Ranji is now seen as somewhat of a tragic figure. Never completely accepted in England, he was upon his return to India, condemned to a marginal existence. And though as a ruler he was kind and benevolent, pursuing good works and looking after the betterment of his subjects, his unwavering loyalty to the idea of

Empire meant that he was largely irrelevant in the context of Indian nationalism. Ranji's last years, to use the phrase that Cardus used to describe his magical batting, were bathed in a "strange light" of ambivalence. He refused to help Indian cricket in any way whatsoever on the flimsy excuse that Duleep (his nephew Duleepsinghji) and he were English cricketers; his behavior invited judgements like A.S. de Mello's that he did "absolutely nothing for Indian sport and sportsmen." Yet outside of the sphere of cricket Ranji espoused causes that were anti-colonial. Thus, he championed the case that Indians should be allowed to become British citizens arguing that the British Empire should treat all its subjects alike. Ranji's contemporary appeal lies in the greatness of his batting. Indian writers return again and again to this figure because Ranji was the first cricketer to demonstrate that the native could match the rulers in cricketing skill. He was as John Lord has written "the first Indian of any kind to be universally known and popular."[14]

How important were the princes to the development of Indian cricket? There is no doubt that the feudal setting of princely cricket was out of tune with the era's democratic leanings. Moreover, the unfortunate convention that the Indian team would have to be captained by a prince led to much rivalry and intrigue among princely contenders and certainly harmed the team's performance. The Maharajah of Vizianagram, known popularly as "Vizzy", took two servants with him for the England tour of 1936 and managed to average only 8.25 in the Test matches. Yet as Mihir Bose has argued it is doubtful if Indian cricket would have developed as quickly as it did without help from the princes. That seems a fair judgement, for the princes can be seen as early capitalists entering a new sector of the economy. Access to unlimited wealth enabled the princes to invest in grounds, equipment, foreign coaches, and foreign tours. These inputs undoubtedly helped the maturation of the Indian game. Princely cricket had another unexpected achievement. As discussed below, while the rest of Indian cricket was organized on a communal basis, it was the princely patrons who consistently fielded the most "secular teams." These contributions have been largely forgotten; the reason behind this amnesia lies in political history. In spite of the pomp and circumstance associated with them, the princely states were insubstantial entities which existed because it suited British policy. After Independence, these states evaporated without resistance and were incorporated into the new nation. The Derecognition Act of 1971 which abolished the privy purse given to ex-rulers was the final curtain on princely India. With that, all memory of this institution, including that of princely cricket, vanished from the nation's consciousness.

Just as the princes took to cricket as part of a larger effort at modernization, so did the emerging middle classes. Of all communities in India the Parsis were the most westward-looking and it is not surprising that they were the first group to take to cricket. In 1848, Parsis established the Orient Cricket Club, the first such institution in India, and a Parsi team was the first Indian team to play against the all-European Bombay Gymkhana in 1877. So devoted were they to the game that Parsis took cricket to the most unlikely of places—a Parsi Cricket Club was formed in Shanghai in 1890! The Parsis were also the first group to tour England, first in 1886 and again in 1888. The second tour featured a bowler who was probably India's first great cricketer—Mehellasha Pavri. On that tour Pavri took an astonishing 170 wickets at an average of 11.66, establishing the fact that cricket was now a "native" game. The Parsis were an elite group largely loyal to the Raj and their cultivation of cricket was a way of establishing the favored status of the Parsi community. Cricket would therefore take on a sacred hue—before the Parsi team left for England, the famous lawyer Pherozeshah Mehta commented that just "as artists go to Italy to do homage to the great Masters.... so now the Parsees are going to England to do homage to the English cricketers, to learn something of that noble and manly pastime in the very country which is its chosen home."[15] This fetishization of the game meant that victory over the colonizers would assume heroic proportions. When, in 1890, the Parsi Gymkhana defeated the touring English team led by G.E. Vernon, the reaction was ecstatic. According to the Parsi captain Framji Patel "the imaginative and emotional Parsee youth felt for a day or two that he was the victor of the victors of Waterloo;" another community leader looked further backwards and saw the triumph as avenging the defeat of the Parsis at the hands of the Arabs in the battle of Nahavand in 621 AD.[16] Although the Parsi community would continue to produce outstanding cricketers for many years to come—Rusi Mody, Polly Umrigar, Nari Contractor and Farokh Engineer being notable examples—Parsi domination of the game ended by the close of the nineteenth century. Other religious groups were quick to follow the Parsi example: Hindus started the Union Cricket Club in 1866, while the Mohammedan Cricket Club was formed in 1883, thus putting in place the communal structure which would govern cricket in India for the next fifty years.

These pioneering clubs, as well as the Parsi, Hindu and Muslim Gymkhanas which were established soon after, were all located in Bombay. There were similar developments in Madras, Poona, and Karachi as well as in many other parts of the country. Given cricket's rising popularity it is surprising that a robust cricketing tradition failed to develop in Bengal. The province was the first British bridgehead in their conquest of India, Calcutta the premier colonial city, and the Calcutta Cricket Club, established in 1792, was the second oldest cricket club in the world after the MCC. Bengalis were the perfect Macaulian subjects, taking to English arts and sciences through movements like Young Bengal and the subsequent "Bengal Renaissance." One would expect cricket to flourish in such a milieu, but though a couple of princely states, namely Cooch Behar and Nathore, did sponsor cricket teams, the game as a whole failed to take root. Appeals to the Bengali's unsporting nature are not sufficient to explain this phenomenon. Macaulay himself had remarked that "whatever the Bengali does he does languidly, his favorite pursuits are sedentary," but such a caricature, common amongst the British, fails to account for the intensity and skill with which Bengalis took up the more physical game of football. It could also be argued that cricket required a level of investment and funding which could only be sustained by wealthy princes or by the rich trading and industrial communities of western India. But Bengal had a high level of native entrepreneurship during this period and consequently there could have been no shortage of capital required to sponsor cricket teams. The real answer may lie elsewhere.

It is pertinent to remember that Bengal was at the forefront of the nationalist movement during the period cricket was being adopted in other areas of the country. Surendranath Banerjea founded the influential Indian Association in 1876 with an aim towards uniting the Indian people around a political program. This initiative led to the formation of the Indian National Congress in 1885. Most importantly, Lord Curzon's decision to partition Bengal in 1905 led to an unprecedented level of political protest in Bengal. A game so strongly identified with European privilege could not have been attractive to a politics of nationalism. The Bengali journal *Sakha* had celebrated the historic defeat of Vernon's team by the Parsis in 1890 by writing that "this victory had made it clear that the Indians had acquired the prowess to counter the colonizers at their own game."[17] Yet cricket could not easily be assimilated into the nationalist program. Calcutta cricket had always been racially exclusivist, and was to stay so—when the MCC toured India in 1926–27, Calcutta was the only venue where they encountered an all-white team (named "Europeans in the East!"). Cricket, therefore, may well have been too strongly identified with the ruling class for it to be adopted by a Bengali middle class devoted to the nationalist cause. Whatever the truth, it is indisputable that, by the turn of the century, football had replaced cricket in the Bengali imagination as the vehicle for demonstrating native prowess. For Bengalis therefore, the foundational nationalist moment in sports history was not the Parsi victory over Vernon's team. That distinction belongs to 28th July, 1911, the day on which Mohun Bagan, a native football club, defeated the East Yorkshire Regiment by a score of 2–1 to win the 1911 IFA Shield final. As a local newspaper commented "It fills every Indian with joy and pride to know that the rice-eating, malaria-ridden, bare-footed Bengali have got the better of beef-eating, Herculean, booted John Bull in that peculiarly English sport."[18] Football was clearly fused with nationalism, but only in the case of Bengal. It is therefore injudicious to claim, as the cricket writer Mihir Bose has done, that "logically, after Independence, football should have become India's number one sport" and that "Had the British been thrown out of India in the violent, revolutionary way proposed by the Indian nationalist Subhas Bose ... football rather than cricket would have become the major game."[19] Bose is guilty of conflating India with Bengal—1911 may have been momentous for Bengalis, but he needs to provide evidence that it fuelled nationalist passions in Gujarat or Madras. Yet Bose is onto something significant when he goes on to observe that "Cricket never became a metaphor for an India vs. England contest as did football."[20] Cricket was never oppositional in the way football was in Bengal. C.K. Nayudu's magnificent innings of 153 against Arthur Gilligan's MCC team in 1926 may have stirred the imagination (though perhaps only that of Hindus since Nayudu was representing the Hindu Eleven) but such triumphs were never incorporated within the discourse of the freedom struggle. Indeed the most popular form of cricket—communal cricket—came to be seen as anti-national by Gandhi and other leaders.

Organized around the annual competition between ethnic groups—the original Triangular played between Europeans, Hindus and Parsis became the Quadrangular in 1912 and then the Pentangular in 1937 with the addition of first the Muslims followed by the "The Rest"—communal cricket defined what the game meant to Indians. The ambiguous status of India as a colony-nation meant that cricket was only sporadically organized around the banner of the whole nation. In all the years up to Independence, only seven Indian teams crossed the waters to represent the country as a whole. Of these, the first two were exclusively Parsi (the very first captained by Dr. D.H.Patel in 1886 bore the colorful name "Parsi Gentlemen to U.K."). Four All-India teams did subsequently tour England, but each team was "chaperoned" by a prince: Patiala in 1911, Porbandar in 1932, Vizianagram (Vizzy) in 1936 and Pataudi in 1946. Though these teams did often include the best players in the nation, they were not truly national teams, being symbolically linked to the princes who led them. On some occasions these teams were not even fully Indian, Vizzy's 1930–31 team which toured India and Ceylon included the immortal Hobbs and Sutcliffe. Nor was there much national cricket played at home. Only three MCC teams (1926–27, 1933–34, 1937–38) came to India in the entire pre-Independence period. The three previous tours by foreigners were very casual affairs, two were private tours led by individuals (Vernon in 1889–90 and Hawke in 1892–93), and the third featured The Oxford University Authentics (1902–03).

In short, cricket was not a national enterprise during the first half of the twentieth century, being organized instead around two alternative axes: princely and communal. While the former version depended on royal patronage, communal cricket was backed by native and colonial groups alike. Thus, Lord Harris, Governor of Bombay and one of cricket's earliest patrons, felt that the Quadrangular would "bring the several races together in a spirit of harmony that should be the spirit in which cricket is played." These sentiments were echoed by leading players. Syed Wazir Ali, captain of the Muslim team in 1940 claimed that "the tournament is not in the least anti-national"; similarly C.K. Nayudu held that it "had fostered healthy rivalry and promoted communal unity."[21] It was only as the nationalist movement gathered momentum that communal cricket began to be seen as undesirable. Gandhi's remark that "I can understand matches between Colleges and Institutions, but I have never understood the reason for having Hindu, Parsi, Muslim and other communal Elevens"[22] was representative of the new sentiment which led to a campaign for the abolition of the Pentangular and the institution of a rival, secular All-India Tournament. Naming the tournament after Ranji was not only an act of homage to one of India's greatest cricketers, but it also implicitly acknowledged the long tradition of secularism within princely cricket. It needs to be stressed here that princely cricket was far more progressive than is often recognized. When Rajendra Singh of Patiala built his cricket team he included Europeans, other princes, as well as the leading Parsi, Hindu and Muslim cricketers of the era. His son, Bhupendra Singh, made sure that his 1911 team to England included members of every community.[23] And when the movement against communal cricket gathered shape, he along with his fellow rulers of Holkar and Baroda forbade players from participating in the Pentangular. The eventual abolition of the Pentangular in 1943 can therefore be seen as a vindication of the principles of princely cricket over its communal counterpart.

In summary then, cricket started as a popular rural game which was subsequently adopted by the Victorian establishment as a means of propagating ruling class ideology. This appropriation happened during the age of Empire, it was therefore inevitable that cricket would become *the* imperial sport. Like most colonial cultural forms it took root in native soil. Cricket in India would be promoted by two unconnected sets of elites—wealthy scions of the princely states as well as the emerging bourgeoisie based in the major cities—and therefore developed in a hybrid fashion. Princely cricket was national in its scope, secular in character, but ultimately too elitist and sporadic to appeal to the masses. Urban cricket on the other hand was enormously popular—as late as 1943, in the face of concerted opposition, the Bombay Pentangular could draw 20,000 people to Brabourne stadium. It was regional in scope, being most popular in western India, and reflecting the political realities of the day, it was strongly communal in its nature. In no way can cricket of this period be considered a national sport, for its patronage, organization and following reflected either an anachronistic feudalism or the destructive energies of sub-national communalism. A very different set of social circumstances that came into being after Independence would make possible a more national articulation of the game.

In the six decades since Independence, the status of cricket has changed from popular sport to national obsession. During the Nehruvian and post-Nehruvian statist era, the game received support and patronage—as did all other sports—from the government. However, even then there were complaints that there was a bias in favor of cricket. As *Link* magazine asked in 1970: "Why this partiality for Test cricket, the running commentary for which is on the national hook up ... Occasionally, the finals of a premier football or tennis or badminton final (sic) get time on AIR [All India Radio], but it is mostly not on the national hook up. Thus a very large number of sports lovers do not get the benefit."[24] The advent and spread of television coupled with India's World Cup win of 1983, catapulted cricket into a different league from all other sports. The following facts speak for themselves: in the late 1960s, the Nawab of Pataudi received Rs. 2,000 for autographing a bat, in the 1980s Kapil Dev earned Rs. 30 lakh for a three-year endorsement, Sachin Tendulkar now gets between one and two crore rupees for a one-year endorsement. His net worth is around Rs. 140 crore while both Sourav Ganguly and Rahul Dravid earn around Rs. 7 crore annually. The BCCI's earnings and television revenues reflect the inflationary spiral. Between 1987 and 1999 the BCCI's annual growth rate in profits was a massive 59%, from Rs. 5 lakh in 1987 to Rs. 8 crore in 1999.[25] The media participates wholeheartedly in selling cricket—in 1999, the BCCI granted television rights for all matches played in India for the period 1999–2004 to Doordarshan for a sum of Rs. 2,240 crore (54 million US dollars). Print journalism is equally biased in its favor—most sports magazines focus primarily on cricket, and some publications like *Cricket Today* and *Wisden Asia* don't cover any other sport. Enthusiasm for the game crosses gender boundaries, it is reported that over 20 million women watched the last World Cup matches played in South Africa. The Indian media is now full of women covering cricket—Mandira Bedi for Sony Entertainment's MAX channel, Sonali Chander and Gaurika Chopra for Star News, Anjali Joshi for cricketnext.com, Maria Goretti and Trishna Bose of MAX, Sharda Ugra of *India Today* and Deepti Menon of Aaj Tak.[26] Even fiction responds to this cricket mania. Inspired by *Lagaan*'s phenomenal success, new film director Raveena Tandon explained her film *Stumped* in the following terms: "Though *Stumped* does not revolve around cricket, it shows the obsession of a nation with cricket and how it minimizes more important aspects of society."[27]

These objective measures of the game's incredible popularity have a correlate in the psychological stance that Indians take towards cricket. Most fans think cricket all the time: the journalist Sandipan Deb recounts how while waiting on a platform in the middle of a cold winter night for a late train, he heard a voice suddenly utter *"Yaar, mujhe to lagta hai India ka is baar chance hai"* (I think India has a chance this time).[28] This disembodied voice symbolizes the ever-present desire for cricketing success that is almost universal. Such fanatic support comes at a price. As Raju Mukherjee has pointed out[29] Indian cricket fans are a singularly ungrateful lot. When India lost to the West Indies a few months after winning the World Cup in 1983, the fans turned on Kapil Dev. They did the same to Sunil Gavaskar in 1985. And when the Indian team got off to a poor start at the 2003 World Cup, the reaction was pathologically aggressive. Fans gathered round Sourav Ganguly's residence in Kolkata yelling obscenities; Hindu extremists in Allahabad attempted to vandalize the home of Mohammed Kaif; and pictures of cricketing heroes were smeared with cow dung and garlanded with chappals. So extreme was the outrage that Parliament had to issue a statement in support of the cricketers and call for measures to protect their homes and families.

A proper analysis of this nationwide obsession needs to locate the phenomenon of Indian cricket in the global context. Though only ten countries play the game at the Test-playing level, cricket must still be considered an international sport. In the past, the game's association with the British Empire gave it a wide geographical reach as well as immense prestige. Even though the world's political hegemony has since shifted to the United States, cricket's standing has not suffered appreciably. Americans may regard the game as quaint and incomprehensible, but still respect it for being an essential part of the Anglo-Saxon tradition. And though the game cannot compete with football or basketball at the international level, it continues to be granted the prestige which it has enjoyed since the middle of the nineteenth century. The story of cricket from the first Test played in Melbourne in 1886 to the present can be briefly summarized as follows: Till the Second World War the game was dominated by two countries—England and Australia—and the contest between them for the Ashes was the most important cricketing event on the calendar. The post-War years saw the rise of the non-white cricketing nations: the West Indies, and then India, Pakistan and Sri Lanka. The West Indies were invincible during the 1970s and 1980s, but have since declined, while the South Asian nations seem to alternate between brilliant and abject performances. New Zealand has, in the last two decades or so, grown into a competitive team, as has South Africa after being readmitted into the international game. Of the two original powers, England suffered a steady decline in the last two decades, but has made a strong comeback, while Australia, in spite of its recent defeat in the Ashes series, remains on top of the cricketing world. Results and rankings, however fascinating, are not of great theoretical interest; the meaning of cricket, I want to argue, can only be got at by an analysis that involves the categories of colonialism, postcolonialism and race. While there were local variations in every country in which cricket was played, we can identify two broad trajectories in cricket history: a game invented in England and then established in the white settler colonies of Australia, South Africa, New Zealand (though cricket was initially popular in Canada, it lost out to more local sports like ice hockey and American style football); as well as a very different version of the sport that developed when played by non-white subjects of the Empire.

Cricket and Race

A brief examination of the history of the game in Australia and the West Indies will help to illustrate this contention. Founded as a colony for relocating criminals and political deviants, Australia's initial settlers were exclusively white. These transplanted Englishmen brought cricket with them, the first cricket game in Australia was played in Sydney in 1803 and club cricket began to be organized in New South Wales around 1830. English sides started touring the country in 1861–62 and in 1877 the match between the touring side led by James Lilywhite and "A Grand Combined Melbourne and Sydney XI" was retroactively named as the first "Test" match. As is well known, the defeat of the English side at the Oval in 1882 led to the comment that English cricket had died and that its "ashes" would be taken to Australia and this event inaugurated a great rivalry and tradition. Australian cricket, like the rest of Australian society, was modeled on the English version. As Richard Cashman has argued, cricket became the dominant summer game because it "addressed the central social and political issue of the day, the relationship between the motherland and colonial Australia."[30] The famous "Mandle thesis"—advanced by the historian W.F. Mandle—argues that cricket provided a vehicle for an emerging Australian nationalism. While it is true that Australians were motivated by a desire to "thrash the motherland"[31] and that the more populist strain in Australian culture poked fun at the Anglophile cricketing establishment, such sentiments were ultimately deferential to the imperial cause. Many Australians refused to relinquish their links to the "home country" and referred to themselves as Anglo-Australians; between 1877 and 1900 five such hybrid players represented both Australia and England.[32] The ideological continuity between the two nations was acknowledged by both sides. The success of Australian cricket was seen by many as proof that British stock could flourish anywhere and that Anglo-Saxon blood had not been thinned in the hot sun! Minor irritants like the Bodyline episode of 1932–33 did not dilute the bond between the nations, as late as 1944 the Australian Prime Minister, watching a game at Lord's, was moved to say "Australians will always fight for those twenty two yards. Lord's and its traditions belong to Australia just as much as to England."[33] Such sentiments explain why Australian troops fought for the motherland in two World Wars and why Australia along with South Africa, New Zealand and England constitutes a white Anglo-Saxon axis that still dominates the cricketing establishment. Given this history it is not surprising that Australia showed great reluctance towards establishing cricketing relations with non-white countries. Australian Board members were loath to allow any senior players to go to India on the private tour organized by the Maharajah of Patiala in 1935–36; and it was not until 1956 that an Australian team would tour India. Australian cricket in its present form must therefore be read in terms of this long history of imperial identification and collaboration. While England itself has responded to the changes in its domestic culture and to the forces of globalization (the choice of the bi-racial Nasseer Hussain as captain of England would have been unthinkable a couple of decades ago), Australian cricket still seems to embody a "White Australian" attitude. This is perhaps not so surprising given the nation's obsession with racial issues from the very beginning of its history. As early as the 1850s, white miners in New South Wales and Victoria protested against the arrival of Chinese laborers, and this anti-immigrant sentiment soon spread to other parts of the country.

The rising wave of bigotry culminated in 1901, when sparked by an incident of 80 Afghans landing on the country's shores, the government passed the Immigration Restriction Act, designed to keep the country as white as possible. This blatantly racist policy utilized a device known as the Dictation Test (borrowed from South Africa) which allowed immigration officers to ask any potential immigrant to write 50 words in any European language—thus a Chinese person seeking to immigrate could be asked to compose a paragraph in Hungarian and denied the right to enter the country if he or she failed! Australian leaders made little effort to hide their racialist sentiments, following the beginning of hostilities with Japan in World War II, the Australian leader John Curtis opined "this country shall forever remain the home of the descendants of those people who came here in peace in order to establish in the South Seas an outpost of the British race."[34] It was only in the 1960s and 1970s that the White Australian policy was finally abandoned. Yet Australia's blind support of Anglo-American hegemony, its current discriminatory policies towards asylum seekers, and the reputed "black list" used by its immigration services for visa-giving purposes, all suggest that the ideology which sustained the policy is still in place. The all-white Australian cricket team even now often seems to display a set of attitudes not far removed from the miners of New South Wales in the 1850s. As a result, in spite of Australia's current domination of the sport, cricket's future as a major Australian sport may be at risk. As Australia becomes more and more multicultural, its non-white population may identify cricket as being a sport meant only for English-speaking Australians of British and Irish descent. As Richard Cashman points out, for the game to have a long and healthy future "it appears necessary that cricket divest itself of some of its imperial legacies and define itself in more global terms."[35]

The story of cricket in the West Indies is a very different tale. The modern history of the region begins when the islands that constitute the Caribbean became European possessions. This happened largely in the seventeenth century—Barbados, for example, became a British colony in 1627. Three processes defined this early history: the extermination of native tribes like the Caribs that cleared the way for European control; the establishment of a plantation economy, mostly growing sugar, by fortune seekers from Britain, France and the Netherlands; and thirdly, the massive (over 10 million) importation of slave labor from West Africa. Cricket was brought over to the West Indies by the moneyed English elite, for whom the cultivation of cricket was a means of establishing a bond with the culture back "home." It is not a coincidence that the four leading British colonies producing sugar—Barbados, Jamaica, Trinidad and Guyana—were also to become the leading cricketing regions in the Caribbean. While cricket was at first played exclusively by the white population, the intimacy of the island setting—Barbados, which would produce Weekes,

Worrell and Sobers, was a mere 166 square miles in area—meant that it wasn't long before cricket had spread to the black population. This is not to say that the game's organization was race-blind. In Barbados, players of all races played together at school, but after graduation players got placed in a highly stratified system that regulated all club cricket: the white elite played for the Wanderers, the second tier of white society was represented by Pickwick, the black elite went to Spartan, while Empire comprised lower class non-whites. The national cricketing scene was even more racialized—only white players were allowed to participate in the inter-colonial Challenge Cup and to represent the very first West Indies teams. So strong was the prevalent prejudice that Barbados would refuse to play against Trinidad in the Challenge Cup if the latter included any black players. When the first English team under Slade Lucas toured the islands, every team it played was composed exclusively of white players. This situation would, however, not last very long. The next two touring teams—one led by A. Priestley and the other by Lord Hawke—performed well, but both lost their games against Trinidad. Observers noted that Trinidad's success was largely due to the prowess of its two black bowlers, and began to call for an integrated team. The cricketing establishment felt compelled to accede to this demand, and when the first West Indian side to tour England was selected, it included five black players in a party of fifteen.[36] This policy did not remove all the inequities associated with the game. Given that black "professionals" were permitted mainly to bowl and to fetch the ball during practice sessions, it is not surprising that most of the early black cricketers, including L.S. Constantine, father of the great Learie Constantine, tended to be bowlers. Moreover, integration did not remove racial hierarchy—right up to 1957, every West Indies team would be captained by a white player.

Victory over the colonial masters was finally achieved in 1950 when the West Indies team in England, helped by the masterful batting of the "three Ws"—Walcott, Weekes and Worrell—and the mesmeric spin bowling of Sonny Ramadhin and Alf Valentine, won the second Lord's Test by 326 runs, and the entire series by a margin of 3–1. The historic Lord's victory was jubilantly celebrated by the immigrant West Indian population; the ground, according to an observer, "exploded in dance, song and bacchanal."[37] The legendary calypso artists Lord Kitchener and Lord Beginner, who were on hand, rushed onto the field and improvised the song "Cricket, Lovely Cricket" which contained the immortal couplet "Those little pals of mine/Ramadhin and Valentine". Kitchener later composed the marvelous call-and-response couplets describing the 1964 West Indies team:

(Bowl Griffith) Bowl, don't
stop at all
(Bowl Griffith) Give him
back the ball
(Bowl Griffith) Sobers and
Hall
(Bowl Griffith) Bring Gibbs
and all.

This rhyming tradition was continued by Relator who reacted to the first West Indian defeat against India with the following words:

and its Gavaskar
We real master
Just like a wall
We couldn't out Gavaskar at all.

The celebrations in rhyme were prophetic. Following the great leadership, first of Frank Worrell and then of Sobers (both to be knighted after their careers were over), the West Indies were to enter a period of invincibility in the 1970s and 1980s under the ruthlessly efficient captaincy of Clive Lloyd and his immediate successors. During these decades, the West Indies, using the radical tactics of doing away with spin bowling altogether and relying in each match on a quartet of very fast bowlers (drawn from a pool that included Roberts, Holding, Garner, Marshall, Patterson, Walsh, Benjamin, Ambrose, Bishop, Davis, and Gray) were close to unbeatable. The year 1950 was for the West Indies what 1911 was for Bengalis, it set in motion a rising tide of nationalist feeling. As Richard Burton observes "It was as though ... Prospero had taught Caliban the use of the bat and ball only to find himself comprehensively 'out-magicked' by his upstart colonial pupil, thus betraying on the cricket field the vulnerability and fallibility that were becoming more and more evident in the governance of the West Indies as a whole: after 1950 it is argued the 'mother country' would never be quite the same again in West Indian eyes."[38] The brutal history of the islands, the ravages and deprivation caused by colonialism, meant that in the West Indies cricket was much larger than a sport. This truth is best summed up by C.L.R. James in this incomparable passage in *Beyond the Boundary*:

> What do they know of cricket who only cricket know? West Indians crowding to Tests bring with them the whole past history and future hopes of the islands. English people, for example, have a conception of themselves breathed from birth. Drake and mighty Nelson, Shakespeare, Waterloo, the Charge of the Light Brigade, the few who did so much for so many, the success of parliamentary democracy, those and such as those constitute a national tradition. Underdeveloped countries have to go back centuries to rebuild one. We of the West Indies have none at all, none that we know of. To such people the three Ws, Ram and Val wrecking the English batting, help to fill a huge gap in their consciousness and in their needs. In one of the sheds on the Port of Spain wharf is a painted sign: 365 Garfield Sobers.[39]

Cricket, then, is a game that can take on multiple meanings. In Australia, cricket remains true to its origins as a flag bearer of Empire and imperialism, its genteel facade barely concealing its inner core of white exclusivity and privilege. In the West Indies cricket is tied up with the passions of anti-colonial struggles, it gives shape and substance to nationalist aspirations, and in drawing from the sound and rhythms of native culture, it becomes a creolized pursuit which helps to bring forth a new manifestation of the Caribbean nation and soul. This double history points to a central truth: *race is the very essence of cricket*. While no sport is free of racism, perhaps no sport is racialized to the extent cricket is. Thus, the major American sports have had a history of excluding blacks from teams, but by the 1960s most professional teams had been integrated. And though blacks continue to be underrepresented in coaching and in front office positions, there is very little overt racism to be found within the NBA (basketball) the NFL (American football) and the MLB (baseball). European soccer is notorious for its virulently racist atmosphere—black players playing in the various European leagues are routinely subjected to vicious abuse from fans. More shockingly, even administrators reflect these prejudices. Hans Kortnig, president of the Austrian club Sturm Graz explained a loss to Manchester United by saying "We lost because we played against Manchester United—not against any Negermannschaft (nigger team)."[40] However, even European soccer is perhaps not fraught with racist politics at every level in the manner cricket is. When England refused to play their scheduled match in the 2003 World Cup at Zimbabwe because of "security concerns" the ICC, which is the highest governing body of the sport, was strangely reluctant to take any sort of punitive action. As an editorial in the Calcutta *Telegraph* wrote "The International Cricket Council is playing Empire, it is not playing cricket ... The special treatment being given to England in 2003 raises the suspicion that the ICC is being run by a small cabal from within the Long Room at Lord's."[41] The syndrome extends to the field as well. Gloucestershire's David Lawrence recalls this about playing in Yorkshire "I was standing on the boundary line and there was a whole section calling me all the names under the sun ... They called me nigger, black bastard, sambo, monkey, gorilla."[42] It is not just the fans who are guilty of such blatant prejudice. In a recent encounter against Sri Lanka, senior Australian player Darren Lehmann caused a furore when he yelled "Black cunt" at Sri Lanka players. Lehmann's action was not atypical, the Australian cricket journalist Malcolm Knox writes "On a tour to India, I heard two Australian cricketers call the locals 'niggers'. I saw Australian cricketers coming across Indians sleeping on a railway platform in Jamshedpur and nudging them awake with their feet in order to take a happy snap."[43]

The constant series of "incidents" which plague cricket, as well as the constant struggle between white and non-white nations for administrative control of the game illustrate cricket's thoroughly racialized nature which, as we have seen, was the result of both colonization and nationalist movements. The historical and social processes set into motion by decolonization added new complexities to cricket's racialist structure. Following World War II, a large number of people from the colonies and ex-colonies came in to Britain to join the workforce. The thriving immigrant communities which sprang up in London, in the Midlands and in various other urban centers, struggled to assimilate into Anglo-Saxon society. The fault line between the new immigrant cultures and mainstream Britain was clearly exposed when "foreign" teams from South Asia or the West Indies came to play cricket. As we have seen, Britons of Caribbean origin rejoiced when the West Indies defeated England in the historic game at Lord's. That celebration set a pattern which saw immigrant communities cheering for their "home" team against England. This behavior would elicit a backlash in the form of the infamous Tebbit test. Proposed by a Tory backbencher named Norman Tebitt after the 1990 Headingley Test where Bradford-based Asians cheered for Pakistan against England, the test posed the question of national identity and loyalty in the following manner:

> When people come to a new country they should be prepared to immerse themselves totally and utterly in that country ... If someone is looking back to the country from where their family came instead of to the country where they live and make their home, you say are they really integrated or are they just living here?[44]

As many have observed, no such demand was placed on Scots or Irishmen who lived in London but still cheered for Scotland or Ireland. Tebitt's question avoids the fact that white majorities in Britain or Australia have been guilty of making the new immigrants feel unwelcome. When Australian-Indian spectators raise Indian flags at cricket matches, they are not being "disloyal," rather, as Malcolm Knox explains, such an act expresses the resentment Indian fathers feel at their sons being excluded from school teams simply because of cultural difference.[45] The same situation occurs in English cricket as well, forcing minorities to organize their own leagues—the Quaid-i-Azam League in Yorkshire and the Inter-Island Amateur Cricket Cup consisting of West Indian immigrants—in order to compensate for their exclusion from mainstream competition.

If, as is being argued here, cricket is crucially about race, how do we explain the enormous significance of contests—between Australia and England or India and Pakistan for instance—that ostensibly have nothing to do with that concept? The Ashes, it must be remembered, got their importance from the politically fraught relationship between mother country and settler colony. With the decline of Britain as a world power, that relationship has very little urgency. Australians now look to America as a role model; the desire to "thrash the motherland" is part of history. Australia's overwhelming superiority over England—they won the last seven Ashes series before the most recent one—is reminder of the fact that the settlers have finally caught up. Furthermore, it could be argued that the Ashes were important as long as the competition could be framed as a tough but friendly fight between fractions of the same hegemonic race. Once, this hegemony was challenged by the emergence of the non-white nations, the Ashes lost their ideological value. If the England–Australia contest has little meaning attached to it today, that between India and Pakistan is problematic for the opposite reason. Any encounter between the two nations—be it sporting, diplomatic or cultural—is so charged that it is impossible to argue that an India-Pakistan match is about cricket. Thus, when India defeated Pakistan in the 1999 World Cup against the backdrop of the Kargil war, it was reported that Indian soldiers let loose round after round of "happy fire." As an Indian colonel explained, "These are the moments when a bit of indiscipline is ok ... This is a fantastic win and will keep us going in Kargil." And when Pakistan (which had gone on to the finals in spite of the defeat against India) suffered a humiliating loss against Australia, there was jubilation all over the country: a participant in a Bangalore victory procession commented "This means they will be thrown out of Kargil also by India." In Calcutta a government employee bursting firecrackers explained, "I am happy because Pakistan lost. They are always our enemy. Look at what they are doing in Kashmir. This is one way how I can express myself with the Indian army."[46] This scenario was repeated after India's comprehensive victory over Pakistan in the 2003 World Cup. As an editorial in the Calcutta *Telegraph* observed, "Only in India, a cricket match between India and Pakistan acquires the dimensions of war minus shooting. Only in India does the prime minister, the deputy prime minister and the army chief send congratulations to the cricket team for winning a cricket match ... The excess of joy being expressed leads one to suspect that a little more than cricket is involved here."[47] That "little more" is an excess or surplus that emerges from the history of the subcontinent. Since every India-Pakistan encounter is read on either side as a Manichean contest between pure good and pure evil, one could argue that cricket in this context functions not as a sport but a bearer of political metaphysics.

In short, then, neither of these two supposed counter-examples refute the thesis that cricket today is fundamentally a site of struggle between the white and non-white nations that constituted the British Empire. It needs to be stressed that race maps onto matters of wealth, and that the entire history of colonialism is reflected in a set of economic inequalities in the present. White and non-white nations fall neatly on two sides of the economic divide. The following are GDP dollar figures for the year 2002:

Australia ($23,030), the UK ($22,801), and New Zealand ($17,494) on one side, Guyana ($4,877), Jamaica ($3,639), India ($2,136), Pakistan ($1,950) and Bangladesh ($1,546) on the other (with countries like Barbados ($14,528), Trinidad & Tobago ($9,575) and South Africa ($8,466) in the middle because of special factors).[48] These figures, and not runs made or wickets taken, give us cricket's real score.

Lagaan and the meaning of contemporary cricket

It is this truth which underlies the extraordinary popularity of *Lagaan*. Ashutosh Gowarikar's great genius lay in intuitively realizing how fundamental race is to contemporary cricket, and then locating his fictional cricket game in a context—colonial India—where race antagonisms could be depicted in a stark and direct way. *Lagaan* is only superficially about anti-colonialism, for the history of Indian cinema suggests that a film based on that theme alone could never perform so well at the box office. Thus, one would have expected a spate of anti-colonial films in the years immediately following Independence, much like the many war movies churned out by Hollywood after the end of World War II. In fact, though, Indian filmmakers chose to focus on other topics. None of the great films of the period—*Awaara, Pyaasa, Mother India, Do Bigha Zamin*—dealt directly with colonialism. In fact it took a westerner like Richard Attenborough to thematize the issue in *Gandhi*, an English-language film whose major impact was in the West. Most current discussions of the film have gone astray by reading *Lagaan* as a text about the past rather than one about the global present. A protracted debate carried on in the pages of *The Economic and Political Weekly*, for example, centered on the contentious but ultimately undecidable question as to whether the film correctly depicted the reality of Indian society in the last decades of the nineteenth century. Nissim Mannathukkaren dismisses *Lagaan* as "a film which ostensibly has the subaltern as the protagonist, [but] ends up reaffirming the hegemonic nationalist project in which the subaltern has no place."[49] Sudhavana Deshpande also criticizes the film for never showing us a subaltern perspective and for projecting a homogeneous picture of village life. Yet, unlike Mannathukkaren he finds the film to be "important and progressive" because it "imagines an India fairly different from the India we have become used to seeing in commercial Hindi cinema for some time now." In *Lagaan* the leading character is a peasant and not rich; the film proposes communal harmony by including Muslim, Sikh, and Christian characters, and gives a sympathetic account of the low caste character. Within the frame of the cricket match the heroics "are performed by the handicapped dalit Kachra, the Muslim Ismail, and the peasant hero Bhuvan."[50] Such an analysis—and Mannathukkaren and Deshpande are two of the many scholars who approach *Lagaan* this way[51]—is too wedded to the cultural politics of representation, that is, with the question as to who is or is not properly depicted within the film text and whether or not the film can thereby be labeled "progressive". This mode of inquiry is unlikely to be productive; firstly, it is fairly apparent that, in spite of some lip service to subaltern and minority groups, the film is grounded in the nationalist secularist vision that characterized Nehruvian India and is therefore progressive to the extent that the Nehruvian program of social management was. More importantly, an analysis based solely on representational issues cannot account for the phenomenal success of the film, both nationally and internationally. The meaning of *Lagaan*, I want to claim, has far less to do with how it depicts nineteenth-century India than with what it tells us about cricket and race in the present moment. That meaning will become clear only if we take a close look at the story the text tells.

Lagaan is, in its essence, a superbly crafted tale of an encounter between Indians and their white rulers, enacted both in the context of the cricket match played between a group of colonial officials and a team of villagers, as well as in the romantic liaison between Bhuvan, the proto-nationalist captain of the native team, and Elizabeth, a visiting Englishwoman whose sympathies lie with the oppressed "natives". The two climactic events in *Lagaan*—the dramatic victory by the native team that saves the village from a draconian *lagaan* (tax), and the resolution of the love triangle between Bhuvan, Gauri (the village belle) and Elizabeth in Gauri's favor—are both structured by the politics of race. Whites lose twice in *Lagaan*, and it is this double reversal which gives the text its power and appeal. It is the film's racial dimensions which explain the enormous success it enjoyed in the West—thus, Blockbuster, the largest video store outlet in America, continued to give shelf space to *Lagaan* two years past its release. Diasporic Indians, in particular, took to the film because it offered a vision of redemption that resonated with their daily struggles as brown-skinned immigrants. *Lagaan*, then, locates cricket in a racialized past to make a point about the racialized present. That it does so with so much success must lead us to conclude that the game of cricket is itself a part of the racial matrix that the film invokes.

The popularity that *Lagaan* enjoyed was in the end a function of the popularity of cricket; we need, therefore, to return to the point where this chapter started: the nation's obsessive relationship with the sport. Almost every writer who has written on cricket has felt the need to address this phenomenon. The noted cricket historian Ramchandra Guha points out "In the years since India became independent in August 1947, cricket has grown spectacularly in mass appeal ... India's most successful cricketers have been elevated to iconic status, worshipped only as film stars and Hindu deities have been. Cricket is not so much India's national game as its national obsession."[52] Arjun Appadurai, in his seminal essay on cricket and modernity asks "Why is cricket a national passion? Why is it watched with rapt attention in stadia from Sharjah to Madras and in every other context as well? Why are the stars of cricket worshipped, perhaps even more than their counterparts in the cinema?[53] Richard Cashman observes that in "post-colonial times [cricket] became the defining sport of the subcontinent" and that "it is ironic that there are now far stronger prospects for cricket on the subcontinent than in England."[54]

Mihir Bose notes that "Cricket, that very English game is now one of the most prized of Indian institutions ... Nothing could be more English than cricket, yet nothing could be more Indian in the way the sub-continent has taken to the game and fashioned out of it something unique and very different to the English game."[55] Explanations of this "national obsession" fall into one of two modes. The first, best exemplified by Ashis Nandy, contests the view that cricket has to be understood through the lens of colonialism. Nandy provocatively asserts that "Cricket is an Indian game accidentally discovered by the English", and that cricket is a cultural import which "meets a vital need of Indian culture, trying to grapple with the modern world and to make sense of that world in terms of native categories." Cricket, according to Nandy, offers Indians "a new and unique means of self-expression"; it does so because "the culture of cricket is more Indian content-wise and normatively." Given that the nation must negotiate modernity through the West, cricket is an indispensable tool because "whereas in politics or in economy it is a complicated affair to conceptualize and institute a 'manageable West' within the Indian culture, in sports such a West is made available in a readymade form through cricket."[56]

What is distinctive about Nandy's position is not his claim that cricket is a means for expressing the nation's encounters with modernity, but rather his insistence that cricket is the national game because its deep structure mirrors that of Indian society. His text is full of supposed homologies between these structures, thus to the Brahminic, the posture of moral superiority and self-control of the gentleman cricketer was bound to be attractive. The Kshatriyas and the Kshatriya-like found him attractive for his defiance of fate, emphasis on style and sense of honour;[57] Indians, Pakistanis and Sri Lankans, who have a greater cultural respect for fate, have usually shown a greater tolerance for draws;[58] The game, like Hinduism, has too many options; it can be played or understood in different ways;[59] True cricket, for those acquainted with Indian classical music, is like an *alap* or an *ativilambit kheyal*.[60] It is hard to know what sense one might make of such a thesis. If cricket is like Hinduism, why is it so popular in Pakistan? And would Nandy have us also say that cricket is a West Indian game "accidentally invented by the English"? Quadri Ismail has complained that "Nandy consistently flouts the protocols of conventional argumentation ... he flitters often from point to point without any effort to connect them; and oftener, makes grand assertions without backing them up."[61] That may well be the case, but more importantly, Nandy's theory has far more baggage than most are willing to carry. Thus, in spite of Nandy's seminal work in other areas, his views on cricket have found very few takers. Only one other writer perhaps comes close to endorsing Nandy's essentialist position. In *A Corner of a Foreign Field*—probably the best book on Indian cricket yet written—Ramachandra Guha confesses that "It is easier to document (and celebrate) the Indian love for cricket than to analyse or explain it"[62] but he falls to the temptation anyway. Thus:

> Five days or thirty hours: an unconscionably long time for an industrial and industrious American, but a bare wink of the eye to the Indian. Cricket fits easily with the rhythms of what is still—in its essence—an agrarian culture, accustomed to thinking in cosmic and calendric rather than clock time. Indians have no difficulty in aimlessly filling up the hours. Consider how they will stop to gaze at the scene of an accident: passengers leaning out of a bus window, the driver too; joined by cyclists, motor-cyclists, car owners and pedestrians: all looking, looking, looking. (An American would rush past without a glance or were his Christian conscience to prompt him, at least get the injured on their way to a hospital).
>
> The uncertainty is gripping, and at the end of the five days there might not even be a conclusion, a 'draw' rather than a win for either side, an outcome that has a curious appeal for the Hindu, many of whose myths stress negotiation and compromise rather than unequivocal victory or defeat.

Cricket watching is a collective and participatory exercise, indulging the Indian taste for chatter and disputation, gossip and debate.

Indians have more time; Indians like doing things together; Hindus don't really mind a 'draw'; Hindus are culturally syncretic and choose to absorb foreign imports rather than reject them: these are the lines on which we might begin to explain the extraordinary Indian love for cricket.[63]

The problem with this approach is that it tends to overlook inconvenient details. Indians do "stop to gaze at the scene of an accident", but Americans too are notorious for "rubbernecking" that is, for turning their necks to look at such scenes—a practice that often leads to long traffic jams and even to secondary accidents. Moreover, Guha fails to address the puzzle why the English— surely the first "industrial and industrious" people of the modern era—happened to devise a game that lasted "an unconscionably long time." Furthermore, how did English lawmakers, unexposed to myths which stress "negotiation and compromise", come up with the notion of a draw? And if cricket is actually Hindu at the deep structural level, then would the many memorable games involving names like Trumper, Hobbs, Hammond or Bradman be mere epiphenomena or *maya*? I would like to argue that there is absolutely *nothing* intrinsically Indian or Hindu about cricket. For if it was indeed so, it would then be a *miracle*, and not merely an *accident* that the game was invented by the English. Rather, as our discussion demonstrated, cricket, from its very inception, was a signifying tool capable of taking on a variety of meanings. This semantic plasticity has little to do with the formal features of the game. Guha is too acute a thinker not to realize this, for in a sentence that follows the last quote given above ("Indians have more time...") he adds the coda that "To these cultural factors we must now add a strictly instrumental one: the motive of national pride."[63]

This sentiment bridges the divide between the structural-essentialist reading proposed by Nandy and Guha to a more discursive-constructivist approach which finds its most sophisticated expression in Arjun Appadurai's essay "Playing with Modernity: The Decolonization of Indian cricket." Appadurai characterizes his approach by observing that while for Nandy "there are mythic structures beneath the surface of the sport which make it profoundly Indian in spite of its Western origins", his own work tries to show "that cricket became indigenized through a set of complex and contradictory processes that parallel the emergence of an Indian 'nation' from the British Empire."[65] Princely cricket was perhaps the first forum where indigenization began, followed by the vernacularization of the game, as in the use of Hindi cricketing terms. These processes help to set up "a complex set of experiential and pedagogical loops ... through which the reception of cricket becomes a critical instrument of subjectivity and agency in decolonization."[66] On the production end, Appadurai points to the role of both the state (through extensive media coverage of the sport) and business corporations (by patronizing individual cricketers) in the development of the game in the first three decades after Independence. In the last two decades, television has turned cricket into spectacle, enabling a rampant commodification of the game. However, none of these factors explain why cricket is the national passion that it is, and Appadurai makes what he terms a "speculative leap" and hypothesizes that "cricket is the ideal focus for national attention and nationalist passion because it affords the experience of experimenting with what might be called the 'means of modernity' to a wide variety of groups within Indian society."[67] To take two of the examples he offers: cricket offers the private sector a means of linking leisure, stardom and merchandise; and to the lumpen youth it gives the sense of group belonging, potential violence and bodily excitement characteristic of football passion in England. Cricket is the premier sport in the country because it meets these and other vital needs, Appadurai concludes his essay with an observation reminiscent of Voltaire's thoughts on the existence of God "If it [cricket] did not exist in India, something like it would certainly have been invented for the conduct of public experiments with the means of modernity."[68]

Appadurai's essay is an elegant example of a fruitful marriage between cultural studies and postcolonial theory whose argument can be briefly summed up as follows: Cricket, at one time a hegemonizing tool for Empire, has over the decades been appropriated by Indians in ways which subvert its original meaning and purpose. The passage of cricket from high Victorian sport to desi *khel* parallels that of the colony to nation. The story of Indian cricket is therefore the story of decolonization. Impressive as this postulation is, two of its aspects should give us pause. Firstly, Appadurai's line of thinking ends up positing an Indian "nation" which seems to be an inclusive and unitary entity. Cricket, for Appadurai, is a means of nation-building which fuses disparate groups into one cricket-loving whole. Recent work on this topic suggests that the opposite may be true. Cricket, according to some contemporary writers creates ideological versions of the nation which define themselves through a deliberate exclusion of marginal groups. Discussing the case of Sri Lanka, Quadri Ismail has argued that "the meaning of cricket cannot be exhausted by nationalism" and that "the current discourse on cricket needs revision."[69] He relates the response given by Lawrence Thilakar, Paris-based spokesperson of the LTTE, who, when asked about his views on the Australia–Sri Lanka World Cup final, replied "All Tamils in the North and East love cricket. It's a part of their lives in school. All the schoolchildren love cricket and football ... I cannot wish Australia to win. At the same time it is difficult to wish Sri Lanka to win."[70] Ismail observes that while Sinhala nationalism demands that all citizens, Sinhalese, Muslim, Burgher and Tamil cheer the team as one, this hegemonic move is disrupted by Tamil nationalism. Indeed, it is possible, as Thilakar's reply suggests, to support a cricket team, but not the illusory nation which that team is supposed to represent. In other words, cricket reveals the fractures of a nation as much as its continuities. Arguing in a similar vein, Ian McDonald suggests that somewhat paradoxically it is "in the context of India's policy of globalization that the 'capitalist modernization' of cricket becomes particularly prone to exploitation by communalist forces."[71] McDonald resurrects a repressed episode of Indian cricketing history that has been long forgotten: the kiss of Abbas Ali Baig. Batting valiantly against the Australians at the Brabourne Test of 1960, Baig, on reaching his fifty, was rewarded with a kiss by a young Hindu woman. The kiss created a scandal, and retribution followed when Baig failed to perform against Pakistan in the following series. Baig went from hero to a Pakistani fifth columnist, was dropped from the national team and ended his promising career in ignominy. McDonald observes that "the scapegoating of Abbas Ali Baig can be seen, not as the expression of a backward and residual force, but as an incipient and modern form of Hindu communalism."[72]

As we see today—whether in the actions of the Shiv Sena whenever matches with Pakistan are proposed, or in the virulent anti-Pakistani and anti-Muslim sentiments displayed by fans at various venues—the globalization of cricket has fuelled communal tensions between Hindus and Muslims. And not even all Hindus may be served well by cricket. As the Dalit writer S. Anand has forcefully argued, cricket in India has been dominated by the upper castes. Thus "Through the 1960s till the 1990s, Test-playing Indian teams have averaged at least six Brahmins, sometimes even nine. And this despite Brahmins comprising a little over 4 per cent of the population."[73] We must then go beyond Appadurai to argue that in an age of globalization, cricket may often serve not to give coherence to the nation but instead to foster sub-nationalisms based on a divisive politics of ethnicity and religion. Appadurai's benevolent characterization of cricket may well be due to his reliance on the functionalist mode of explanation that he employs. Appadurai reduces cricket to a list of purposes or functions that it fulfils, thereby locating it entirely within a rational domain. It needs to be asked however whether such a strategy is sufficient to account for what Appadurai himself terms "a national passion". Passions and obsessions are fuelled by contradiction and lack, and if Appadurai's analysis "does not go as far as it might," it is because he makes no use of such categories, relying instead on the explanatory powers of a utilitarian calculus. How then do we analyze cricket? The best place to start is not with the record television audiences that cricket draws, or the stellar contracts signed by superstars like Tendulkar, but instead on instances of silence and lack:

> As a direct—though paradoxical—corollary of cricket being our only chance to have a crack at world domination ... we Indians are not the least bit interested in domestic cricket. No one except rookie sports reporters go to watch a Ranji Trophy match.[74]

> Was a Mumbai Ranji player ever introduced as a "local hero"? If we so love cricket, why can't we name all the 11 players who play for Mumbai or Delhi? Because, in reality, we do not care for sports or our sportsmen. We only love heroes. And heroes are only those who represent us in the league of nations.[75]

> The new Ranji season started on a dull, drab November morning, and at Delhi's Ferozeshah Kotla, when play got under way, the setting for cricket was far from perfect ... the cricket arena is decidedly unattractive. As Ranji has no sponsorship, there are no advertising runners round the field, no banners on the sight screen, no hoardings in sight. There are no crowds either—on day one of this season, as Delhi played Railways in the elite group, there were not enough people to fill a first class coach of a train.[76]

These subjective impressions are backed up by objective data. The following set of figures showing daily attendance in Ranji and Duleep Trophy matches for the 1999–2000 season (when cricket hysteria was at least a decade old) are: In Bangalore between 2000 and 6000, in Kerala around 1000, in Mumbai around 200–300 (for zonal league matches), in Chennai between 200–300, in Goa and Delhi between 50–60.[77] What these figures irrefutably demonstrate is that far from being an "Indian sport", cricket seems barely present at the domestic level. Consider the sporting scene in Bengal. As is well known, sport in Bengal is synonymous with the rivalry between two institutions—Mohun Bagan and East Bengal. The enthusiasm surrounding games between these teams is legendary, the 2000 East Bengal-Mohun Bagan football match in the Super League Derby, for example, could draw a crowd of 80,000. Fans in Kolkata are no less devoted when it comes to international cricket— Eden Gardens regularly produces the largest gates in India for Test and one-day matches. Quite astonishingly, no one shows up when Mohun Bagan and East Bengal play each other at cricket! How does one explain this negation? We can take our cue from Manu Joseph's observation that cricket's function is solely to represent us in the "league of nations." In other words, cricket is not internal to the culture; it has no meaning whatsoever as domestic sporting practice. Rather, its place is beyond the boundary, located at the point where nation meets the world. The domestic game is insubstantial because it is a mere rehearsal for the show that really matters. In the end, all cricket is international cricket.

We need, finally, to identify the specific ways in which cricket helps to create a global nation. Globalization is commonly thought of as consisting of the following set of components: a set of economic processes like offshoring, business process outsourcing, and bodyshopping whose material consequence is the rise of global delivery centers in siliconized cities like Bangalore and Hyderabad; the political regulation of economic policies in developing nations through the agencies of institutions like the IMF and the World Bank; the informational networking of the entire globe enabled by cable and satellite television and by the Internet; and the rise of a spectacular consumer culture facilitated by advertising and mass media. If globalization is in these instances characterized by different modes of excess, it is at the same time a condition of lack. A poll conducted in 2003 by *The Hindustan Times* to measure the attitudes of Indian youth, found that more than half the respondents would prefer to live in another country.[78] The desire to be elsewhere, to be one's own other, is symptomatic of an evacuated self, of a hole in the heart. And since the "another country" where these young people want to be are the white nations of the western world, globalization at a psychic level can be said to be partly constituted by a racialized lack. Such a diagnosis might explain the existence of "Western" bars in Japan where local patrons go dressed in boots and cowboy hats, or the practice, in contemporary China, of naming and modeling local suburbs after those in California. Cricket, too, is part of this complex. Born in the colonial era, Indian cricket in its early days was simply a matter of imitating the ruling class. Because of its communal character it never enjoyed the nationalist moment that it did, for example, in the West Indies. In the era after Independence, cricket began to grow in popularity and importance but it shared the stage with other sports and had not reached the status of a national obsession. This was no doubt partly due to the abysmal level of competence (losing 0–5 in a series was almost a normal outcome) of our cricketers at the international level. More crucially, cricket was not the site of lack that it would be in the age of globalization. Postcoloniality, can in retrospect, be seen as a period which placed great faith in an Indian way of doing things. This third way—associated with concepts like non-alignment, the public sector, and socialism—insulated us from the processes of late capitalism already in place in the western world. With the collapse of the Nehruvian project by the 1980s, the nation had no other choice, as it were, but to rejoin capitalism at the global level. That primal moment of reentry (symbolized by the word "liberalization") instituted an ontology of lack whose cultural manifestations compose the frenetic mediated space of consumerism that we inhabit. The hysteria over cricket is thus the tremor of the liminal, of the pangs of passage from one order to another. And in its other aspect, cricket is also retribution, the Battle of Plassey reconstituted as a battle over Lord's. In the last analysis, then, cricket plays out the vicissitudes of the nation's psyche as it negotiates the long journey from colony to global power.

2
Tragedy in Two Acts
The Sudden Death of Hockey and Football

At the time of Independence, a triumvirate of team sports dominated the Indian sporting scene: cricket with its rich tradition of Pentangular and Test matches; football which by then had flourishing tournaments like the Durand, the Rovers and IFA Shield; and hockey, the game that had brought the Indian team the most glory and international recognition with the astonishing victories in the Olympics of 1928, 1932 and 1936. Cricketers like Nayudu, Merchant and Mankad may have been household names but so were hockey stars like Dhyan Chand, Roop Singh and K.D. Singh "Babu." By the end of the century however, cricket had completely outstripped its two competitors in terms of fan interest, sponsorship and media coverage. Today hockey and football have shrinking fan bases, attract very little money, and get scant coverage on television and other media. The decline of hockey and football and their relegation to the status of second class sports has typically been blamed on bad management and lack of corporate sponsorship. According to this line of argument, these sports would be restored to their former glory if organizations like the IHF and the AIFF would change their antiquated mindsets and if corporate managers would change advertising policy and begin to divert sponsorship funds from cricket to needier sports. It is my argument in this chapter that such an analysis is unduly optimistic and based on an inadequate understanding of the role and meaning of these sports in contemporary India. Indeed, if the current forces of liberalization and globalization continue to hold sway, my own analysis suggests that hockey and football will remain second class sports in the years to come and may become even more insignificant.

Hockey has had the paradoxical status of being unloved in spite of the great achievements of our teams. Asked in 1932 if he would release funds for the Olympic team, Mahatma Gandhi replied "What is hockey?"[1] In this respect at least, all Indians are Gandhian now. It is doubtful whether the average person can name the entire national hockey team. As Shekhar Gupta of the *Indian Express* writes "Our kids are not lining up to collect posters of Pillai, Prabhjyot, Dileep Tirkey, Jugraj Singh. Nor are advertisers vying to sign them up to sell soap, shampoo, shaving creams, even *gutka* and *paan masala*. In fact, many of you might still not have heard these names."[2] To take a random example that illustrates the neglect of this once-popular game: the May 21–27, 2003, web issue of *Sportstar*, a leading sports magazine, contained 13 pieces on cricket, four on football and only one on hockey. As an anonymous writer on the website *bharatiya.com* puts it, sports magazines exhibit a herd mentality in promoting cricket at the expense of all other Indian sports. Thus, when India won the three-nation Hockey Challenge in Australia, *Sportstar* "whose business is to cover sports, totally ignored the tournament ... while the first leg of the Hockey Challenge was going on in Perth it featured a cover story on the 'Accidental Chucker in Cricket' and during the second leg its cover story focused 'on how New Zealand captain Stephen Fleming is similar to another Australian captain Mark Taylor.' Are these worthy of fawning cover stories?" Broadcast media has reflected print's lack of interest in hockey, both ESPN and Star Sports regularly

favor American football and basketball, New Zealand rugby and
Formula One racing, over Indian hockey. The Indian team's
victories in Sydney and in Hamburg in 2003 were not shown on
television. As a TV executive explained "We wanted to show the
matches, especially the ones featuring India and Pakistan, but no
sponsor was willing to bear the expenses."[3] And the administrators
of the game have shown little initiative in improving conditions.
Thus, while the cricketing body BCCI decided to pay every player
participating in the domestic Ranji Trophy a match fee of Rs.
35,000, the captain of the Indian hockey team gets nothing for
representing the country. And when hockey players tour abroad
they get a meager daily allowance of 20 dollars; in comparison
Indian cricketers receive fees of 2,800 dollars for a single one-day
international, and an out-of-pocket allowance of 60 dollars a day.
Unlike cricket or even football, Indian hockey's domestic structure
is virtually non-existent. Top teams compete in an informal circuit
of a handful of tournaments. There is no "National League" as
in football, and the national hockey team no longer has a sponsor
after oil major Castrol, in a cost-cutting measure, withdrew support
in May 2003. The rest of the world plays on artificial turf, but
there are only 15 such surfaces in India.[4] And while the BCCI is
introducing the Cricketer's Insurance Scheme to replace an already
existing benevolent fund, the Indian Hockey Federation neither
has a benevolent fund, nor a player insurance scheme, and,
to make matters worse, rarely organizes benefit matches for
retiring players.

Hockey: The Glory Days

Like almost every other modern sport—barring the American
ones—hockey was "invented" in 19th century Britain. While
historical records show that some form of field hockey was played
in both Ancient Egypt and Greece, the antecedents of modern
hockey lie more directly in the version of the sport prevalent
in 17th and 18th century England. Hockey as it was played then

consisted of whole villages playing the game, the objective being that of hitting the hockey ball into the opposing village's common ground. Teams consisted of 60 to 100 players and games went on for several days. As in so many other spheres of public life, Victorian discipline reined in and codified this chaotic practice sometime in the mid-nineteenth century. The first rules for hockey were written in the 1860s at Eton College, and the game was promoted as an alternative to football for cricketers seeking a winter sport. Modern hockey was, from its very beginning, parasitic on the major sports. Thus, the two clubs responsible for the development of the game were named the Blackheath Football and Hockey Club and the Teddington Cricket Club. It was at Teddington that some of the crucial innovations were made including that of substituting a rubber cube by the modern sphere-shaped ball. A movement for a governing body was led by the Teddington Club and resulted in the formation of the British Hockey Association in 1886. The Association was initially confined to wealthy London suburban clubs along with Trinity College Cambridge. This restricted milieu meant "that ladies could take up a game that had achieved social respectability but was not yet widely known as a specifically male sport."[5] The very first international hockey match was played between England and Ireland in 1890 and by 1908 the men's game had been included in the Olympics. Though hockey was dropped from the 1912 Stockholm and the 1924 Paris Olympics, the founding of the International Hockey Federation in 1924 put the game on firmer ground. Starting from the 1928 Amsterdam games, men's hockey has been played in every Olympics; women's hockey was introduced in 1980 and has become a regular presence at the international level. The game now has global reach—the current nations ranked in the top ten of men's hockey include four from Europe (Germany, Netherlands, England, Spain); three from Asia (Korea, Pakistan, India), one from South America (Argentina) as well as Australia and New Zealand.[6] In spite of the rapidity with which it was organized and spread across the globe, hockey did not become a popular sport in the country of its birth. Football too had begun as an elite sport, but it quickly transformed itself into a game for the masses. Hockey clearly failed in this regard; hockey teams did not galvanize entire cities in the manner of clubs like Liverpool or Manchester United, and the game never enjoyed the passionate following that filled the terraces of football matches every Saturday. The reason for this may lie in economics; the British working class probably lacked the time and the disposable income to patronize two different team sports. More curiously, hockey failed to become an elite sport like cricket or rugby. Its rapid popularity among women probably had the effect of diminishing its appeal to upper class males, and the fact that it was not well patronized by public schools and the universities meant that its status as an upper class sport was placed in jeopardy. In fact, within a few years of its birth, modern hockey was literally consigned to a "no-man's land," becoming a game for middle class women and a handful of middle-class men. Devoid of either snobbery or passion, hockey came to be characterized by the dour pragmatism associated with philosophies of health and self-improvement. That connotation has been hard to shed; and even though the country is currently ranked in the world top ten in both the men's and women's sections, British hockey continues to be a most unglamorous pursuit:

> In England it [hockey] is a popular family oriented sport, played mainly in the clubs by both men and women. The game is well-liked in many schools, particularly in the independent sector and offers a lifetime of both sporting and social opportunities for players, officials and administrators alike.[7]

> Waltham Forest is a friendly field hockey club in North East London with 3 men's and 3 women's hockey teams, as well as a mixed side ... We were established in 1989, and play field hockey in Walthamstow, North East London. The hockey we play is competitive yet fun! The teams cover a wide range of playing abilities and we encourage players of all standards to join.[8]

The wholesome and stodgy picture evoked by these descriptions is even truer in the American context. Hockey was introduced to the

US by an English physical instructor named Constance Applebee at the very beginning of the twentieth century. Applebee had been attending a seminar at Harvard University and was appalled by the mild parlor games that passed for exercise among young American women. She organized a game behind the Harvard gymnasium; this first hockey match staged on American soil, held in 1901, proved very popular and soon the sport spread to most of the prestigious women's schools in the region.[9] Men's hockey did not start till much later, the first match between teams from Westchester and Philadelphia took place in 1928. The US did field a men's team at the 1932 Los Angeles Olympics—the team finished third in a three-team tournament losing 9–2 to Japan and 24–1 to India. That loss proved to be a bad omen; hockey never succeeded in attracting American men, being considered too effete and precious by a machismo culture which valued brute contact sports like American football and ice hockey. Hockey was gendered more strongly in America than in Britain, and has remained till today a college sport played almost exclusively by women.

Hockey came to India through the agency of army officers who introduced it in the 1880s. The game spread quickly, and Indians showed a remarkable aptitude for the game, even changing the shape of the stick so that the ball could be dribbled more easily.[10] The Indian Hockey Federation was founded in 1925, and the country made its international debut at the 1928 Amsterdam Olympics. Led by Jaipal Singh (and by Eric Pinniger in the finals) the team, which included the legendary Dhyan Chand, won the gold medal by beating Holland 3–0 in the final. So outstanding was the Indian performance that a Dutch journalist wrote, "The Indian ball seems ignorant of the laws of gravity. One of those tanned diabolical jugglers stares at the ball intently; it gets upright and remains suspended in the air. This is no longer the game of hockey. It is a juggling turn. It is splendid."[11] India would win five more Olympic gold medals—in 1932, 1948, 1952, 1964 and 1980—but soon after Indian hockey would go into a precipitous decline from which it is yet to fully recover. Since its last victory in the boycott-ridden Moscow Olympics of 1980, India has failed to win even a bronze medal in the sport it once dominated. World Cup results (the World Cup in hockey was inaugurated in 1971) show a similar trend—after winning the bronze, silver and gold in the first three tournaments, the team has finished 10th, 5th, 9th and 10th in the last four World Cups. It ought to be obvious that any analysis of Indian hockey must begin by addressing this dramatic drop in our performance. We need therefore to start our inquiry by asking two simple, almost childish, questions: why were we so good at hockey, and why have we declined so much?

Three sorts of answers have traditionally been offered in response to such queries. The first explanation demystifies the golden age by arguing that Indians were invincible only because the opposition was not serious about playing hockey. This theory of *relative* excellence may have applied in some cases, but it is hard to accept the assertion that all the Indian teams from 1928 to 1964 failed to meet *absolute* standards of excellence. The Dutch journalist quoted above was not the only foreigner to be dazzled by the magic of Indian hockey. After India's outstanding performance at the Los Angeles Olympics, a correspondent observed:

> All the color, glamour and pageantry of Rudyard Kipling's India might well have found its incarnation in the personnel of the Indian team which is to represent the land of Mahatma Gandhi. So agile are the members of the team that they can run the full length of the hockey field, juggling a small wooden ball with the flat of a hockey stick.[12]

This may have been orientalist rhetoric, but the tribute by Los Angeles journalists who voted the Indian team's showing as the "most outstanding exhibition of skill in any sport" removes any doubt about the intrinsic worth of the Indian team. Moreover, the Indian team was winning matches as late as the early 1960s against teams from Australia, Great Britain, the Netherlands and West Germany. Given the fact that the Indian team consistently won almost all its matches against the best international competition for over forty years, we must conclude that something was very right about Indian hockey in this period.

A second school of explanation grants excellence to early Indian hockey and claims that its decline occurred because it did not adapt itself to the evolution of modern hockey. The changes in playing surfaces, in rules and in styles of play, it is argued, helped the European nations catch up and eventually surpass subcontinental hockey. Thus Sandip Singh, sports journalist, observes that most Indian players lack the stamina to withstand the pace of the game on synthetic surfaces. This happens because "Indians grow up on grass fields and the switch to playing on synthetic pitches is not always easy and this only takes place at an advanced stage, quite often only when players reach national level."[13] There is considerable truth to such a line of argument. Most decision and rule-making bodies in international sports are controlled by the western nations. Quite predictably therefore, changes in the game tend to favor the styles and cultures of these nations thus making dubious the notion of a level playing field. Yet this fact alone is not sufficient to explain the dire straits that Indian hockey finds itself in. Cricket too has evolved under the demands of modernity—the introduction of the one-day game being the most significant—yet Indian cricket has had no difficulty in adapting to such changes and in achieving success at the international level. Moreover, such an argument is unnecessarily defeatist, for it seems to suggest—in a manner redolent of economic discussions concerning tradition and modernity—that the postcolonial nations are destined not to achieve parity with the West. Such a stance is not well-founded; the amazing success of the Indian software industry is an illustration that development is possible everywhere regardless of previous status. Indeed, results in recent hockey tournaments suggest that the Indian team may be finally closing the gap between teams like the Netherlands, Australia and itself.

The third and most persuasive analysis of hockey's status comes from those who approach it from the perspective of economics and management. The basic argument here is that in the post-Independence period hockey lost out to other sports in terms of its capacity to attract corporate sponsorship. Cricket is the villain of the piece here, for it is seen as having drawn away potential players and fans as well as siphoning off most of the available sponsorship revenues. Thus Sandip Singh observes:

> With cricket taking over as the national sport since the late 1960s, hockey is no longer glamorous. The number of boys and girls playing the game diminished drastically as it was no longer fashionable.[14]

And Dhanraj Pillai, India's only hockey superstar complains:

> I don't know why corporates do not show interest in hockey despite our repeated success. Cricket has enough resources. It is time money came to hockey and other sports. How can you expect an Olympic medal without financially backing the sport? "[15]

Most observers of the contemporary sports scene in India would agree with Pillai that cricket sucks away a disproportionate amount of available sponsorship, leaving sports like hockey and football to beg for survival. But those who blame cricket must explain why sports funding in India is a zero-sum game where cricket's gain entails an equivalent loss for other sports. As Navroze Dhondy, an advertising executive, rightly points out: "Every big country has at least three major sports; India is the only aberration in the world. There is space in India for at least two more sports to get a big chunk of the business and the fan following."[16] The crux of the problem lies not with cricket's drawing power but with hockey's (or football's) lack of "glamour". Advertising does not flow to these sports because they are not seen as attractive enough in terms of cultural appeal and therefore of revenue-generating potential. Pointing an accusing finger at cricket is not enough, only an analysis which takes into account hockey's various meanings as a cultural text will be able to discern why the game has failed to attract fans and investors. Those who diagnose the current situation as a management problem tend to focus on faulty decision-making as the source of the problem and refuse to adequately acknowledge the role of culture in determining a sport's fate, thus inhibiting the scope and power of their analysis. Sandip Singh exemplifies this tendency when he accuses politically motivated administrators of playing a major part in the game's demise "by playing politics in the regions, in terms of selecting players, coaches and management."[17] No one would demur with Singh's contention that such considerations have harmed Indian hockey, but it is incumbent on him to explain why only hockey succumbed to these evils. After all, cricket too has been beset by the worst sort of politicking but has still attained unprecedented success. A similar flaw in reasoning mars other contemporary analyses of modern hockey. Thus Harsha Bhogle diagnoses hockey as suffering from "three viruses that seem to have proprietary rights over Indian sport: pompous federations, abominable television and the inability to see the difference between philanthropy and sponsorship." Bhogle too blames the game's administrators for its inability to duplicate cricket's success:

> Actually India needs to rediscover another sport and might well have had, if the custodians of other sports had not made it so easy for cricket. If there is only one marketable sport in India, it is partly because the BCCI sold itself hard and because the others sold themselves short. Cricket needs a rival but the others are unwilling to play that role. They may talk about it, but playing it is a different matter.[18]

According to Shekhar Gupta, Indian hockey's decline coincided with the arrival of live television and big sponsorship money. Sponsors needed stars to sell their products, but hockey lacked visible names like Gavaskar and Kapil Dev. Thus, at the crucial moment when advertising money began to flow into sports via the medium of television, hockey lost out to cricket because of its lack of star figures. Rather than admit any shortcoming in the game itself, Gupta blames those who managed hockey for letting this opportunity slip by: "The hockey establishment too was happy to let things drift. If there was anything they hated more than losing, it was the hockey star. So the moment one reared his head, it was squashed. And the basic principle of modern sports is, no stars, no cash."[19] Like Singh and Bhogle, Gupta's analysis begs a crucial question, namely why cricket bosses did not behave like their counterparts in hockey. Gupta has to resort to conspiracy theories, because, like the others, he is loath to admit that the real problem may lie with the nature of the game.

Communal Hockey

The failure of hockey to establish itself as a major sport is a function of its meaning in the context of Indian modernity. We have seen that hockey was a second class sport when it was brought over by the British in the late nineteenth century. Its reception in India was quite different from what it was in western contexts. Hockey would not become a sport for women as it did in the United States, since the Indian social milieu precluded team sports for women. Instead, hockey was enthusiastically taken up by minorities within Indian society: Anglo-Indians, Muslims and Sikhs. Many of the earlier players came from the public schools, a fact that may explain the large presence of Anglo-Indians. As a British observer recalled, "in the 20s and 30s practically the entire Olympic teams representing India were composed of young men from hill schools, St. George's, Oakgrove, Bishop Cotton's, etc."[20] The composition of the 1928 Olympic team bears this out:

Jaipal Singh (captain), Broome Eric Pininger (vice-captain), Shaukat Ali, Richard Allen (goalkeeper), Dhyan Chand, Maurice

Gately, William James Goodsir-Cullen, Leslie Hammond, Feroze Khan, George E. Mathins, Rex A.O. Norris, Michael E. Rocque, Nawab of Pataudi, Frederick S. Seaman, Kher Singh, Syed M. Yusuf.

Except for Dhyan Chand, the entire team consists of minority players! Judging by first and last names, nine out of the 16 players are Anglo-Indians/Christians, four are Muslim and two are Sikh. Things would remain the same for the 1932 team captained by Lal Shah Bokhari (who migrated to Pakistan and would later become that country's High Commissioner to Sri Lanka): eight Anglo-Indians/Christians, four Muslims, two Sikhs, with Dhyan Chand and his brother Roop Singh being the only two Hindus. The 1936 Berlin squad showed a gradual increase in the number of Muslim players:

Dhyan Chand (captain), Richard Allen (goalkeeper), Ali Iqtidar Dara, Lionel C. Emmett, Paul Peter Fernandes, Joseph Galibardy, Earnest John Goodsir-Cullen, Mohammed Hussain, Syed Mohammed Jafar, Ahsan Mohammed Khan, Ahmed Sher Khan, Mirza Nasir-ud-din Masud, Cyril J. Mitchie, Babu Narsoo Nimal, Joseph Philips, Shabban Shahab-ud-din, Gurcharan Singh Garewal, Roop Singh.

The communal break up of this squad, which would be the last team representing undivided India at this level of competition was: seven Anglo-Indians, seven Muslims, one Sikh and three Hindus. Counting by communities may seem to be a dubious methodology; my purpose here is to demonstrate that while it is commonly known that early Indian cricket (in the period 1886–1944) was organized and played along communal lines, Indian hockey can also be described in similar terms. While in cricket, teams were constituted on communal lines—Parsis, Hindus, Muslims— in hockey the entire pool of hockey players was determined by communal origins. In the period up to Independence, Anglo-Indians and Muslims were the two communities that provided almost all of India's notable hockey players. With the coming of Independence and Partition a great majority of these players were lost due to migration; the resultant void was filled by athletes from another minority community: Sikhs. The change in the ethnic composition is strikingly brought out by the 1964 Olympic team which won gold in Tokyo: ten Sikhs, two Anglo-Indians/Christians, three Hindus and one Muslim. Sikhs would continue to dominate the team for a couple of decades, causing jokes like the British cartoon whose caption read "Singh passes the ball to Singh who passes to Singh." By the turn of the millennium things had changed again, as evidenced by the team which represented India at the 2002 Kuala Lumpur World Cup:

Baljit Singh Dhillon (captain), Jude Menezes, Devesh Chauhan, Dileep Tirkey, Lajarus Barla, Kanwalpreet Singh, Jugraj Singh, Sukhbir Singh Gill, Ignace Tirkey, Selvaraj Thirumalvalavan, Arjun Halappa, Baljeet Singh Saini, Dhanraj Pillai, Sabu Varkey, Daljeet Singh Dhillon, Deepak Thakur, Prabhjyot Singh, Bipin Fernandez.

Tribals are the latest minority group to succeed at hockey. Dilip Tirkey, a tribal from Orissa, has captained the national team, and as Shekhar Gupta asserts in praise of hockey "when do you see an Oraon or a Santhal or a Manipuri becoming the captain of the national team? In hockey, just try to keep them out!"[21] Hockey, then, must be understood as a game primarily played by minorities—Anglo-Indians, Muslims, Sikhs, tribals. Why was this so? Any account of Indian hockey must come to terms with the extreme paucity of data and analysis concerning the social factors that constituted the game. The reading of hockey that I provide below must be seen as largely speculative, intended more to provoke questions than to provide any definitive answers.

The context of late nineteenth-century India entailed that every sport was inserted into the politics of colonialism and nationalism. Cricket, as we have seen in the previous chapter, was conceived of as a means to achieve modernity, and to challenge colonial authority. The game was doubly political, not only did it articulate the passions of the colonized vis-à-vis the British; it simultaneously became the mirror for the struggle between Hindu and Muslim nationalisms. Football was also seen as an instrument of nationalist consciousness, especially after Mohun Bagan's historic victory over an English team in the finals of the 1911 IFA Shield trophy. Hockey's early history seems to be far more passive. In a period when all sports—from bodybuilding to cricket—were intensely political, it existed in the negative, so to speak, as a mere game. Indeed, the fact that it was so enthusiastically embraced by the Anglo-Indian community, may suggest that its politics, if any, was of a loyalist stripe. The absence of politics may explain the tepid nature of the domestic game; in spite of India's spectacular performances at the international level, there is little evidence to show that local tournaments could command the level of attendance and involvement associated with Bombay cricket or Calcutta football.

The relative silence surrounding hockey enables an alternative reading, one at odds with nostalgic and misplaced descriptions of hockey being India's "national sport." Far from being "national," hockey has been that Indian sport within whose frame the category of "nation" has been continuously interrogated and destabilized. As we have seen, the story of Indian hockey, from its very inception, has been the saga of the exploits of successive groups of minorities. Each chapter in this saga constitutes a politics of negation, of bringing into question the idea of nation as imagined by a dominant group of nation-builders. There is, unfortunately, very little work which has examined the ideological constructions which sustained the Anglo-Indian community in the decades leading up to Independence. Indian by skin and culture, yet compelled by genealogy and colonial politics to owe loyalty to an idea of Britain, Anglo-Indians were subject to an irreconcilable contradiction whose only resolution was tragedy. Those who migrated to Britain or Australia never quite found "home" to be what they had imagined; those who stayed behind saw their unique culture fray and fade away, a process memorably portrayed in Aparna Sen's *36 Chowringhee Lane* (1981). For a while though, Anglo-Indians had prospered as agents of colonial administration—in the railways, customs, police and in the schools—and in this duration the community's athletic prowess was expressed through the medium of hockey. The early history of hockey in every region of the country bears the stamp of this engagement:

> Any evaluation of the fecundity of hockey in Chennai is incomplete without acknowledging the glorious role played by the Europeans and the Anglo-Indian communities. From the days of Cullen, Tremenere, Hart, and Summerheys, to the golden age of Eric Blankley, Gilbert, Richtor, down the era of Jimmy Carr, Cunnigham, Joe D'Costa, and the Pears brothers, competitive hockey in the 1930s and 1940s mirrored the craft in full bloom of pure skill and artistry.[22]

This is a roll-call of names totally erased from our consciousness and utterly lost to our collective memory. The historiography practised by the dominant culture has been a highly selective one preserving only those who are thought fit to be national heroes. We have commemorated the exploits of Dhyan Chand and Roop Singh, and rightly so, for these were great players, scoring between them 25 of the 35 goals scored by India at the 1932 Olympics. But what of Richard Allen who kept goal and conceded only three goals in three Olympics? Or Eric Pinniger, who captained India in the finals of the 1928 Olympics and Leslie Hammond who played in both the '28 and '32 teams? The erasure of these names is part of the forgotten history of the Anglo-Indians as a whole.

Anglo-Indians took to hockey and made it their game partly because it was the one major sporting pursuit unconnected with the freedom movement that dominated the entirety of life in late colonial India. This movement, though ostensibly a struggle on behalf of the whole nation, increasingly came to be dominated by leaders representing the upper segments of the Hindu majority.

The profound ambivalence and anxiety which the Anglo-Indians felt towards this tendency, and which caused them to excel in the "apolitical" sphere of hockey, was undoubtedly shared by Muslims as well. In fact, Muslims were far more outright in rejecting majority politics, creating the Muslim League in direct opposition to the Hindu-dominated Congress Party, thus setting in motion a current of Muslim separatism which was to find fruition in the creation of Pakistan. Muslim participation in sport had already been politicized with the introduction of a Muslim team in the Quadrangular Cricket Tournament of 1912. However amicable the personal relationships between Hindu and Muslim sportsmen or fans, communal cricket was in effect a sundering in advance of a nation yet to be born. The founding of Mohammedan Sporting, a football club representing all the Muslims in India, was another instance of Muslim separatism expressed in sports. No comparable development took place in hockey, partly because Muslims, like Anglo-Indians, put a claim on hockey and made the game their own. By 1936, as we have seen, a large percentage of the best Indian players tended to be Muslim. Partition would cause a severe drop in the number of Muslim players, though Hindu-Muslim rivalry in the sport would be reconfigured through the hockey rivalry between India and Pakistan. Perhaps as a consequence of this, the participation of Indian Muslims in the game began to fall drastically after Independence. This decline is partly explained by the unfair manner in which Muslim players were treated; the great Inam-ur-Rehman, for example, was left out of the team to play Pakistan because his loyalties were questioned by some. Not surprisingly, Indian Muslims started to desert the game at which they had once excelled. Though the recent years have seen the emergence of stars like Aslam Sher Khan, Mohammed Shahid and Zafar Iqbal, by and large Muslim participation in the sport has declined drastically, to the extent that the 2002 World Cup did not have a single Muslim player on it. The wholesale disenfranchisement and marginalization of India's Muslim population in the years after Ayodhya have had their echoes in hockey's playing fields. Similarly, the Sikh dominance of the sport which occurred in the years immediately after Independence peaked sometime in the 1970s. To some extent the agitation and violence that caused such havoc in the Punjab over the issue of Khalistan must have had some role to play in the relative decline of Sikh participation in the sport. And as we pointed out earlier, at the present moment, hockey's major stars are coming from yet another marginal group—the tribals.

Hockey turns out to possess quite an extraordinary history. A succession of marginal groups, none of whom belonged squarely in the middle of the nation, took up hockey and played it with such a degree of skill so as to make world champions of a nation not known for its accomplishments in any kind of sport. Yet the fact that it has always been a game played almost exclusively by minorities may have also contributed to its almost downright rejection by the Hindu majority. A game belonging to those who were situated at the fringes of the nation could only have caused a deep disquiet amongst those others who held the reins of power and privilege. Hockey constituted a challenge and a threat to the nation according to upper-caste, upper-class Hindus. Gandhi's indifference to hockey was therefore symptomatic of the nation's ultimate indifference to its sub-nationalities. Thus, in spite of bringing gold and glory in the international arena, hockey was never accepted as a legitimate game by India's emerging elite. Born and nurtured under British patronage, hockey managed to survive as a major sport after Independence only because of bureaucratic inertia. The Congress government that came into power under Nehru in 1947 inherited the statist characteristics of its colonial predecessor. The fact that the colonial state had sponsored all the sports implied that the new government would continue to grant patronage in the same manner. The union and state governments, regulating bodies like the IHF (Indian Hockey Federation), AIFF (All India Football Federation), the BCCI (Board of Cricket Control of India) and the IOC (Indian Olympic Committee), and governmental institutions like the Railways, Indian Airlines, the Border Security Force and Customs became instrumental in organizing tournaments, sponsoring teams, and paying for players and coaches. As in other instances of the public sector, this economy was top-driven, governed not by the profit motive but by bureaucratic logic. This led to systematic irrationalities and inefficiencies—for example, a large number of "officials" accompanying a few athletes for foreign tours—but it also ensured that the less popular sports could continue to get funding regardless of their profitability.

This state of affairs began to give way to a new order sometime in the 1970s. The expansion and influence of television made possible the marketing both of goods as well as sports itself. In cricket, Kerry Packer's revolution of one-day cricket was the signal that the game had entered the society of the spectacle, to use Guy Debord's memorable phrase. Hockey was not destined to share in the coming boon. Firstly, the game had little glamour at the international level and therefore could not be capitalized the way cricket could be. Of course other low-status sports like badminton and table-tennis ("low" in the sense that they have not had much of a following in the capital-rich West) have flourished elsewhere, especially in Asia and in northern Europe. Hockey's dismal fate has more to do with its minority status, unloved by the elite it proved unattractive for the investing classes. As the Dalit writer Siriyavan points out tellingly, "Dhanraj, Thirumavalavan, Jude Menezes, Lazarus Balra or Pargat Singh are unlikely to win the confidence of the publicity managers of Pepsi or Coke. Add to this the fact that cricket players tend to be a fairer lot compared to our hockey players. Art and cinema have always promoted an Indian brand of racism that excludes the darker looking majority."[23] This deep-rooted prejudice against the sport became crucial when governmental patronage began to be replaced by market forces. Without any more safety nets to protect it, hockey went on a vertiginous free fall, reaching rock bottom. Its abject condition today is illustrated by a report that the former Olympian Sylvanus Dung Dung had been considering selling off his gold medal just in order to make ends meet.[24] Hockey's decline is a function of the transition from a secular state socialism to a casteist and communal capitalism. The brutality with which it has been discarded is reflective of the unmerciful processes of consumerism and globalization.

Football and the Nation

To some extent the history of football in India recapitulates that of hockey. Like hockey, Indian football too had a version of a "golden era," though its achievements were far less modest. The Indian football team first started playing international matches in the 1930s with tours of Malaysia, Singapore, Japan and China. The 1948 London Olympics was the first major international tournament for the team—playing mainly barefoot on a cold and wet surface the Indian players lost a close match to France by 2–1. In 1956, India finished fourth, losing to Yugoslavia after leading 1–0 until the final ten minutes. And at the 1960 Rome tournament, India drew with France (1–1) and lost narrowly to Peru (3–1) and the powerful Hungarians (2–1). Within the context of Asian football, India's performance was even more noteworthy. India won the gold medal at the 1952 Asian Games held in New Delhi, but Indian football's most glorious moment came in 1962, when playing with a number of injured players against the favourites South Korea, the Indian team emerged victorious by a margin of 2–1. The country produced a host of talented players in this period all of whom were selected to play for the Asian All-Stars: Jarnail Singh, Chuni Goswami, P.K. Banerjee, T. Balaram, Peter Thangaraj, Altaf Ahmed, Yusuf Khan and Prasun Bannerjee.

These early successes could not be sustained, and a process of decline, which seemed almost scripted in its predictability, set in by the end of the 1960s. Indian players seemed to lack ambition— Mohun Bagan's legendary inside-left Chuni Goswami received an offer from Totenham Hotspur but chose to stay back in India, as did the 1970s right-winger Surojit Sengupta when given the chance to play as a professional in the UAE and Kuwait. It was not until Baichung Bhutia joined the English second-division team Bury in 1999 that any Indian footballer had a professional career abroad. Indian officialdom was equally unenterprising, and lacked any kind of managerial imagination. For years, officials decreed that domestic matches be played for only 70 minutes, causing Indian teams to tire out when playing in normal 90–minute international matches. The administration of the game has been half-hearted— in the 1960s about 125 domestic tournaments were held every year, there are currently only two dozen. The Indian team's recent performance has reflected the sport's bad management. India has never made it to the World Cup finals and has not qualified for the Olympics since 1960. The last time the Indian team appeared in a quarter-finals match at the international level was at the Asian Games in 1982. Not surprisingly the sport has steadily lost popularity. Traditional football centers like Hyderabad, Bangalore and Chennai are no longer attracting fans and the sport is now confined to a handful of states like West Bengal, Goa, and Kerala.[25]

The history of Indian football—with its dual themes of promise and decline—seems to resemble that of Indian hockey. This similarity, however, is purely formal—an investigation of football's specific history shows us that its role within the colonial social formation was very different from that of hockey, as was its meaning for the culture at large. We must turn to the history of the game to properly understand its specific meaning. Football, or more specifically Association football, was initially an English game played by the populace against the wishes and interdictions of the ruling powers. Thus, the English monarch in 1349 banned football as being "dishonest, unthrifty and idle" and north of the border, James I of Scotland passed an act in 1424 stating "That na man play at the fute-ball." Like most other games, it was codified and given its modern shape in the nineteenth century. Street football was firmly repressed (a law passed in 1834 made it a criminal act), and the first steps at nationalising the game were carried out in the public schools—the rules of Rugby would of course give rise to another variety of football. The old boys from these schools were largely instrumental in the development of rules and organization. The first combined rules for football were drawn up by the Old Etonians in 1846, and another version in 1848 (The Cambridge Rules) by a group of Old Harrovians who were at university. In 1863 a number of these old boy clubs got together in London to create the Football Association.

Interestingly, football became popular much later than cricket. While cricket was drawing large crowds at the beginning of the nineteenth century, football had little or no following. Writing in 1801 on the sports and pastimes of the English people, Joseph Strut could say "The game was formerly much in vogue among the common people, though of late it seems to have fallen into disrepute and is but little practised."[26] By the end of the century however, football was the number one sport in the country. This rapid growth in popularity was possible only because the game suited the needs of a modern society. Football initially prospered in the emerging industrial cities, especially in the north of England. It was decidedly an urban phenomenon—of the 12 teams that formed the Football League in 1888, all except two came from towns of over 80,000. Many football teams grew out of the bonds developed in urban social spaces like pubs, or were directly connected to work. The most famous instance of the latter was the founding of a club by the working men of the Dining Committee of the Lancashire and Yorkshire Railway. The club, founded around 1880, was known as Newton Heath, and was later to become Manchester United.

Football was tailor-made for the needs of nineteenth-century Britain. Industrialization had dislocated large segments of the rural population and put people in urban settings which were largely anonymous. And as Tony Mason has pointed out, factory production led to a much clearer demarcation between time that was work and time that was not.[27] The new modes of economic production and organization and the growth of urban centers led to a demand for leisure and the development of a mass leisure market. A sport like football was necessary in order for working class men to temporarily escape the brutality of factory life; it enabled people to retain a sense of place (many clubs bore place names); it provided strangers with a source of talk; and it helped foster both local and national identity through the instrument of the national league. Football's value was recognized by employers; in 1860 a provision was made for a Saturday half-day for skilled workers (soon extended to all workers). Not surprisingly, Manchester, the center of the cotton industry, was the first major British city to grant the shorter Saturday to all workers. Football was supported in this manner because it was seen as an activity which would keep the workers off the street and thus function as a means of containment of the working classes. As Lord Birenhead observed, were sports to be abolished "it would bring upon the masses nothing but misery, depression, sloth, indiscipline, and disorder."[28] Football was also instrumental in giving the new urban working class a sense of place and identity. The practice of football—the regular weekly matches—coverage in local newspapers, conversations amongst fans, all contributed to a sense of being from a particular town and place. This identification was heightened when the local team reached the upper levels of tournaments and perhaps won a cup, the entire town turned out in celebration in the manner which has since become standard.

Soldiers in the British Army brought the game to India in the last decades of the nineteenth century. Calcutta, the capital of British India at the time, had the largest garrisons and not surprisingly it was there that football made its greatest impact. The game was soon taken up by civilians and within a few years numerous clubs representing various segments of the white population had sprung up: the Calcutta Football Club was established in 1872, the Dalhousie Club in 1878, followed by Calcutta Rangers, Police, Customs, Howrah United and the Armenian Club. The Trades Cup, a knockout tournament, was established in 1889, it was soon to be replaced by the prestigious IFA Shield which was instituted after the formation of the Indian Football Association in 1893.

From its very inception, football was embroiled in the complex web of colonial politics. As Paul Dimeo has argued the colonial system was naturally inclined to exclude Indians from the social realm. Football was no exception, thus in the early days "the Anglo-Indian clubs were chary of including a footballer who was not fair-skinned."[29] Yet the very nature of colonial society made contamination inevitable. As one private in the Royal Scots described:

> In the evening we used to have a chat with the Gurkha boys. We would invariably find them playing football and they would immediately split up and demand that we should join them. From then on it was everyone for himself with about forty Gurkhas on each side, each having two or three British ranks playing with them ...[30]

Indeed, as Dimeo goes on to point out, a certain section of British administrators felt it was "part of their imperial duty to help Indians to 'improve' themselves and deliberately set about encouraging Bengalis to engage in games."[31]

This interest was reciprocated by many Bengalis who realized the importance of participating in the colonizer's sports. Most of these sporting pioneers came from the ranks of the dominant *bhadralok*. Tony Mason has rightly speculated that while we do not know much about the social origins of Bengali players, it seems likely that they were drawn mainly from the educated lower-middle and middle classes, groups without whose existence and positive support the British Empire in India could not have been sustained.[32] Educational institutions were instrumental in fielding the first native teams—Presidency College FC was the first in 1884, followed quickly by Sibpur Engineering College, Medical, St. Xavier's and La Martiniere Colleges. These were followed by the sports clubs—Sovabazar (1885), which in 1892 became the first native team to beat a British club, Mohun Bagan (1889) and Mohammedan Sporting (1891). Bengalis may have taken to football with such enthusiasm in order to prove a point. In spite of often being loyal and indispensable agents of the Raj, Bengalis got little respect from their colonial rulers; the Bengali babu, described as weak and effeminate, became a figure of mockery and caricature. As many historians have pointed out, the threat posed by Bengali nationalism accounted for the intensity of the ridicule they were subject to. At the same time though, Bengalis internalized these denigrating descriptions of themselves. Thus, it became imperative for the purposes of nationalism that Bengalis demonstrate a physical virility that would serve as a signifier of political and moral worth. In other words, if Bengalis were to lead the nationalist struggle they had to be good at football. The proof of excellence had to wait for a while, since the white sporting establishment was loath to allow native teams to participate in tournaments. Thus when the IFA Shield began in 1893 only one Indian team was allowed entry. It wasn't until 1909 that Mohun Bagan, the leading native club, was permitted to participate. Two years later, after having defeated St. Xavier's (3–0), Rangers (1–0), the Rifle Brigade (1–0) and the 1st Middlesex Regiment (1–1, 3–0), Mohun Bagan found itself in the final of the tournament with a chance to vindicate Bengal's reputation. On the historic day of July 28, 1911 a Mohun Bagan team supposedly composed of "low-lying people in a low-lying land" defeated the "crack" East Yorkshire Regiment by 2–1 to win the IFA Shield. When the referee blew the whistle to announce the end of the match, "shirts, hats, handkerchiefs, sticks, and umbrellas started flying in the air."[33] The victory was not just a matter of winning a football game, what was at stake here was something much larger. The *Indian Mirror* claimed that the Japanese victory over Russia "did not stir the East half as much as did that of Mohun Bagan over the East Yorks" while *The Nayak* declared that:

> Indians can hold their own against Englishmen in every walk of art and science, in every learned profession, and in the higher grades of the public service…It only remained for Indians to beat Englishmen in the peculiarly English sport, the football

... It fills every Indian with joy and pride to know that rice-eating, malaria-ridden, barefooted Bengalis have got the better of beef-eating, Herculean, booted John Bull in the peculiarly English sport.[34]

In Bengal, football had become nationalism. Mohun Bagan's victory came in the wake of the agitation against the proposed Partition of Bengal and the intensification of *swadeshi* terrorism all over Bengal. The British no doubt saw this defeat at the hands of a "subject" people as a threat to the myth of white supremacy. In fact, the English hockey team, which had won gold at the 1908 and the 1920 Olympics, withdrew from the 1928 tournament after scouting reports convinced them that they would be no match for the Indians. As it turned out, the British shifted their capital from Calcutta to New Delhi precisely the very same year that Mohun Bagan won the IFA Shield. This may have been pure coincidence but as Ramchandra Guha perceptively points out "it is highly likely .. that to pre-empt further humiliation the British ... moved the seat of power away from Bengal, away from its skilful footballers and its bomb-wielding nationalists. The link between sporting prowess and militant anti-imperialism was thus undermined."[35] This link was to be further weakened when the epicenter of the nationalist struggle moved away, under the leadership of Gandhi, from Bengal to western India. The epiphany of 1911 was thus lost forever.

Though football would no longer be a vehicle for the freedom movement, it soon came to be identified with another type of politics. As mentioned earlier, the emergence of a separatist Muslim politics led to the communalization of both cricket and football. The All-India Muslim League, which had been formed in 1906, was indicative of a rising demand within the Muslim community for an independent political future. The League supported the British government's decision to partition Bengal into two provinces, one of which would have a Muslim majority, and thus came into direct conflict with a Hindu leadership which wanted to preserve the status quo. The League would also fight for the principle of separate electorates, a dream realized by the passing of the Morley-Minto Act. The founding of the Mohammedan Sporting Club was in keeping with this logic of separatism and the club came to be seen as the representative of every Muslim on the subcontinent. Because of its symbolic value, Mohammedan Sporting became the first Indian team with a truly national following, and was consequently able to attract Muslim talent from all around the country. The great team of the 1930s which won the Calcutta league for five years in a row (and was also the first Indian club to win the Durand Cup in 1940) was a case in point. Fullbacks Juma Khan and Bachi Khan came from Peshawar and Quetta, goalkeeper Usman Jan was from Delhi, and the star centre-forward Rashid was from Ajmer.[36] The team's many victories contributed to the sense of Muslim pride, but not everyone saw them as benign achievements. As one writer put it "with each victory, a communal wedge was driven deeper into Calcutta football if not into Calcutta society."[37] It is difficult to predict exactly what shape football would have taken had India remained undivided. Partition, and the consequent decline of Muslim political power, took the luster away from Muslim football. The secular ethos dominant in the country in the first three decades after Independence compromised the club's identity. Talented Muslim players like Mohammed Habib or Syed Naeemuddin chose to play for "Hindu" clubs like Mohun Bagan and East Bengal, conversely, Mohammedan Sporting opened its doors to non-Muslim footballers. The club's weak finances hampered its ability to obtain the best talent, and its status changed from champion to also-ran.

Region and identity

Following its nationalist and communal phases, football in Bengal was to be reincarnated yet again, this time as an expression of ethnicity. Even those slightly acquainted with the game know that modern Indian football can be reduced, in the ultimate analysis,

to the rivalry between two Calcutta clubs—Mohun Bagan and East
Bengal. Over the decades there were plenty of other teams which
could match the Big Two in skill and ability: Andhra Pradesh Police,
Leaders Club, BSF, JCT Mills, (currently known as JCT Phagwara),
Indian Telephone Industries (ITI) Integral Coach Factory (ICF),
Vasco, Mahindras, Dempo. None, however, possessed the glamour
and drawing power of the Calcutta teams. Over the years, almost
all the great Indian football players (with exceptions like Yusuf
Khan or Inder Singh) have worn the famous maroon and green
or the red and gold, enabling these clubs to be successful in a way
no other Indian football team club has ever been. The dominance
of Calcutta football was a result of the large salaries they were
able to pay their players. This economic prowess was, in turn, made
possible by a fanatical fan following which not only generated
large revenues at the gate, but, more importantly, fueled the desire,
within the Bengali elite, to put money into the sport. What
differentiated Calcutta football and ultimately made it superior
to its counterparts in other states, was the brute fact that Bengali
fans, were quite literally, ready to die for their teams.

The ferocious binary constitutive of Calcutta football came
into being in 1924 with the founding of the East Bengal Club.
Mohun Bagan was the preeminent Bengali football club of that
time, having won the IFA Shield and countless other tournaments.
The club's fan base came from the indigenous population of *ghotis*
(West Bengalis) and its patrons included most of Calcutta's native
aristocracy. Formed in conscious opposition to Mohun Bagan, East
Bengal was meant to represent newly-arrived *bangals* or migrants
from the eastern part of Bengal (now Bangladesh). Anxious about
rising Hindu-Muslim tensions in Muslim-majority East Bengal,
Hindus from the region began a westward migration which would
last till until the Partition and ultimately involve the transfer of
almost 4 million people from east to west. This immigrant
population constituted a distinct sociological group which stood
culturally at odds—in manners, accent or food—with the previously
settled denizens of Calcutta and its environs. This antagonism

got articulated by the means of football, the many differences between *bangals* and *ghotis* got ritually "played" out on the green soccer fields of the Maidan. The social strains between these two ethnic communities got exacerbated after the Partition when millions of refugees moved to Calcutta. Living in destitute conditions on the platforms of railway stations, and dependent on a government dole for survival, these new *bangals* would come to constitute a volatile, plebian fan base for East Bengal. Older fans of Calcutta football will no doubt recall that throughout the 1950s, and the 1960s (and even into the 1970s) every fixture involving Mohun Bagan and East Bengal had the city teetering on the edge of violence. This intense rivalry and the concomitant supremacy of Calcutta football would last almost till the end of the millennium. By then several countervailing forces had tended to diminish the importance of Calcutta football and reduce its significance as a cultural phenomenon. Firstly, intermarriage and cultural diffusion had erased many of the differences between *bangal* and *ghoti* thus removing the objective ground for rivalry between the teams. That both Mohun Bagan and East Bengal are today under the same ownership is an ironic acknowledgment of this convergence. Secondly, the emergence of well-funded professional teams in other parts of the country—FC Cochin in Kerala, Churchill Brothers in Goa, BMFC in Mumbai—meant that soccer talent was more evenly distributed across the country. And finally, the massive spread of television in the 1980s brought international football into every living room. Maradona and Ronaldo began to appear on calendars and posters, and the World Cup and the English Premier League replaced local soccer as the staple viewing fare.

In its heyday Calcutta football exhibited two peculiarities which help us get to its kernel. British football was based on teams that represented very specific locales—Arsenal, or Leeds or Liverpool. The Calcutta League was presumably modeled on the British one, and one would have expected a tournament composed of teams from Burdwan, Durgapur, Asansol and other mofussil towns competing against clubs from Calcutta. No such league came to fruition nor one which fielded teams from Calcutta's own geography: Shyambazar, Ballygunge, Jadavpore, Kasba. Rather, the entirety of the Calcutta game collapsed into the binary logic of Mohun Bagan versus East Bengal. All other clubs—Aryans, Sporting Union or George Telegraph for example—became ghost teams with no supporters, having the purely formal function of providing an opponent for the Big Two. This phenomenon, which we may term cultural monism, is a common feature of postcolonial societies. The gathering of all music under the voice of Lata or Kishore, of all heroics under the sign of Bachchan or Shah Rukh, of all cricket under Tendulkar or Sehwag, of all politics (till recently at least) under the Nehru-Gandhi dynasty—signify a recurrent tendency at play in the realm of the popular. This is not the proper place to attempt an explanation of so complex and profound a phenomenon. What we can observe is that in the realm of football, the desire to collapse everything into One signifies a collective desire to preserve the psychic valence of the contradiction between Mohun Bagan (MB) and East Bengal (EB). The necessity of the opposition indicates that this is not mere sport we are talking about, but rather a ritual of great significance. In his seminal work *The Savage Mind*, Claude Lévi Strauss has drawn an illuminating difference between sport and ritual. Within the framework of modern sports opponents are considered equal until they meet in a sporting contest. The "result" in such a match is the device by which a hierarchy of superior-inferior is introduced. Ritual, on the other hand, reverses the logic of sport. It begins with two sharply divided halves which stand in a relationship of great antagonism to each other, through the process of ritualistic contest this opposition is cancelled, revealing the truth that these supposedly distinct halves actually are both parts of the same tribe. The human psyche's need for ritual is so deep that it is present in the most "modern" of societies. American sports may be the most rationalized sports culture in terms of training methods, salary structures, coaching strategies and the use of corporate money. In spite of the staggering media hype which surrounds them and the superb athleticism displayed on the field, the biggest events like the Super Bowl or the World Series in baseball are played with a degree of calculation and emotional reserve quite surprising to observers from other cultures. The greatest displays of passion and emotions are found not at the professional level but instead in a context whose meanings are exclusively shaped by the logic of ritual. The great annual football contest between the Ohio State University and the University of Michigan is a case in point. The entire season is spent in talking about the big game, and for coaches, players and fans alike, victory in that encounter makes or breaks a game. Alumni travel hundreds, even thousands, of miles to attend the game, fans boo and jeer at each other, insults are traded, and the result in the match leads to ecstasy or despondency. Yet no enmity is produced, rather a feeling of togetherness, a coming together of collegians who share the commonality of geography (the American midwest in this case) and culture.

To extend Lévi Strauss' analysis, ritualistic rivalry is constituted by means of the following paradox: the more the displays of hatred against your opponent, the more the joy and sorrow associated with victory or defeat, the less the real desire to vanquish and conquer. The entire power of rivalry is dissolved if the opponent turns out to be fundamentally inferior. Ritualistic battle is radically unlike real war, for underlying it is a craving to be defeated by the rival. To be never defeated would be the death of rivalry, which is why one yearns to be defeated by precisely that opponent who one pretends to hate. Ritualistic rivalry thus uses the subterfuge of hatred in order to express and create solidarity. The rivalry between Mohun Bagan and East Bengal was ritualistic in the sense just outlined, because its real function was not to sharpen the antagonism between two social groups but rather to fuse them into one Bengali identity. Two facts justify this conclusion. Firstly, the emotional intensity surrounding the big match was always far in excess of the actual social tensions between *ghotis* and *bangals*.

This surplus is an indicator that the binary was being pressed to do some other work beyond reiterating a contradiction. When there is no such surplus, when the contradiction of ritual is no wider than the contradiction of the social, then ritual becomes an impossibility. That is why it is so hard to hold a cricket match between India and Pakistan, because the real of the social has intervened in the space of ritual. Real enemies do not play together, they go to war.

The real function of the football mania constructed round the opposition between two ethnically marked clubs was the articulation of modern Bengali identity. To support Mohun Bagan (and thus be in a relation of passionate negation to East Bengal) was not really to support "Mohun Bagan" or identify with *"ghotis"* but rather to announce Bengaliness. That is why it was possible for two brothers from the same family to support different clubs. By the 1950s the binary had become a formal one, unrelated to ethnic content. The negation of the disjunctive is the real culprit here: not to support either Mohun Bagan or East Bengal would be tantamount to being a false Bengali or a non-Bengali. It is to be noted that Bengalis were probably the only ethnic group among whom a negative descriptor had the force of positive identification—a non-Bengali was not just a logical term but rather a cultural type who was the other of the Bengali. By organizing the entire Bengali population into two footballing moieties, football served as a means of expressing a specifically Bengali identity. Tagore and Rabindrasangeet, the films of Uttam Kumar and Suchitra Sen, *rosogolla* and *sandesh*, processions and *Lal Salaam*, and football on the Maidan—these were what it meant to be Bengali in the post-Independence years. If that football has lost its appeal today—graffiti in the slums now celebrate international heroes like Maradona or Ronaldo—it is because Bengali identity itself is undergoing a radical erasure. The economic decline of the state, Marwari domination of capital, the mass emigration of natives out of the state, the overwhelming influences of global consumerism, all these have contributed to a crisis in Bengali identity. Consquently, football, which was such a crucial component of that vanishing identity, is now losing its importance.

Football in Bengal, then, passed through three successive stages. It initially served as a vehicle for nationalist pride, then went through a communal phase which embodied the politics of Muslim separatism. In its most recent stage, football became a site for the working out of modern Bengali identity. Indian football may have found its greatest success in the Maidan, but the fundamentally regional character it acquired in Bengal undoubtedly hampered its development as a national game. Football became so identified with Bengal and Bengalis that its reputation may well have acted as a disincentive for other regions to develop strong football traditions. In fact, the story of football in Goa—the only other true center of soccer apart from Bengal—bears a strong resemblance to the one just told. If Calcutta football was exclusively for Bengalis (its constitutive binary can be seen as anti-national in that it made it impossible for a non-Bengali to enter that binary space), then Goan football too was intimately tied up with the troubled issue of Goan identity. In his succinct analysis of Goan football, James Mills argues the "game is now embedded in Goan culture precisely because it has been so closely related to Goan history."[38] Mills shows that the development of football has been closely tied to certain key processes and institutions that have shaped Goan history. The Catholic Church, which played a crucial role in Goan social life was instrumental in introducing and promoting the game in the late nineteenth and early twentieth centuries. Football became an integral part of Goan life, played not only by Christians but by Hindus as well. A second impetus to Goan football was provided by the large-scale migration that occurred in the first few decades of the 20th century. Goan emigrants, especially those in Bombay, organized football teams like the Young Goans which regularly competed against local teams, thus stimulating the growth of the game. Emigrants continue to play a role even today, and in 2000 there was even a Goan World Cup played between different Goan communities from around the world. Large-scale investment in football clubs occurred in the 1950s when the Portuguese decided to industrialize Goa in a last-ditch attempt to maintain control over the colony. The new economic policies saw the rise of large industrial houses like Salgaocar and Dempo, who would go on to finance highly successful teams that bore the company name. The period had an international flavor; many foreign clubs, including the famous Benifica Club, visited the colony to play in exhibition matches.

After the Indian Army ended Portuguese rule in 1961, Goa went through a period of uncertainty about its status and identity. Football played a significant role in these deliberations. Dayand Bandodkar, who as Chief Minister led a movement for Goa's merger with Maharashtra, used football as an instrument for mobilizing public opinion. He organized a new football tournament named after himself and patronized the Panvel Sports Club. All this was to no avail, the referendum of 1967 rejected Bandodkar's merger plan, thus ensuring that Goa would eventually win statehood for itself. Those fighting for a separate Goan identity included B.M. Parkkot, who had first successfully established Salgaocar and then taken over control of Vasco. Parkkot's efforts to maintain the independence of the Goan Football Association was closely linked to the local population's desire to maintain Goa as a distinct political entity. Goa finally became a state of the Indian Union in 1987; the new Goan government celebrated the ascension by building the new Fatorda stadium, meant to serve as a symbol of football in the state. Mills' account of Goan football shows us that the game's immense popularity can only be understood by looking at the specific events of its regional history. The alienation of the region first from British and then independent India meant that "being Goan" was a problematic project. Football played a crucial part in the development of a specific Goan identity, helping to differentiate Goans from their more numerous neighbors to the north and south. The case histories of Bengal and Goa demonstrate that football has succeeded in those contexts where it played a role in the articulation of local identity. Conversely, it has failed to prosper in those regions which may have had an abundance of footballing talent but where the crucial link between sport and identity politics did not obtain. In most of southern India football was nurtured and kept alive by governmental patronage but never succeeded in producing the fan involvement necessary to sustain a sport once market forces came into play. In Hyderabad, for example, football was originally patronized by the royalty and then by the government. The city's premier team, Hyderabad City Police, won the Rovers Cup five years in a row in the early 1950s under the great coaching of A.S. Rahim. As Novy Kapadia has pointed out, the club's style of functioning reflected the idealism of the immediate post-Independence era, in the willingness of players to play for no monetary reward, and to sacrifice and work for great ideals.[39] The growing commercialization of the game, spurred by the large salaries offered to talented players by the Calcutta teams, made such a value system quite anachronistic. Consequently, the team could not survive beyond the 1960s. Teams that shared the same set of values like HAL (Hindustan Aeronautics Limited) and ITI (Indian Telephone Industries)—both from Bangalore—and ICF (Integral Coach Factory) from Chennai suffered the same fate. The south had once produced some of the very best players in the country—the 1948 Olympic team had six players from Mysore—but today the entire southern region, except for Kerala, has lost its enthusiasm for the game.

The failure of football to take root in the south underscores the fact that football's intrinsically regional nature comes in the way of its development into a truly national sport. The creation of the National Football League and the large influx of capital provided some of the ingredients necessary for growth, but football's fundamental problem remains to be solved. The National League was introduced in the mid-nineties with a Rs. 20 million sponsorship from Philips India, and from Coca Cola. There was a simultaneous boost in corporate ownership when Vijay Mallya, the beer magnate, bought both Mohun Bagan and East Bengal and Mohammedan Sporting as well, thus putting three of India's oldest clubs under one common ownership. Commercialization led to the establishment of India's first purely professional teams: FC Cochin, Kerala, funded partly by expatriates in the Gulf, and BMFC which was established by Bengali businessmen based in Mumbai. The inflow of corporate money has led to a great increase in the number of foreign players and a huge increase in players' salaries: East Bengal paid Baichung Bhutia Rs. 20 lakh for a single season, the Brazilian Jose Barreto earned double that amount with Mohun Bagan. However, the efforts to modernize football stalled almost as soon as they started. Mallya's UB group reduced their commitments to the Calcutta clubs drastically after the first season (from 27.5 million rupees to 12.5 million per team), and withdrew its sponsorship of the Federation Cup. Philips pulled out of sponsoring the National League, and explained its decision to return to cricket by claiming that "Cricket is a ready recipe that works. It is a great media event ... this alone makes tremendous marketing sense."[40] Philips' decision makes sense if one takes into account the results of a survey conducted in several Asian countries by A.C. Nielsen in 1999. While football was by far the most popular sport in a majority of countries, only 3 per cent of Indian respondents—compared to 82 per cent for cricket—listed it as their top sport.[41] This statistic dramatically underscores football's chronic inability to compete with cricket at the national level.

As I have shown, football developed as a regional sport and in spite of attempts over the years to popularize the game, its reach remains confined to a handful of states. Attendance figures for the 1999–2000 National Football League matches provide definitive proof of this proposition. The biggest gate of the season was, quite expectedly, at Kolkata (East Bengal vs. Mohun Bagan, 50,000), Kochi in Kerala and Margao in Goa came next (FC Cochin vs. Churchill Brothers 35,000; Salgaocar vs. Mohun Bagan 25,000). The figures for Bangalore (ITI vs. FC Cochin, 15,000) show the dip outside the triumvirate of Bengal, Kerala and Goa. What is truly shocking are the figures for Mumbai and Punjab. Only 3,500 attended the Mumbai match between Mahindras (a top Mumbai team) and Mohun Bagan, and only 2,000 in Ludhiana watched JCT Mills play Mahindras. In spite of the many great players produced by the Punjab—Jarnail Singh and Inder Singh to name only two— as well as in the Mumbai region, football has limited appeal in these areas. Clearly, football has lost out to cricket as far as Mumbai goes, and to hockey and cricket in the case of Punjab.

The uneven development of football—its immense popularity in Bengal, Goa and Kerala and its mysterious failure elsewhere in India—raises interesting questions about the nature and interrelationships between Indian states. There is within Indian scholarship a very serious lacuna regarding the category of the "state." The logic of statehood as we know it today was formally established by the States Reorganization Act of 1956. A movement for the constitution of states on the principle of language had gathered strength immediately after Independence, and had led to the formation of the Telegu-speaking Andhra Pradesh and the Tamil-speaking Madras states in 1953. The passage of the Act led to the creation of Kerala as well as the redrawing of the boundaries for Andhra Pradesh, Mysore and Bombay. The fears of the minority Gujarati population led, in 1960, to the bifurcation of the state of Bombay into Gujarat and Maharashtra. The initial period of state-formation came to an end in 1966 when Punjab was divided into Hindi-speaking Haryana and a rump bearing the original name. Recent years have seen the incorporation of Sikkim as a state of the Union, the coming into being of the "seven sisters" in the north-east and the emergence of the breakaway states of Jharkhand, Chattisgarh and Uttarakhand. A copious amount of scholarly works exist on various aspects of these states, especially within the disciplines of developmental economics, political science and sociology. Interestingly enough there are very few modern histories of individual states—a fact which reflects both the commitment shared by most contemporary scholars to a nationalistic construction of "India", as well as to a fundamental difficulty in articulating the identity of "Bihar" or "Karnataka." Most academics have treated the states as "givens" and thus have not interrogated the parameters upon which states have been constituted. My suggestion is that we can use football as a springboard for an inquiry into the fundamental nature of states within federal India. What for example explains the incredible lack of interest in the Santosh Trophy, a tournament which pits each Indian state against another? Not only is there no audience for a match between Assam and Gujarat, there is hardly any interest even when football-crazy states play each other. Bengalis, whose very life is called into stake when East Bengal plays Mohun Bagan, seem not to care even a little bit whether Bengal triumphs over Kerala or Goa. The absence of passion surrounding the Santosh can only be explained by the non-relation that has historically obtained between the different states of the Union. Though Indian politics since Independence has been volatile and vigorous, most of it has been conducted through categories other than that of the state—religion, caste, class. Indeed, except for the occasional conflicts concerning water or some other resource, the states have existed in political indifference towards each other. The reason for this detachment has to do a lot with the statist nature of the Indian government in the decades following Independence. Given that most important economic and political decisions were taken at the central level, and the servile nature of the Congress governments at the state level, the state as such was not an effective unit of political or social action till at least the mid-seventies. What these later developments demonstrate is the following: under statism the states had no independent mode of existence. Though linguistically different, each state was very dependent on the center and was constituted as no more than a mere appendage. That being so, the relation between states was equally unimportant, reducible to the bureaucratic octroi levied at the borders. This lack of contradiction or antagonism between the states explains why sports tournaments organized as competitions between teams representing states—the Ranji, the Santosh and the Rangaswamy— have never aroused much passion. In the last three decades however, states have begun to acquire more distinct identities. Three factors have contributed to this emergence. First, the assumption of power by non-Congress governments in a majority of states has meant that state policies and the ethos of governance are no longer decided by a monolithic centre. Andhra Pradesh (till recently) under Rama Rao, Tamil Nadu under Jayalalitha, Bihar under Laloo Yadav and now Nitish Kumar and Gujarat under Narendra Modi possess distinct identities in a way earlier state governments did not. Secondly, liberalization has meant that economics has begun to influence culture, thus Bangalore's (and by extension Karnataka's) globalized yuppie culture has come into being as a consequence of its software industry. Finally, the dispersal of populations under diaspora, has, in a paradoxical way, led to the crystallizing of local identities. Thus, the cultural practices of the Gujarati communities in Africa, UK and the US have contributed to a sharper sense of what "being Gujarati" entails. If in the middle of the twentieth century, all states were considered equal and fundamentally the same but for the accident of language, today local cultures are far more crucial as is the sense of difference between states. What consequence this will have for the future of football is still unclear.

We can attempt to sum up the essence of Indian football in the following manner: While football was briefly used as a site of resistance against colonialism, it lost that function early on in its history. It then became instrumental in forging Muslim communal identity as well as ethnic identities in a few regions of the country. Football's profoundly regional character is a limitation with regards to its becoming a truly national sport. Like hockey then, football seems to be condemned to live on as a minor sport.

3

Hindi-Pop

The Quest for Modernity in Film Music

In October of 2002, Anthony Kornarens, a lawyer representing music composer Bappi Lahiri, filed a case in the Los Angeles district court seeking to halt sales of "Truthfully Speaking," a rhythm and blues album recorded by Truth Hurts under the auspices of Aftermath Records. The suit, which named the famous hip hop producer Dr. Dre as a defendant, claimed that one of the tracks on the album—the Top Ten hit, "Addictive"—had lifted four minutes of a tune composed by Lahiri without prior permission. That song—"Thoda Resham Lagta Hai"—had been performed by Lata Mangeshkar for a relatively unknown 1980s Hindi film (*Jyoti*, 1981). The song's notoriety is solely a product of its subsequent fate within the frenzied circulation of cultural commodities that characterizes the global marketplace. Twenty years after its initial release in India, "Thoda Resham" got remixed by DJs in the US and became a big hit on the club circuit. DJ Quik, whose remix version would become part of "Addictive," recounted the serendipitous way in which he stumbled onto the song:

I woke up one morning ... I turned on the TV and landed on this Hindi channel and just turned it up real loud ... there was a commercial on, and I just got up and went into the bathroom and started brushing my teeth. I'm brushing, and before I knew it, I was grooving.... [The beat on the TV] was just in my body. I went back in there and looked at the TV, there was a girl on there belly-dancing, just like real fly. So I pushed record on the VCR.[1]

With that push of the VCR button, a forgotten song from an obscure Hindi film got transformed into a cult song in American dance clubs. The song's trajectory would not end there. Harry Anand, a Mumbai-based producer, decided to remix "Addictive," adding on lyrics by Dev Kohli and using a vocalist called Shashwati. Anand claimed that he had never heard the Lata original—he changed his stance subsequently—and argued that all he was trying to do was to improve on "Addictive". Whatever the truth, this new version, released as "Kalyon ka Chaman," also became a huge hit, this time in India and in Europe. This last twist had no bearing for the case being heard in Los Angeles. In that court, the lawyer for Lahiri accused the American producers of the unfortunately named "Truthfully Speaking" of "cultural imperialism" and stated, "It's our opinion that the label simply took for granted that Hindi music was something they didn't need to pay for, that it could simply be used at will."[2] The federal judge hearing the case disregarded the defence's argument that the plaintiff was trying to cash in on Dr. Dre's celebrity status and issued a court order prohibiting sales of "Addictive" unless and until Bappi Lahiri was listed on the song's credits.

The situation here is full of irony, for the alleged victim in this case has enjoyed a notorious reputation as a plagiarist himself. Summing up Lahiri's career, a columnist on the website *www.musicindiaonline.com* says "In the '80s, Bappi's fortunes took a turn for the better, albeit with the help of straight lifts like "Hari Om Hari" (*Pyaara Dushman*, 1980), "Mere Jaisi Haseena ka Dil" (*Armaan*, 1982) and disco numbers like "Rambha Ho" (*Armaan*),

"Disco Station" (*Hathkadi*, 1982) and "I am a Disco Dancer" and "Koi Yahan Naache Naache" (*Disco Dancer*, 1982). Known as the Disco King at his peak, the poor man is generally considered the Master Plagiarist."[3] Lahiri's sources were often easily identifiable— "Hari Om Hari" was an exact copy of "One Way Ticket" by Eruption, while "Koi Yahan Naache Naache" was directly lifted from the Buggles' historic song "Video Killed the Radio Star"— thus solidifying his reputation as a maestro of "borrowed" art. Peter Manuel, author of the influential work *Cassette Culture*, notes that "The amount of plagiarization within film music has greatly increased since the early 1980s ... by far the leading offender, and the primary butt of criticism, has been film-music director Bappi Lahiri."[4] And cultural critic Subhash Jha bitterly observes "Off goes the composer, hunting for pop-rock tunes to pilfer from English, Swedish, African and Pakistani charts ... This, then, is the tragedy of film music today. A tragedy engineered by Bappi Lahiri almost single-handedly."[5] These charges haven't weighed too heavily on Lahiri himself. In response to an interviewer from the *Economic Times* who, while discussing the Los Angeles case concerning "Addictive," had pointed out that he himself had lifted scores of music, Lahiri had this to say:

> I have lifted tunes occasionally—just like any other Indian director. But I haven't stolen an original piece and made a video out of it. For, this constitutes an infringement of copyright. Even SD Burman, RD Burman, Shankar-Jaikishen and Laxmikant-Pyarelal have lifted tunes from the Beatles, Tequila and others. The trend was set even before I was born. So, it is unfair to accuse me. Anyway, we don't have any original composers today. Music directors ape RD Burman and me.[6]

Criticism regarding his lack of artistic originality has not hurt Lahiri's career nor diminished his significance. His output has been unimpeded, he has, to date, composed over 4,000 songs for over 500 films, and got his name included in the *Guinness Book of World*

Records for having penned 180 songs in one calendar year. Lahiri's reach is worldwide: the website *www.talentworld.biz* features a young Uzbeki man called Arthur Mullokondov who knows every single Bappi composition by heart, the Chinese awarded him their Gold Award for *Disco Dancer*, and he is a legend among diasporic Indians. While promoting the cultish Bollywood Disco Night held annually in Manhattan, New York's premier desi deejay DJ Rekha writes, "I always wanted to do a night focused on filmi music, but it wasn't till last spring that the words Bollywood Disco popped into my head. It all made sense. The music of Bollywood that I was most in love was the disco sounds I grew up on—Helen, *Qurbani*, Amitabh and of course Bappi Lahiri."[7] And the noise surrounding the "Addictive" affair has thoroughly revived Lahiri's flagging career. He has signed a multi-record contract with Serious Music, an American record company, which released "Bappiwood Remixes." This was followed by "Bikram Lounge," a multicultural effort that fuses Indian classical with world music, has songs sung in Arabic and Spanish, and features artists from all over the globe.

To encounter "Bappi" then, is to touch upon a node in a vast network of connected disparate musical traditions and practices. This point of intersection where West meets East, classical fuses with the popular, and folk becomes mass, is thoroughly hybrid and lacks all essence. It has no specific geographic location, no single historical origin, and no attachment to strict rule or dogma. It is shamelessly promiscuous in its borrowings, nonchalant in the way it combines forms, and exuberant in the multiplicity of its productions. Understood in this sense, "Bappi" refers not to a person but rather to an entire way of music-making, and stands in for the totality of Indian popular music: Hemant Kumar and Geeta Dutt, Lata and Kishore, Biddu and Alisha, Apache Indian and A.R. Rahman. Further, "Bappi" points us to a new way of conceptualizing the popular, one at variance with those found in western accounts of the subject. The popular has typically been theorized in terms of a two-tiered "vertical" model of cultural

production: an elite culture associated with the aristocracy and
sections of the bourgeoisie occupying the top, and popular or
mass culture associated with peasantry and the proletariat at the
bottom. Whatever the political implications of such a model—
some seeing the popular as the primary site of capitalist
manipulation, others thinking of it as a repository of revolutionary
action—it is in either case sharply distinguished from high cultural
forms and thought of as a distinct domain of cultural practice.
It is my claim that such a model is quite inappropriate for the
purposes of understanding popular culture in India. As the analysis
of "Bappi" suggests, it is far more useful to think of the Indian
popular as constituted by lines of "horizontality"—export and
import, imitation and emendation, sampling and remixing,
Hindu and Muslim, eastern and western, durbar and tamasha,
high and low. To understand the western popular is to follow the
logic of its negotiations with what is *above*, to comprehend the
Indian popular is to trace the patterns of its interactions with
what is *alongside*.

By a happy coincidence the difference in these notions of the
popular is mirrored by the characteristics that distinguish the
Indian system of music from the western one:

> Hindustani music is a *melodic* system, and in this sense the
> relationship between tones is linear and horizontal in contrast
> to the Western harmonic system in which the relationships
> between tones could be said to be governed by the hierarchical
> and vertical.[8]

This fundamental difference was the source of many cross-cultural
misunderstandings; imperial emissaries serving in the subcontinent
were especially prone to the temptation of judging Indian music
by western rules of aesthetics. John Hawd Watson, agent for the
Gramophone and Typewriter Company in Kolkata, wrote to his
superiors in London on the advantages of entering the recording
business in India, even while asserting that "the native music is

to me worse than Turkish but as long as it suits them and sells well what do we care?" The Company heard Watson's pleas and the very first commercial recordings of Indian music were made on November 8, 1902 under the supervision of a certain Fred Gaisberg. The sessions utilized the services of two *nautch* girls named Soshi Mukhi and Fani Bala who sang bits from the popular theater shows of the time. Gaisberg turned out to be no more enlightened than his colleague at the gramophone company. He was self-reflexive enough to observe that,

> We entered a new world of musical and artistic values. One had to erase all memories of the music of European opera houses and concert halls: the very foundation of my musical training was undermined.

He nonetheless could not refrain from voicing his disapproval of native musical practices:

> Our first visit was to a native "Classic Theatre" ... quite arbitrarily there was introduced a chorus of young nautch girls heavily bleached with rice powder and dressed in transparent gauze. They sang "And Her Golden Hair Was Hanging Down Her Back" accompanied by fourteen brass instruments all playing in unison. I had yet to learn that the oriental ear was unappreciative of chords and harmonic treatment and only demanded the rhythmic beat of the accompaniment of the drums. At this point we left.[9]

These dismissive remarks not only illustrate the truism that Indian music is inaudible to an ear trained exclusively in western musicology, but also suggest the need to develop a theory of Indian popular music which is based on a proper understanding of the ground it springs from. The rest of this chapter will attempt to develop such an analysis by looking at the main currents of Indian popular music over the course of the twentieth century. I begin by looking at accounts of popular music proposed by western thinkers, only to argue that these be abandoned in favor of a theory that is more attentive to indigenous factors.

Debating the "Popular"

Theories of popular music have traditionally been of two sorts, depending on their evaluation of the role of the popular. The first tendency, most notably exemplified by the work of the German philosopher Theodor Adorno, dismisses popular music as being banal in its form and content, commercial in its origin, and detrimental in its effects. Popular songs, it is held, are standardized in format, repetitive in structure and do not require any effort on the part of the listener. Popular music is essentially trivial because it is the product of a "culture industry" which is bound by the logic of commodity production. By churning out identical and replicable "songs", the music industry ensures continuing profitability for itself. But commercialization serves a second, more ideological, function. In concert with other forms of mass-produced leisure, popular music acts as a form of distraction, thus making certain that the working-class and other poorer sections of the population remain oblivious to the kind of exploitation that underlies the capitalist form of production. Popular music, along with the rest of popular culture, is "escapist" because it provides illusory gratification and diverts attention from the real conditions of our existence. Such music has the most harmful effects on its audience for it produces listeners who are obedient, pseudo-individualistic and eager to conform and therefore "constitutes the dregs of musical history ... it is catharsis for the masses but catharsis which keeps them all the more firmly in line."[10] Adorno, a practitioner and aficionado of classical music, was inclined to the view that truth in art could only be found in the autonomous products of elite culture. Thus of Beethoven he could write:

> By exposing some irreconcilable dichotomy within itself, Beethoven's late music could call attention to the concurrent external disintegration of human integrity, to the enslaving dehumanizing compartmentalization (for example, into individual and social identities) forced upon man by society.[11]

Adorno's enthusiasm for Beethoven and for high culture in general had its own dark side, for it came with a fear and loathing of anything that was popular or different. Thus "negro jazz" had no real variety because it utilized "certain well-defined tricks, formulas, and clichés to the exclusion of everything else...The eunuch-like voice of the crooner on the radio, the heiress's smooth suitor, who falls into the swimming pool in his dinner jacket, are models for those who must become whatever the system wants." On modern dance he was even more vituperative:

> Their ecstasy is without content.... The ecstasy takes possession of its object by its own compulsive character. It is stylized like the ecstasies savages go into in beating the war drums. It has convulsive aspects reminiscent of St Vitus's dance or the reflexes of mutilated animals.... The same jitterbugs who behave as if they were electrified by syncopation, dance almost exclusively the good rhythmic parts...[12]

Adorno is a paradigmatic figure because he is the most rigorous exponent of what was, in the early years of radio and television, a widespread stance towards popular music. His line of thought would find especial favor amongst the bureaucracies who ran the broadcasting systems in several countries across the world. Thus Adorno's disdain for Americanization (which, in his eyes, was synonymous with the popular) was echoed by a British establishment thoroughly scared of "vulgarity" and the "jungle music" of "negro orgies." The perceived threat to "British values" called for defensive measures, the effort on this score was led by the BBC, which under the legendary stewardship of John Reith, saw itself as a bulwark against Americanized mass culture. Even as rock and roll was beginning to shake up the world of western music, the BBC stuck to its practice of broadcasting only that music which was deemed to be edifying for the public. Thus two of its three main channels—the Home Service, Third Programme and Network 3—were entirely devoted to "serious," that is classical, music. The Light Programme was the only channel that targeted a younger audience, but it too eschewed the new sound in favor of more sedate forms like jazz and folk. All through the 1950s, the BBC's bureaucratic elitism was instrumental in keeping artists like Elvis Presley, Jerry Lee Lewis or Chuck Berry off the airwaves, even as their records and acts became phenomenally popular amongst British teenagers. It was only with the rise of a rock and roll youth culture epitomized by the Beatles and the Rolling Stones, and the ensuing loss of listeners to rival radio stations, that the BBC relented and began to modify its broadcasting policies.

A very similar battle regarding the popular would be enacted in India as well. Established in a colonial context, Indian broadcasting shared many of the structural and ideological features of its British counterpart. The very first radio broadcasts in the country were made from privately owned stations in Bombay and Calcutta in 1927, but the airwaves were soon monopolized by the government with the setting up of All India Radio in 1936. As may be expected, the AIR approached the business of media in the stiff, paternalistic manner characteristic of all governmental agencies. The following description is a succinct statement of how the organization has always perceived of itself: "Since 1957, the service is known as Akashvani, and at present, functions not only as a means of wholesome entertainment, but also as a medium to educate and inform people in every nook and cranny of the country."[13] This utilitarian doctrine found a perfect zealot in the person of Dr. Balkrishna Vishwanath Keskar, Minister of Information and Broadcasting from 1952 to 1962. A great devotee of classical music, Keskar felt that it was the government's duty to ensure that the public was exposed to the right sort of music:

> The object is to encourage the revival of our traditional music, classical and folk. The Radio is fulfilling that task for the nation and I can say with satisfaction, that it has become the greatest patron of Indian music and musicians, greater than all the princely and munificent patronage of former days.[14]

Under Keskar's tutelage AIR developed a list of 7,000 "approved" classical artists who appeared on radio; as a result half of all the music broadcast was classical music. Keskar's contempt for more popular forms of art and music rivaled Adorno's. Of filmmakers he opined "Producers in this line should have a certain background of culture ... At present there is hardly a standard maintained by many of the productions we see on the screen." He thought even less highly of film music, maintaining that it appealed to no one "except for raw and immature people like children and adolescents."[15] Keskar, however, was not destined to win the culture wars. Unable to digest AIR's stern diet, the public turned to Radio Ceylon, a commercial radio station broadcasting out of Colombo, which was only too willing to provide Indian listeners with the music that they wanted. Landmark shows like the Binaca Geetmala hosted by the charismatic Ameen Sayani played the latest hits from Hindi films and for a while Radio Ceylon became synonymous with Indian popular culture. In the end, the government conceded defeat. In 1957, it decided to set up a new channel called Vividh Bharati which would broadcast "popular music and light entertainment" for the entire nation.

Keskar's campaign of cultural indoctrination failed because it was based on the premise that the only culture worth disseminating was that practiced by the elite. Keskar was, no doubt, influenced by western theories, which, as we have seen, tended to plot culture on a vertical axis representing social hierarchy. The notion that there were two kinds of culture—one for the elite and another for the masses—arose with the formation of capitalist societies. Previous to the modern age, difference in social rank did not entail any great difference in cultural terms. In feudal Europe, for example, lord and serf existed in a highly proximate and intimate manner, sharing one common culture. Thus, "In Ferrara in the late fifteenth century the Duke, joined in the fun, going masked in the streets and entering private houses to dance with the ladies. In Florence Lorenzo de Medici took part in the carnival ... Henry VIII went to the woods on May Day, just like other young men.

The Emperor Charles V took part in bull-fights during festivals."[16]
This egalitarian culture was destined to vanish once the manorial
system came to be replaced by capitalist modes of production and
consumption. As a result of this transition, the land-owning classes
succumbed to the bourgeoisie, the peasantry was transformed
into a ghettoized urban working class, and a new middle class—
composed of bureaucrats, professionals, small businessmen—
began to emerge as the most important bearer of modernity. The
material arrangements of the capitalist economy dictated that
there was little intercourse between the classes; the impersonal
and disciplinary space of the factory was, for example, the only
point of contact between owners, overseers and workers. An urban
geography of neighborhoods defined by social class and lifestyle
illustrated the growing gap between the various classes. The
middle classes were especially keen to distinguish themselves from
what they saw as the rough and coarse aspects of working class
culture, and put a lot of effort into creating exclusive domains
of artistic practice and consumption. The fate of Shakespeare in
America succinctly illustrates the process of cultural gentrification.
As Lawrence Levine has shown, Shakespearean drama was at one
time an integral part of American popular culture—plays like
Hamlet and *Macbeth* were staged along with fire-eating and juggling
acts and were attended by loud and vociferous crowds who weren't
reluctant to boo incompetent actors off the stage. By the middle of
the nineteenth century however, these same texts had been adopted
by the middle class as exemplars of "high culture" and were
transformed into austere instruments of education and propriety.[17]

The very processes that gave rise to modernity caused a split in
the concept of culture and led to the postulation of elitist cultural
theories which plotted aesthetic value along a vertical axis of low
to high. So crucial is the concept of "verticality" to contemporary
western thought that it also underlies the other contemporary
account of modern culture, one that is expressedly anti-elitist in
its formulation. This latter approach, whose disciplinary name is
cultural studies, draws from the work of the Marxist philosopher

Antonio Gramsci and sees the popular not just as the product of a manipulative capitalism, but more crucially as a contested territory where dominant and oppositional values symbolically engage each other in a struggle for hegemony. In other words, popular culture is a dynamic and shifting space where above meets below, and where high and low clash. Such a theory has an implicit aesthetics—the good or valuable artwork is one that expresses the condition of the oppressed and the marginal—and therefore reaches conclusions regarding the popular which are radically different from those that follow from elitist perspectives. In the case of popular music for example, what Adorno (or Keskar) would consider the repetitive and mind-numbing drone of a depoliticized mass, becomes, for cultural studies, an emancipating sound of resistance and freedom. In the section below, I look at contemporary accounts of what was perhaps the most dominant form of popular music in the twentieth century—rock and roll. Cultural studies can indeed be misled by its own progressivism into erroneous aesthetic judgement; I argue that models structured around verticality are highly inappropriate tools with which to study Indian popular music.

For most commentators, three aspects of rock and roll make it the exemplary instance of the oppositional and liberatory role of popular music: its origins in marginal music forms, its role in the formation of subcultures and its redefinition of pleasure and sexuality. According to the standard histories, rock and roll emerged as a fusion between two older forms of American music. As rock critic Simon Frith observes, "The formula rock n' roll = blues + country is deeply entrenched in rock history."[18] The blues originated in the American South at the end of the nineteenth century, it was a music created by a desperate black community struggling to survive in the years following the Civil War. Though slavery had been abolished as a result of the Union's victory, the economic and social condition of blacks saw very little improvement. The promise of "forty acres and a mule" was never fulfilled; most ex-slaves were forced to become sharecroppers working for white farmers, and were thus condemned to a lifelong cycle of poverty and debt. Blacks also faced virulent forms of racism typified by the Klu Klux Klan and the Jim Crow laws which instituted strict forms of segregation. The blues were an expression of black consciousness trying to come to terms with the harsh realities of its material existence. Though different versions of the form were played all over the South, it was in the Delta, a land of vast alluvial plains filled with cotton plantations, that the blues emerged in its purest and most striking form. As the story goes, W.C. Handy, a professional black musician, who led a successful group which played ragtime and light classical music, was waiting for a train in a small Mississippi town called Tutwiler:

> The train was nine hours late, and sometime during the night a black man in ragged clothes sat down beside him and began playing a guitar, pressing a knife against the strings to get a slurred, moaning, voice-like sound that closely followed his singing. Handy woke up to this music, and the first words he heard the man sing were "Goin' where the Southern meets the Dog". The line was repeated three times, answered in each case by the slide guitar.[19]

What Handy described as "the weirdest music I ever heard" was the sound of the Delta blues. Immortalized through the work of Charley Patton, Son House, Blind Lemon Jefferson and the incomparable Robert Johnson, the acoustic Delta blues would constitute the foundation of much of American music in the twentieth century. Like any artistic form, the blues reflected the history of its makers, and as the material conditions of African-Americans changed, so did the blues. The first few decades of the twentieth century saw a massive migration out of the south, as blacks moved by the thousands to the industrial north in search of employment and a better life. The grit and grime of urban life called for a different kind of music. Playing tough and demanding audiences in bars and honky-tonks in cities like Chicago, Detroit and St. Louis, black musicians were forced to play faster and louder, plugging their guitars into amplifiers to create the "electric blues." This new music, given shape by such giants as Muddy Waters, Howling Wolf, John Lee Hooker, and B.B. King, would in turn, influence the entire generation of white musicians who defined the music of the 1960s: Eric Clapton, Jim Morrisson, the Rolling Stones, and Led Zeppelin.

The second source for rock and roll lay in the music of the Appalachian hill country. The poor white settlers who populated this remote region, had, by dint of their isolation, preserved the traditional musical forms brought over to America by their British ancestors. This pristine music, consisting mainly of exquisite lyrical ballads, had lain unnoticed until discovered by record executives roaming the backwoods in search of new material. Known pejoratively at first as "hillbilly music", this music would become famous all over the world as "country music." Influenced by the blues, country music was raw and down to earth; full of plaintive lyrics that spoke of simple joys and sorrows with great artistic integrity. Made popular in the 1920s and 1930s by stars such as Jimmie Rodgers, the Carter Family and Bob Wills and the Texas Playboys, this music had, by the early 1950s gained even more momentum through the work of artists like Bill Monroe and Hank Williams Sr. These two great strains of native music—blues and country—would, in the early 1950s come together to form the basis for rock and roll. The very first songs recorded by Elvis Presley in 1954 for the historic Sun Sessions clearly demonstrate rock's twin heritage. "That's All Right" is pure blues, in fact when the song was first aired on a mainstream radio station, hundreds of incensed white listeners called in to protest the playing of "nigger music". "I Love You Because," on the other hand is pure country, as is the bluegrass number "Blue Moon of Kentucky". Elvis was a musicological as well as an economic miracle in that he managed to fuse older white and black sounds and give the resulting mix a totally contemporary feel. Elvis would go on to have *thirty* #1 hits, selling millions of records in the process, and his enormous popularity was the main factor which helped rock and roll—known originally as rockabilly—outgrow its regional and racially divided roots in the south and become a global phenomenon.

The "low" origins of rock and roll gave rise to the notion that popular music is an instance of cultural politics, a means by which various underprivileged or unassimilated sections of society have expressed their marginal status. The canonical history of the genre goes something like this: early rock and roll expressed the frustration of white teenagers growing up in the straitlaced 1950s; soul music reflected the aspirations of a disenfranchised black community; 1960s rock was the voice of flower power, free love and the peace movement; punk articulated the raw energies of the British working class and alienated teenagers growing· up in barren suburbs; grunge gave words to the hopelessness of Generation X; and rap enunciated the anger and negative energy of the African-American ghetto. Such a narrative not only prioritizes "political" music at the expense of more mainstream genres like R&B, doo-wop, disco, funk and synthesizer pop, it also conveniently overlooks how this "oppositional" music very quickly became integrated with the marketplace. The standard reading of rock and roll highlights the truth that the whole analytical framework of cultural studies is dependent on a notion of verticality which sees the popular as an eruption from below. Can such a perspective be employed in developing a theory of Indian popular music? We can answer this question only after we delineate a "cognitive map" that enumerates the different genres of popular music, their logic of production and consumption, their relationship to each other, and their location within both the nation as well as the global system. What I hope to do in the following pages is to briefly sketch out the contours of such a map and suggest some possible ways in which we can begin to conceptualize the function and meaning of popular music in contemporary India. My central argument in what follows is that Indian popular music needs to be conceptualized as being constituted along an axis of *horizontality* rather than the vertical one that has been used to analyze western cultural production. To put it differently, Indian popular music must be seen as *spreading across* different segments of Indian society rather than being located at one particular level that *stands above* or *below* other such layers. Like cricket or Hindi film, Indian popular music has always cut across categories like caste, class or religion that are otherwise divisive in their effects. To analyze Indian popular music is tantamount then, to studying the culture of the entire nation.

The Birth of Film Music

Two genres, both ancient in lineage, lie at the edges of the ensemble that is Indian music. Classical music, which found fruition in the courts of Mughal India, has stayed alive till today, albeit as the pursuit of a tiny elite. At the other end of the spectrum lies the music of the rural hinterlands—songs sung at harvest time, at religious *melas* and *pujas*, at births, weddings and deaths, in short, all the various musics that fall under the rubric of "folk". Classical music enjoys the patronage of both the government and the social elite, its prestige has been further enhanced by its dissemination at a global level through the efforts of artists like Ravi Shankar and Ali Akbar Khan. Folk music too has grown glamorous through the same processes: continuously mined by the tools of anthropology, more and more folk music appears in parades, in arts festivals, and in the culture-hungry circuits of foreign capitals. How does one make sense of these two prestigious forms—one supposedly "raw", the other simmered for centuries and cooked to perfection? To understand the meaning of classical music in contemporary India, one ought to resist the temptation to treat it as the repository of some "higher" value, but instead take a more materialist perspective and inquire into its sociological function. The origins of what we call classical music can be traced back to Amir Khusrau (1253–1325), who is credited with the invention of the sitar, and perhaps to an even earlier era of Hindu temple singing. Later exponents include Tansen (1508–1600), one of the *Nava Ratnas*

(Nine Gems) in Akbar's court, and Thyagaraja (1760–1848), the famous Carnatic saint-musician. Patronized by royalty and nobility, this music was elitist in character and in structure. It had an elaborate temporal dimension, with typical performances often stretching for many hours. It was formally complex—as early as the thirteenth century the great scholar Sarangadeva could list as many as 264 ragas in his musicological treatise *Sangeet-ratnakara*. Also it involved a highly mannered mode of listening and appreciation in keeping with its aristocratic audience. In more recent times classical music became institutionalized through the *gharanas* and was largely supported by the rulers of princely states like Gwalior, Indore, Mysore and Patiala. After Independence, the role of patronage passed on to the Indian government, which, as we have seen, became a vigorous champion of the form. Over the course of the twentieth century classical music produced a galaxy of stars who gained national repute: Allauddin Khan (sarod), Bade Ghulam Ali Khan (vocalist), Ravi Shankar (sitar), Ali Akbar Khan (sarod), Alla Rakha (tabla), Bismillah Khan (shenai), the Dagar Brothers (vocalists), Hari Prasad Chaurasiya (flute), Vilayat Khan (sitar) and V.G. Jog (violin)—to name only a few exponents of north Indian music. Many of these musicians became prolific performers at the international level, helping Indian classical music gain respectability and fans—of whom Yehudi Menuhin and George Harrison were among the most prominent.

How relevant is classical music today? As any music theorist can demonstrate, the music is complex and rich at a purely formal level. And though its reach is minuscule in comparison with more popular forms, it has an appreciative and enthusiastic following in the major urban centers, enjoying enormous prestige amongst the intelligentsia. None of these factors, however, are sufficient to establish classical music as true contemporary art. The complexities of the *thaats*, ragas and *talas* may be a matter of fine art, but how significant is the resulting beauty? The sounds developed in the courts of a distant feudal aristocracy cannot be adequate to the cacophony that characterizes contemporary India: Ayodhya and Gujarat, Agnis and nuclear bombs, supermarkets and fast food chains, Shah Rukh Khan and Sachin Tendulkar, Naxalites and the Ranbir Sena, cyber cafes and chat rooms, bodyshopping and outsourcing, landless labor and female infanticide. Just as no one demands that a performance of Beethoven's Eroica reveals any truth about the contemporary West—one lets Madonna or Eminem do the talking—so it would be unfair to demand of a *khyaal* sung by Bade Ghulam Ali Khan (a man whose universe was the princely state of Patiala)—that it transcend its own space and time and speak convincingly to the present. That being so, we need to pay more attention to the cultural politics associated with classical music than to its aesthetic splendors. It is very clear that the patronage and consumption of classical music is strongly linked to an elementary logic of elitism: that of prioritizing the effort involved in "appreciating" the art form in order to elevate its significance. Classical music is held to have high aesthetic value because it is "difficult to understand." What this formulation conceals is that this "difficulty" is ultimately only equivalent to a specific set of material resources—leisure time, private tutors, music schools and expensive concerts—which are necessary in order to become an informed listener. Classical music is necessarily restricted to a small privileged group, and those who uphold it as a repository of truth are therefore committed to the questionable assertion that a practice that excludes a majority of people can function as universal art.

Though folk music has no such pretensions, it too is equally implicated in the politics of above and below. The discovery and celebration of folk music originated from the anthropological impulse to get to the "essence" of man that arose at the beginning of the modern period. As Peter Burke has observed, "It was in the late eighteenth and early nineteenth centuries when traditional popular culture was just beginning to disappear that the 'people' or 'folk' became a subject of interest to European intellectuals."[20] The term "folk" first came into circulation in Germany when

J.G. Herder gave the name *Volkslied* (folksong) to a collection of songs he made in 1774. Herder's neologism expressed an idea shared by many others: the modern world had lost its moral integrity and spirituality, modern art was too sophisticated and therefore corrupt. True wisdom and morality lay with common peasant folk, who though poor and uneducated, lived close to nature and had preserved the simple truths of man's primitive ways. Coming as it did in the high noon of the Enlightenment, this philosophy of the folk was a romantic construction that was at bottom a reaction to the rampant industrialization that was sweeping across western Europe. Wordsworth's "leech gatherer," the figure in the poem "Resolution and Independence" who represents the stoic, unchanging essence of man, was the romantic fantasy which compensated for the real economic ravages depicted in Oliver Goldsmith's "The Deserted Village." What was true in the West was valid in the empire as well. Colonialism granted a certain measure of industrialization to the colonies, at the same time, the needs of colonial administration were behind the desire to scrutinize and classify the "folk" of the land. As has been well documented, colonial anthropology was mainly responsible for the modern nomenclature for the caste system as well as for the elaborate lists of "tribals" and "aboriginals." The slow pace of colonial development meant that neither the peasantry nor rural culture disappeared as had happened in the case of Europe. But the cult of the folk was inherited from the British, and came to the fore in the postcolonial period when industrialization instituted by the Nehruvian state raised fears that folk culture may become extinct. Seen now as an "endangered species," folk music, much like *sastryiasangeet*, came to enjoy the patronage of both government and the social elite.

Though the rural may now be an endangered category, the music associated with the countryside has had considerable influence on the evolution of modern Indian music. In Bengal, for example, the music of the *bauls*—travelling bards who roamed the hinterland— was a deep source of inspiration for the province's most famous poet and songwriter. On hearing the now famous tune *"Amar Moner Manush Ye Re"*, Rabindranath Tagore would write "The words are very plain, but in conjunction with the tune, their meaning flashes up in unexpected brilliance ... like the sobbing air of a child who cannot find its mother in the dark."[21] Tagore's music incorporated many *baul* themes, and his play *Phalguni* features a blind *baul* who is the only character who understands the mysteries of life. So great was this influence, that one scholar described Tagore as "the greatest of the *bauls.*"[22] Tagore's use of *baul* material may seem to be an act of appropriation—he was, after all, a westernized bhadralok zamindar whose only contact with folk culture came about as a consequence of his appointment as administrator for his family's extensive estates in East Bengal. Yet Tagore may be less guilty than he seems at first glance. The *bauls* inhabited and performed in a very specific area—mainly in the remote district of Birbhum. They earned a living by traveling from village to village, performing at festive occasions and receiving alms for their singing. Their songs, accompanied by distinctive instruments like the *ektara*, reflected their Vaisnavite origins, many recounting the amorous exploits of Lord Krishna. By incorporating these themes and styles into modern Bengali music, Tagore was not only paying homage to *baul* art but also signaling the truth that such localized art needed to be inflected with contemporary accents if it was to be appreciated by a larger audience. Tagore's intuition was well-founded; all ethnographic studies have reiterated the fundamental truth that folk music is the most context-specific and therefore the most limited of all art forms, consisting as it does of distinct music appropriate for particular occasions and places. Edward O. Henry's well-known study on Bhojpuri music, for example, elaborates this truth in detail. Some Bhojpuri genres belong exclusively to women: wedding songs, songs sung when a woman gives birth to boys (*sohars*), recreational songs known as *kajalis*, rice-transplanting songs, milling songs and songs of lament. Others, like *harikirtans*, devotional songs addressed to Ram or Krishna, are sung only by men.[23] And then there are genres which are even more specialized: field hollers known as *khari biraha* sung exclusively by men of the cow herding and sheep herding castes, epic ballads called *Alha* sung by members of the Muslim *nat* caste and bhajans sung by mendicants known as *jogis*.

Henry's discussion of Bhojpuri illustrates the more general truth that in the pre-capitalist world all music (except that patronized in the courts) was mapped onto the practices of everyday life. The music of a particular community could therefore only co-exist with its culture. Thus folk music is literally mundane and non-transcendental. This is both its strength and its limitation and explains why, despite the piety surrounding it, it can often be unappealing to modern ears:

> ... in the U.K., people might point to Gaelic songs and industrial songs ... These it is argued, are not, like disco (and pop music in general), produced *for* the people, but *by* them. The problem is that we don't live in a society of small, technologically simple communities such as produce such art. Preserving such music at best gives us a historical perspective on peasant and working-class culture, at worst leads to a nostalgia for a simple, harmonious community existence that never existed. *More bluntly, songs in Gaelic or dealing with nineteenth-century factory conditions, beautiful as they are, don't mean much to most English-speaking people today.*[24]

What Dyer says about British folk music in the quote above is equally true for Bhojpuri songs. A Bhojpuri song, cannot by its very nature, transcend the culture it comes from. This is a kind of "iron law" that applies to all folk music including urban music. To use a contemporary example, most British punk music from the 1970s (a form grounded in the lives of unemployed white working class males) sounds repetitive, boring and irrelevant today even while being fetishized by music critics in the manner folk music often is. Bhojpuri and punk both exhibit the "boringness" of purely immanent art forms, that is, of art which is too closely tied to life. If by transcendence we mean the property of exceeding the ground or conditions of production, then it is no heresy to suggest that a disco number by Bappi or Biddu is far more transcendental than Bhojpuri or *baul*. As proof of this consider Henry's observation that:

> the All-India Radio station in Varanasi transmits a considerable amount of music including classical Hindustani, folk and popular music. Popular music, *consisting largely of film songs*, is enjoyed more by the younger people. Young men sing snatches of it to each other on their evening rambles around their village, and boys and girls alike make up their own verses to film song tunes.[25]

One must caution though against an overly anthropological reading of the sort implied by Henry. Just because these young men have begun to hum lines from film songs on their evening rambles around their village it does not follow that film music is contemporary folk music. Film music is not embedded in daily life in the manner of Bhojpuri folk music; in fact quite the opposite is true. Filmi *geet* gets its power from being deterritorialized and decontextualized—it belongs to but is not contained by the parameters of local life. The lack of location is a function of what might be called Hindi film music's "inessence," its absolute hybridity. Film music is flux rather than form; it is a bubbling mixture of influences which never stabilizes into sediment. It is syntactic rather than semantic. This insubstantiality permits film music to be popular in the way classical and folk music are not. The latter are art forms which are external to the field of the popular even though they may sometimes influence it. Classical music is an elite form, it is music from above, and its meaning is exhausted by the role it plays in elite-formation, whereas folk music originates with peasants and tribals, it is music from below, and it circulates as a symbol of "authentic" culture. Sociology aside, both forms live on by being appropriated by popular music. The failure of these forms has philosophical reasons: for classical music, the dubious claim that only one particular form can apprehend the universal; for folk, the futile attempt to find transcendental meaning in mundane sounds.

Hindi film music *is* Indian popular music, and any analysis of popular Indian culture must try and explain its fundamental nature. Hindi film songs' delirious lack of substance can elicit puzzlement,

> Cine music is a curious and somewhat bizarre blend of East and West: choppy and hyperactive melodies, often in oriental scales, are belted out by nasal singers over Latin rhythms and an eclectic accompaniment that may include rap set, electric organs and guitars, violins, xylophones, celeste, bongos, sitar, tabla, or bamboo flute.[26]

and sometimes even downright hostility:

> On the whole, Indian film music has certainly had some very undesirable effects. Most of it is not so much Indian as a form of commercial hybridization from various sources. This orchestrated mush has been blaring away in thousands of villages for over a generation and has now started to influence the folk music of the peasants. This music springs from the very soul of the people and it would be a gigantic tragedy if the concoctions of the smart musicians in the Bombay studios were to injure so rich a folk tradition.[27]

The tenor of these remarks—not far in spirit from Keskar—are typical of western observers obsessed with "the wonder that was India" but prevented by that very passion from perceiving the India of the present. To dismiss Hindi film music as "orchestrated mush" is to forgo the means by which to analyze contemporary India, for it, along with cricket, television and Bollywood movies, comprises the four cornerstones of Indian popular culture.

Music was an integral part of Indian film from the very beginning. The very first sound film *Alam Ara* (1931) had about a dozen songs, *Indrasabha* released in 1932 had 72! When the Wadia brothers dared to produce a film—*Navajawan* (1937)—which contained no songs, so great was the hostility to this lack that they had to screen a trailer seeking to explain the absence of the "song-cushions."[28] Film production in this early period was organized under a studio system dominated by three companies: New Theatres, Prabhat and Bombay Talkies. New Theatres, established in 1931, was based in Calcutta; it had on its staff famous directors like Debaki Bose (*Vidyapathi*), and the legendary Pramathesh Nath Barua (*Devdas*) as well as actors like K.L. Saigal and Kanan Devi. The Prabhat Film Company was based in Pune (it later moved to Bombay) and one of its leading lights— V. Shantaram—was instrumental in producing the very first gramophone record of Indian film music (*Sairandhri*, 1934). Bombay Talkies was founded by Devika Rani and Himansu Rai, and its stable of artists included some of the greatest names in Indian cinema—Ashok Kumar, Raj Kapoor and Dilip Kumar. Because music was so essential to the process of moviemaking, each studio maintained a roster of music directors who were under exclusive contracts and composed only for the studio that employed them. Thus New Theatres had Rai Chand Boral, Timir Boran and Pankaj Mullick; Prabhat employed Govind Tembe, Keshavrao Bhole and Master Krishnarao; while Bombay Talkies relied almost exclusively on Saraswati Devi.

In the early years, music composed by these resident directors tended to be very derivative of traditional forms. Since Indian film itself had developed from theatrical forms like *nautanki* (U.P.), *tamasha* (Marathi) and *jatra* (Bengal), it is not surprising that music directors would turn to indigenous sources for inspiration. Many songs in these early years were in the light-classical *ghazal* form, or used the *dadra* metre; their instrumentation was also traditional consisting of the tabla, the *tanpura* and the harmonium. The Bombay studios were the most conservative in the matter of musical taste. Saraswati Devi had learnt classical music under Pandit Vishnunarayan Bhatkhande, and her scores reflected her training. Most of her work for Bombay Talkies was classical-influenced and she took great pains to ensure that every musician employed by the studio was a master of some classical instrument. The Prabhat trio—Tembe, Bhole and Krishnarao—

were also classically oriented, though their music also showed the influence of Marathi folk music and Urdu *ghazals* and *quawwalis*. The truly significant innovations in film music were to come from Calcutta. Musical practice at New Theatres was quite different from that cultivated at the Bombay studios. Though New Theatres had its share of classical-based songs—K.L. Saigal's *thumri* "Babul Mora Naihar Chuto hi Jae" was a national hit—its musicians were far more influenced by western music. This fact fostered a culture of experimentation and innovation which would produce striking results. Thus Pankaj Mullick used Tagore's compositions in his film scores and incorporated the vibrato—a western vocal technique—into his songs. Rai Chand Boral introduced western instruments like the organ and the piano, and his score for the film *Bidyapati* is the first example of the use of chords and western harmonic principles. Boral was also responsible for the first use of playback in Indian film—in the film *Dhoop Chaon* (1935) directed by Nitin Bose. As the story goes, Bose overheard Pankaj Mullick singing along with an American song that he was playing on the gramophone. The moment was serendipitous—Bose reasoned that Mullick need only lip-synch the lyrics for an audience to believe that he was the real singer, and thus was born that uniquely Indian device of playback singing. This "invention" symbolized the fertile interplay between western and Indian traditions that characterized the musical culture of New Theatres.

There was in the decades of the 1930s and 1940s an "invasion" of indigenous Indian music by western-influenced Bengali modes of musical experimentation. This was in keeping with the cultural hegemony that Bengal enjoyed over the rest of India. Bengal was at the forefront simply because, of all the Indian cultures, it was best able to articulate an incipient version of Indian modernity. Gokhale's famous statement "What Bengal thinks today, India thinks tomorrow" summed up Bengal's advanced location. The very fact that Bengal was "backward" in terms of high Indian culture enabled it to be home to the most "forward" of cultural formations.

Indigenous north Indian culture was far too colored by feudal stylistic forms for its music to be an expression of the contemporary. The westernized film music created first in Bengal proved irresistible to audiences because, as the writer Hameedudin Mohammed observes, "the only music available to the masses was either the devotional music of *kathas, kirtans* and *bhajans* or the *quawwalis, mushairas* or shenais".[29] Mohammed's observation suggests that traditional music—and to his list we need to add folk music and the music of the theater—was quite unable to satisfy the needs of the broader audience.

The Sounds of Modernity

This unsatisfied demand was to be met by artists working in Bengal who came up with the musical tools with which Indian modernity could be articulated. This "Bengali invasion" predates the more famous "British invasion" of rock and roll. One could argue that music directors like Boral, Mullick and Biswas performed the same function that the Beatles and the Rolling Stones were to fulfill thirty years later in a more global context. Anyone who follows western popular music must wonder why English bands like the Beatles and the Rolling Stones could have such a huge impact on what was essentially an American art form. The answer lies in the fact that no particular musical idiom present in America in the 1950s and early 1960s was sufficient to express what may be called the sounds of modernity. Rock and roll, as we have seen, was born from a fusion of black blues rhythm and blues and white country music. Created essentially by poor southern whites, this early rock and roll—known more specifically as rockabilly—was a very temporary formation. First of all, the fusion was never stable; it always threatened to split into its constituent parts. Thus in Elvis Presley's classic Sun recordings (often referred to as the text which gave birth to rock and roll) the blues and the country influence are separate: "That's All Right Mama" is black music, "Blue Moon" is white. This split in Elvis's repertoire was to be generalized in just a few years with rock and roll leaving its black influences largely behind in the lily-white pop of teen idols like Rick Nelson, Fabian, Bobby Vinton, Bobby Vee and others. Secondly, rockabilly as a sound (except in the transcendental case of Elvis) was dated even at its birth, it never was fully modern. Thus, even a major artist like Jerry Lee Lewis was popular more in the American South and today sounds distinctly unmodern unlike performers who came just a few years later. Compared to America, Britain had a thin tradition of popular music: music hall (which was already dead by the 1950s), some crooning and the odd genre known as skiffle (whose most famous practitioner was Lonnie Donnegan). Most British pop musicians—Cliff Richard being the most notable—produced faithful and pale imitations of American material. The Beatles and the Stones changed all that by producing a music which was strikingly original and modern. They were able to do this because of their very distance from the sources of rock and roll. Unburdened by any musical native tradition, and equidistant from country and blues, pop and R&B, the Beatles stitched together all these various idioms—white ballad music ("Yesterday"), British music hall ("Yellow Submarine"), Southern rockabilly ("Hippy Hippy Shake"), black rhythm and blues ("Money"), teen pop ("All My Loving") into an idiolect which would come to stand for the modern.

The Beatles combined all the various strands of American music to create a truly modern international pop sound; years earlier the musical directors at New Theatres combined aspects of western music with the whole range of Indian musical forms to produce the sound of Indian modernity. The innovations in Calcutta stimulated change in Bombay musical production as well. Singing styles changed in response to technology and modern sensibility. The softer style of singing for the microphone developed in America by singers like Whispering Jack Smith and Rudy Vallee and later perfected by Bing Crosby and Frank Sinatra was made popular in India by K.L. Saigal. Another innovation was the introduction of large orchestras consisting mainly of western instruments like violins, violas, cellos, pianos, organs, flutes, cymbals, drums, and harmoniums. A similar change could be seen in the case of women vocalists as well. Women singers had traditionally sung in a dramatic, throaty style inherited from the culture of *mehfils* (musical soirees) and nautch girls. Nurjahan (who migrated to Pakistan after Partition) inaugurated a narrower, more restrained vocal style which was then perfected by the queen of Indian vocalists—Lata Mangeshkar.

In her study of Hindi film songs Alison Arnold states that the period 1931–1955 marked a dynamic, even revolutionary period in the history of Hindi film music. Over these two decades film music directors worked creatively towards establishing an acceptable, identifiable, national, popular film music. By 1955 they had achieved this goal. Arnold goes on to argue that though the genre has exhibited increasing westernization and use of western technology since then, developments since the 1950s have been largely cosmetic, and Hindi film song has remained fundamentally unchanged. There is a great deal of truth in Arnold's observation. As seen above, many of the stylistic features associated with present-day Hindi songs were already in place several decades ago. Moreover, all the major playback singers of the post-Independence period—Manna Dey, Hemant Kumar, Talat Mahmood, Mohammed Rafi, Mukesh, Kishore Kumar, Geeta Dutt, Lata Mangeshkar and Asha Bhosle—had all started recording as early as the 1940s. Composers like Naushad, O.P. Nayyar, SD Burman and Shanker-Jaikishen had also established themselves by the mid-1950s. The next two decades would see the emergence of most of the other big names in Hindi film music: Laxmikant-Pyarelal, Kalyanji-Anandji, Rajesh Roshan, Bappi Lahiri and RD Burman. For Arnold, none of these directors introduced anything radically new into the technique, style and content of the Hindi film song. The only change she notes is in the direction of noisier and faster paced music enabled by technological features like multiple stereo, echo chambers, reverberation and distortion techniques, feedback, staggered tracks, multiple overdubbing, compression, high-speed effects, filtered sounds and the electronic amplification of all types of musical information.[30] This may well be true if one is looking at film music from a musicological perspective like that of Arnold, but what is passed over in this account is the cultural impact of this new bout of westernization and hybridization. If Hindi film music had articulated Indian modernity in the 1930s and 1940s, it rearticulated it one more time in the 1970s.

Once again, Bengal played a crucial role in this process, helped by two Bengali expatriates—Kishore Kumar and Rahul Dev Burman. Born in Khandwa in Madhya Pradesh, Kishore Kumar started singing in Saraswati Devi's chorus in Bombay Talkies, where his elder brother Ashok Kumar was a top star. Though well known as Dev Anand's singing voice, it was only after he teamed up with RD Burman (often as the singing voice for Rajesh Khanna) that Kishore became synonymous with the very voice of Indian modernity. What is unique about this achievement is that Kishore Kumar was entirely untutored in music. All the other male playback singers of his generation had an acquaintance with classical music— Mohammed Rafi had trained under the great Bade Ghulam Ali Khan, Manna Dey with Aman Ali Khan, while both Mukesh and Mahendra Kapoor were versed in light classical music. Kishore's lack of training caused him to be initially shunned by musical directors and to be ignored by award-granting juries. Kalyanji (of the duo Kalyanji-Anandji) once said that Kishore's skills lay more in mimicry than in technique, but Ashok Kumar was surely nearer the truth when he asserted that "Kishore's voice hits the mike, straight, at its most sensitive point—and that's the secret of his success as a singer without peer!"[31] It was precisely this raw directness and the accelerated tempo in his singing voice which made Kishore the ultimate symbol of modern Hindi film music. Earlier playback singers lacked his zip; thus Rafi, who sang playback for Shammi Kapoor in films like *Junglee* (1961), *Jaanwar* (1965) and *Kashmir Ki Kali* (1964), could never find the pitch to match Kapoor's frenetic modern heroics. Rafi belonged to an earlier time, and though technically proficient, his sedate style evoked the world of courtly sophistication and not the images we associate with Shammi Kapoor—driving recklessly up the hills (and running into Sharmila Tagore) in *Kashmir Ki Kali*, or returning home in a motorcade to assume the crown in *Rajkumar* (1964).

Kishore started as playback singer for Dev Anand—with *Ziddi* in 1948 and continued to be Anand's voice until his own death. This association was not entirely fortuitous—Kishore's voice was a perfect match for the cocky, light-hearted, urbane characters Dev Anand had popularized. But his real breakthrough came in 1967, when SD Burman made him sing "Roop Tera Mastana" and "Mere Sapno ki Rani" in *Aradhana* (1969). "The whole nation was enthralled by his sensual vocals ... after that, there was no looking back."[32] It was however the work he did with SD Burman's son which would guarantee Kishore's immortality. That inimitable partnership was to produce some of the greatest music in contemporary times, in the songs from films like *Padosan* (1968), *Amar Prem* (1971), *Hare Rama Hare Krishna* (1971), *Yaadon Ki Baraat* (1973), *Sholay* (1975) and many others. Rahul Dev, also known as Pancham (a nickname reputedly given to him by Ashok Kumar) had worked from a very early age as assistant to his father and had also trained for a while under Ali Akbar Khan. Yet like Kishore, he was not burdened by fealty to any sort of tradition. As he observed about himself:

> I don't say I am a knowledgeable man when it comes to raags. I don't say I tried to do so and so song in Raag Darbar or attempted some difficult raag in another song. Whatever comes to my head I compose.[33]

The seminal partnership between RD Burman and Kishore Kumar changed the face of Hindi film music and gave Indian modernity an utterly contemporary voice. The Kishore-RD sound—with its multicultural influences, its frenetic pacing, its youthful exuberance and upbeat rhythms—encapsulated in advance and foretold the new globalized India which was yet to come into being. This music represented a complete rupture with the music of the "golden age" associated with composers like SD Burman, Naushad, O.P. Nayyar, Ghulam Mohammed, and Shanker-Jaikishen. When teenagers in Mumbai or Toronto congregate today in discotheques it is RD they groove to, Kishore they sing with. Why are RD-Kishore still relevant while Naushad or Ghulam Mohammed are not? Because the life-world evoked by the latter has vanished into the past. The music of the golden age was created within the context of a very particular formation—the postcolonial state that came into being with Independence—and its aesthetic features are intimately connected with the nature of that formation. The need to understand the specificities of this aesthetic as well as that of its successor calls for a discussion of the Indian state after Independence.

The Nehruvian postcolonial state is typically analyzed in one of two ways. A triumphalist free market account—specially popular in the wake of liberalization and the rise of Hindutva— sees the entire era as being inefficient and corrupt and impeding the country's progress because of its misguided commitment to socialism and secularism. The orthodox Marxist analysis, in a characteristically formulaic manner, sees the Nehruvite state as "the organ of the class rule of the bourgeosie and landlords, led by the big bourgeoise, who are increasingly collaborating with foreign finance capital."[34] Both these descriptions fall prey to cynicism and are guilty of too easy a dismissal of the achievements of the era. While the license raj did indeed encourage corruption and stagnation, it was instrumental in establishing an infrastructure— through investment in heavy industries, transporation and education—which later enabled the economic boom of the nineties. It also had a commendable record in looking after minority rights and interests. Again, while the various Congress governments often surreptitiously sided with the ruling groups and classes, many governmental policies—the abolition of privy purses, the nationalization of banks, or the introduction of reservations—sought to remove societal iniquity. The project of nation-building had been initiated with the optimism and innocence characteristic of all beginnings. Nehru reflected the mood of the country when he wrote in 1955 that:

> Even though we have a multitude of problems, and difficulties surround us and often appear to overwhelm, there is an air of hope in this country, a faith in our future and a certain reliance on the basic principles that have guided us so far. There is the breadth of dawn, the feeling of the beginning of a new era in the long and chequered history of India.[35]

Under Nehru's leadership, the country eschewed the path of capitalist development for one of socialistic transformation. This project was based on a planned economy dominated by heavy industry and the public sector and an ideological commitment, in the words of the historian Bipan Chandra, to a "greater equality of opportunity, social justice, the ending of the acute social and economic disparities generated by feudalism and capitalism, and the application of the scientific approach to the problems of society."[36] Though redolent of the Soviet and Chinese models, the Indian experiment avoided all forms of totalitarianism, embracing instead democratic values of free elections, freedom of speech and minimal interference in the areas of religion, culture and private life. Indeed it may be said to be one of the very few instances of "socialism with a human face." Such a program proved increasingly difficult to execute, and by the mid-1960s the country was in a severe crisis: inflation was high, foreign exchange reserves had sunk to perilously low levels, and failures in the monsoons raised the possibility of widespread famines. Economic failures led to social and political turmoil. There was a marked rise in communal tensions, and social protests and movements grew increasingly violent—in Naxalbari, Gujarat and finally in Bihar under the impetus of Jayaprakash Narayan's "Total Revolution." The imposition of the Emergency in 1975 was merely an admission that Nehruvian socialism was not sustainable any more. The country silently abandoned its socialist principles under the force of these circumstances. Land reforms and community development went into abeyance and were replaced by an agrarian capitalism made possible by the "green revolution." Planning lost its crucial role, the Fourth Five Year Plan was postponed and the Planning Commission lost all its power and became reduced to a mere advisory body. And in a humiliating measure, the government was forced to devalue the rupee under pressure from the United States and the World Bank. The setbacks suffered by the system led to an isolation which bordered on the paranoid. The banking, coal and insurance industries were all nationalized in the early seventies, while the passage of FERA (Foreign Exchange Regulation Act) in 1973 made "India one of the most difficult destinations for capital in the world."[37] The quasi-socialist state hobbled along until it reached a point of no return in 1991. Faced with the prospect of defaulting on international loans, the Congress government led by Narasimha Rao started the process of reforms which came to be known as liberalization. India's tryst with socialism was over.

It is the pathos of Indian socialism which provides the ground for the sublime music of the golden age. The fragility and nebulousness of the postcolonial formation imbues the aesthetic of the music with a sense of passing and sorrow. The sense of inhabiting a place which is always vanishing and perhaps already gone gave songs like "Baharon Phul Barsao" (*Suraj*, 1966), "Dost Dost Na Raha" (*Sangam*, 1964) or "Chalo Dildar Chalo" (*Pakeezah*, 1971) their unparalled beauty. The essence of these songs, then, was one of *nostalgia for the present*. The peculiarity of the postcolonial socialist state, its suspension in a time which was outside of the present, was the objective correlative and the material source for this aesthetic. What Kishore and RD did was to introduce an entirely new regime of sound and significance into the domain of Hindi film music. A song like "Mere Samne Wali Khirki Mein" (*Padosan*, 1968) is firmly located in the here and now, its lyrics signifying a materiality of presence, its rhythms pounding out the trajectory of desire. It is truly contemporary and this music is immanent to an order of reality which is both tangible and attainable. The joyous yelps of *Padosan* predict the jouissance of lifestyle that the liberalization of 1991 would inaugurate. The French theorist Jacques Atali had once written that music is prophecy; it makes the future audible. The music of Kishore and RD proves Atali right, for it foretells a future that would come to pass.

Kishore Kumar and RD Burman may well have been Bengal's last gift to Indian modernity, thus bringing to a close a long process of diffusion that started as early as the 1830s with thinkers and activists like Raja Rammohun Roy and Iswarchandra Vidyasagar, and included seminal figures of modern India such as Bankim Chandra Chattopadhay, Rabindranath Tagore, Swami Vivekananda, Sri Aurobindo, Surendranath Bannerjea and Netaji Subhas Chandra Bose, Jagadish Bose, Satyen Bose, Suniti Chatterjee, P.C. Mahalonobis, Satyajit Ray and Mrinal Sen. Bengal was the epicenter of the colonial state, and from it blew the winds of change. The innovations at New Theatres and their subsequent adoption in Bombay film music illustrate the one-way relationship that existed between Bengal and the rest of India. The nature of development in independent India would radically alter this scenario: the rise of Gujarat, Maharashtra and Punjab and the simultaneous economic decline of Bengal would put an end to Bengali cultural hegemony. Kishore-RD is therefore a double-edged trope—signifying both the coming of a global Indian modernity as well as the eclipse of Bengal. It is not accidental that in spite of their incredible impact all over the country, neither Kishore nor RD were much loved in Bengal itself. They could never rival Hemant Kumar (known better in Bengal as Hemanta Mukhopadhay) or Manna Dey, nor did RD's compositions become the defining tunes of the era as they were to be in the Hindi music world. Both were *probashis*—Bengalis born and raised outside of Bengal—and perhaps this lack in "authenticity" contributed to the tepidity with which they were received in the land of their forefathers. More importantly though, the sounds they created had left Bengal behind. Kishore clearly was the Indian Elvis—his voice encapsulated the brazen yearning of a liberated sexuality and an insistent urgency which demands its object right now. The new paradigm of voice and soul that Kishore, in tandem with RD, created was very far removed from the sedate and repressed patterns of Bengali *bhadralok* culture.

Bengali music reached its zenith in the 1950s and 1960s, coinciding with the golden age of Hindi song. For Bengalis of that time, as well as for subsequent generations, nothing is perhaps more beautiful than the music of that era which is still known as Adhunik Gaan, literally "Modern Song." Bengal had enjoyed a rich musical tradition stretching back to the nineteenth century: the classically based songs of Ramnidhi Gupta known as Nidhubabu's *tappa*; religious genres like *kirtan* and *shymasangeet* (songs devoted to Kali); the work of individual composers like Rajnikanta Sen (1865–1910), Dwijendra Lal Roy (1863–1913), Atul Prasad Sen (1871–1934) and Nazrul Islam; and the rural music of the *bauls* and other folk groups. By Independence most of these genres were exhausted and incapable of serving as vehicles of expression for the new urban generation which was coming into being. The religious genres were popular with women and with the lower classes but were too limited in scope to appeal to urban youth. Classical music had by then reached elite status and had no relation with the popular. *Bauls* were becoming an exportable item (a sure sign that they were irrelevant in their native milieu) and whatever energy remained in rural music had been sanitized into a modernized version which the AIR referred to as *"palligeeti."* This was in keeping with the patronizing term *"kisan"* by which rural India was sentimentally trivialized by Indian political discourse.

Only one out of the many musical forms of early modern Bengal survived as living music in the post-Independence era. Rabindrasangeet, by far the most prestigious of all Bengali genres, had by then reached canonical status and was one of the crucial constitutive tools of Bengali *bhadralok* culture. Much more so than classical music—which had never had more than a handful of devotees—Rabindrasangeet operated much as classical music and the opera do in the West, by defining and separating the elite from common folk. Rabindrasangeet embodied three crucial characteristics which underlie *bhadralok* subjectivity—individualistic western Romanticism, religiosity and secular nationalism. It expressed with great precision the restrained and orderly pleasures of the middle classes, and encapsulated the very essence of that Brahmo sensibility which came to dominate Bengali culture as a whole. In establishing its hegemony, Rabindrik ways effectively marginalized the excesses of both the *chotolok* or the lower classes (*jatras, khemta* dancing, *sawner gan*) and feudal cultures (*jalshaghars, baijis*). By the time of Independence this process of hegemony was complete. A partial challenge to this dominant culture came from the theatrical and musical productions that were centered around IPTA (Indian People's Theatre Association). But, by the late 1950s, this movement was a spent force. The true opposition to Rabindrik culture came from outside, from the ubiquitous and overwhelming presence of Hindi film music. The all-India reach of Vividh Bharati ensured that the "vulgar" would once again find its voice. The rhythms and beats of Hindi music—especially of Kishore Kumar and RD Burman—challenged the stiff propriety of Rabindrik culture, and had by the 1970s, conquered the Bengali masses.

Adhunik music, created mainly in the two decades after Independence, was never oppositional to mainstream Rabindrik culture nor was it ever implicated in the cultural politics of high versus low. Though there existed an unwritten rule against recording in both genres—Hemanta Mukhopadhay was a notable exception—the ideologies and practices underlying the production and consumption of Rabindrasangeet and Adhunik were exactly the same. The rhythmic structures of Adhunik music were restrained, sedate and *bhodro* (civilized). And its practitioners as well as its consumers were roughly equivalent in class and cultural background to those who patronized Rabindrasangeet. Adhunik differentiated itself from Rabindrasangeet by eschewing all religious and nationalistic themes; its lyrics focused exclusively on one topic—romantic love. Like the songs of the Hindi golden age, Adhunik seems to stand alone, unconnected to the world at large, analyzable only into a list of exquisite songs and a roll-call of magical names: Hemanta, Manna, Shyamal, Lata, Sandhya, Arati. Here then is an astonishing paradox: in spite of being burdened with conventional, and even banal, rhythmic structures and lyrical content, Adhunik music managed to produce a body of melodic masterpieces which will forever endure in the minds of Bengalis. Songs like "Hoito Tomare Jonno" (Manna); "Nijhumo Sandhaye" (Hemanta); "Shediner Shona Bhora Sandhaye" (Shymal) and "Aro Koto Deen" (Arati) can rank with the best in Hindi music (the songs from *Pakeezah*, say) or the greatest examples of western pop (the Beach Boys or the Beatles). They comprise art of the highest order.

Adhunik song is perhaps the purest genre in all of contemporary Indian music. Though a majority of Hindi songs explored the travails of romantic love, many others had patriotism or religion as a theme, invoking *desh*, bhagwan and Allah in their verses. This was the crude, propagandist and inferior aspect of Hindi film music, deriving from the contemporary statist ideology of secular nation-building. While the production of popular art was never controlled from above—thus thankfully sparing us from songs about the Bhakra Nangal Dam or The Integral Coach Factory—popular music was often inflected with the pomp and circumstance of a desi raj where the state was larger than life and supreme in all matters. The films of Manoj Kumar are the most obvious example of this tendency. Bengali Adhunik, however, disavowed any relation to the social, and was entirely defined by the parameters of the romantic: stars, clouds, twilight, the beloved's glance and the inevitable sorrows of love. This narrow focus was partly enabled by its conditions of production. Unlike Hindi music, Bengali popular song was not parasitic on film; the music industry was an autonomous entity and released records of modern music on an independent basis—especially on the occasion of Durga Puja. Bengali films did contain music, though not to the extent that Hindi films did. This music, known as *Chayachabir Gaan* (songs from film), was formally not very different from Adhunik, though it occasionally favored rhythm over melody (in many of the comedic songs of Manna Dey for example). This happened because film music must perforce accompany and be congruent with scenes involving the larger space of the social. With no such obligation, Adhunik song was free to pursue its private obsessions. Utterly beautiful, but frozen in time—that's how one can best describe the enchanting world of Adhunik songs. These are the songs of swans that have no wings to fly, the signaling of imminent demise. Whose death? That of Bengali culture as a whole. Once Bengal's symbiotic relationship with the British ended, it had no real place in the project of postcolonial modernity. Its industry destroyed by a persistent class-struggle and a consequent flight of capital; its politics rendered impotent by a parochial and idealistic devotion to outmoded social theories; its brainpower drained by a steady emigration to lands far away; its autonomy compromised by the virtual takeover of all wealth by a minority community—Bengal at the beginning of the millennium stood emaciated and empty. Bengali literature ground to a halt, Bengali film and televison was maudlin and impoverished, and there was little development in Bengali cuisine or fashion. If Adhunik songs are so memorable today, it is because they foretold in the most exquisite manner a stalled and barren future that has subsequently come to pass. As the song by Hemanta so lyrically put it, *"Tarar aar por nei, nei kono thikana,"* there is no future, no address.

Bengalis attach to Adhunik because it represents a world that fell off from the plane of history. The event is not an unique one— the story of western popular music in India also provides us with a similar example. For over thirty years at least, a certain kind of pop song, characterized by a sugary sentimentality that bordered on kitsch, circulated on the Indian airwaves as carriers of pleasure and desire: "Tell Laura I Love Her" by Ray Peterson, "Distant Drums" by Jim Reeves, "Lemon Tree" by Trini Lopez, "Wooden Heart" by Elvis Presley, "Evergreen Tree" by Cliff Richard, "Spanish Eyes" by Al Martino, "Fernando" by Abba, "Seasons in the Sun" by Terry Jack. Played over and over on programs like Musical Bandbox in

Calcutta and Date With You in Delhi, these songs became staples of growing up for successive generations of teenagers and acquired a timelessness that objects belonging to memory possess. This is not the place to attempt a comprehensive explanation, but I would like to point out a possible line of inquiry. For Indian listeners melancholy pop songs evoke the Raj and its remnants in postcolonial India: hill stations and boarding schools, missionaries and convent education, Christmas Eve bashes and Charity Balls, *khansamas* and *baburchis*, mulligatawny soup and trifle pudding, Park Street and Connaught Place. This world, and the Anglo-Indian community which is so strongly associated with it, was doomed when the country achieved Independence. These sentimental tunes are then a dirge for a vanishing order; their form expresses an aesthetic of ruins.

When the West eventually became articulated by means of the global instead of the colonial, this music was driven out by the much more upbeat sounds of disco and the 1980s pop of Madonna and Michael Jackson. The immense success of *Saturday Night Fever* (1977) was a measure of disco's worldwide influence. "Disco Dancer" released in 1982 was a smash hit, establishing Bappi Lahiri as a top music director. Due to the endless fast-paced and dance-oriented numbers that he churned out, Lahiri came to be known as the Disco King, though that title actually belongs to one of the most astonishing figures in Indian music history: Biddu. Hailing from Bangalore, Biddu played in a Rolling Stones influenced pop group before deciding to emigrate to Britain in the late sixties. While passing through Beirut he heard "Reach Out, I'll Be There" by the The Four Tops. It was the first time he had ever heard black music, and became an immediate convert. This story reveals the silent apartheid practised by the Indian recording industry and All India Radio all through the 1950s and early 1960s. Except for very white-sounding artists like Nat King Cole and Eartha Kitt, black singers were effectively banned from the Indian airwaves. The generation that grew up after Independence had no exposure to the electrifying blues of Muddy Waters or John Lee

Hooker, the shouts and whoops of Ray Charles or Little Richard, the dulcet voices of Sam Cooke or Solomon Burke. It is therefore a testament to Biddu's musical intelligence that he was to absorb and master the rich beats and rhythms of black music. After arriving in Britain, Biddu worked ordinary jobs—once as chef at the American Embassy—and in time managed to save enough to rent studio time and release his first single. That record did not do much, nor did subsequent releases; most of them were produced by small labels and sold in the region of five thousand copies. In 1974, Biddu was looking for a singer to record a lush ballad called "I Want to Give You my Everything" written by Steve Weiss, the man who also wrote Glen Campbell's classic "Rhinestone Cowboy". Biddu recruited Carl Douglas, a transplanted Jamaican singer he had gotten acquainted with a year earlier. The Weiss song was intended to be the A side of the disc and Biddu asked Douglas if he had something to record on the B side. As Biddu recalls "He rattled off about four to five songs ... one had the lyrics for Kung Fu Fighting. Since it was going to be a B side I said 'Fine, we'll have a song called Kung Fu Fighting.' So I started working out some melody for it. Nothing was taken very seriously ... We put a lot of 'hoos' and 'haas!' like someone giving a karate chop."[38] The public took the record very seriously indeed—"Kung Fu Fighting" topped the charts in both Britain and America, eventually selling an astonishing nine million copies. Biddu had found the golden touch. In 1975 the single "Summer of 42" (from Biddu Orchestra's LP "Blue Eyed Soul") climbed to #14 on the British charts, and the following year he had another #1 hit when he produced "I Love to Love" for vocalist Tina Charles. In 1977 he added veteran Jamaican soul singer Jimmy James to his stable and produced two more disco classics "I'll Go Where your Music Takes Me" and "Disco Fever."

What followed was a remarkable saga of return. Approached by Hindi film-maker Feroze Khan to compose the score for "Qurbani" Biddu recruited a 15-year-old Pakistani girl Nazia Hassan who was living in Britain. Hassan's rendition of the song "Aap

Jaisa Koi" gave birth to the genre known as Indipop and brought to Indian music an international feel and beat which had never been heard before. The team comprising Biddu, Nazia and her brother Zoheb then released "Disco Deewane" which can justifiably be termed India's first pop record. The album was released in 14 countries and became the biggest Asian pop record until then. The same team replicated its success with three further releases: "Star" (1982), "Young Tarang" (1984) and "Hotline" (1987). Biddu then adopted new proteges each of whom achieved phenomenal success under his production and musical guidance: Shwetta Shetty with the "Johnny Joker" LP in 1993, the superlative "Made in India" by Alisha Chenoy (1995), Shantanu and Sagarika Mukherjee's "Naujawan" (1996), Sonu Nigam and Sansara with "Yeh Dil Sun Raha Hai" and "Habibi" in 2000. This astonishing sequence of successes might be termed the third wave of modernization, this time with a global touch.

While the musical experimentations of New Theatres or RD Burman pulled strands of western musicality into the domain of Indian music, Biddu's music incorporated international ideas and pushed Indian music outwards in the direction of world music. Biddu himself was the trailblazer who created the space for a wave of stars whose music now constitutes a significant body of work which lies alongside the more traditional space of filmi music. By the end of the nineties Indipop artists like Alisha Chenoy, Daler Mehdi, Sharon Prabhakar, Lucky Ali, Shaan, Baba Sehgal, Sonu Nigam and others had captured ten per cent of the Indian music market. Together these artists represent every possible style and influence: classical, light classical, bhangra, disco, rap, reggae, ghazal, as well as the entire tradition of Hindi film song.

At the beginning of the new millennium then, Indian popular music is characterized by an astonishing level of hybridity which reflects the cosmopolitan face of contemporary India. This is in keeping with our observation that popular music is constituted in India not along vertical lines of hegemony and opposition, but horizontally with lines of influences continuously extending into and out of musical space. These vectors flow in both directions: from the outside to inside as well as vice versa. In colonial and postcolonial formations, most lines of influence ran from west to east. Generations of Indian composers from Tagore to RD Burman had adapted the basic structures of Indian music in order to produce a music which would be adequate to modernity. This is no longer the case in a globalized world. If the period of nationalism and colonialism witnessed the erasure of the local under the pressure of the national and the imperial, globalization is all about the eruption of the local into world space. Thus regional accents and inflections are becoming increasingly more visible. Restaurant cuisine—which for decades was only Mughlai cuisine—has now developed a hundred tastes. *Oh Calcutta* serves classic Bengali dishes for expatriates in Mumbai; *Teej* provides Rajasthani food in Calcutta. Movies reflect this trend as well: Bhansali's *Devdas* has smatterings of several Indian languages, *Calcutta Mail* identifies its protagonists not just as Hindi-speaking but specifically as Bihari.

Thus the processes of advanced capitalism and globalization have led to a vernacularization of the aesthetic. No single artist symbolizes this better than India's current musical hero A.R. Rahman. Born into a musical family—his father K.A. Sekhar worked as conductor in Malayalam movies—Rahman started learning the piano at the age of four. His father's death when he was nine put the family into penury, and as a mere child of eleven he joined a local troupe as a keyboard player. He was soon accompanying stars like Zakir Hussain and Kunnakudi Vaidyanathan on trips abroad, and eventually received a scholarship to the Trinity College of Music at Oxford University from where he obtained a degree in western classical music. After returning to India he was associated with various troupes as well as with local rock bands, and then had a five-year stint in the advertising industry composing over 300 jingles. His big break came when the director Mani Ratnam signed him on to compose the score for the film *Roja* (1992). Rahman's compositions (including the hit song "Tamizha Tamizha") took the music world by storm, and *Roja* won every award in music that year. In the next few years Rahman would write the music for several blockbuster films; the soundtrack for the film *Bombay* (1995) sold more than 5 million copies. Since then Rahman has redefined Hindi film music. His intensely personal style based on his superb sense of rhythm appealed to an international audience. David Byrne of Talking Heads was so impressed by Rahman's music that he insisted on recording some sessions with him. Rahman's biggest achievement on a global scale came in 2002 when Andrew Lloyd Weber chose him to compose the music for his production of *Bombay Dreams* (2004). Today Rahman's appeal seems endless, it extends from the villages of Tamil Nadu to cutting-edge rap artists like Jay Z.

Eclectic, multicultural, in love with all traditions though not awed by any, and filled with resonances of modern India's contradictions and vitality—A.R. Rahman is the perfect symbol for popular music in India today. This music is regional and national, local and global, traditional and modern. It is neither the music of subcultures or marginal groups, nor that of the avant-garde or the elite. Played in the bazaars of small towns as well as in the clubs of New York, it exceeds the boundaries of the nation and becomes a truly global art form. As India grows from a "Third World" postcolonial nation to a world power, its popular music too is keeping pace.

4

A Boy, a Girl and a Tree

Song and Dance in Bollywood Cinema

Though Bollywood is undoubtedly the most widely circulated representative of India's popular culture, it is yet to gain the respect that such a popular art form deserves. There is a widespread belief, common among Indian intelligentsia, that Bollywood films are devoid of any aesthetic value. Of the various components that make up the standard Bollywood film, one feature in particular— the song-and-dance sequences which are present in every film— draws special ire. Pointing to the blatant "unrealism" of these musical interludes—the many changes of costumes within the frame of a single song, the sudden shift of locales from verse to verse, the depiction of armies of extras swaying and dancing along the hero and the heroine—critics contend that song-dance sequences symbolize, in a condensed fashion, what is wrong with Bollywood films as a whole. The vulgar use of sexuality and the ostentatious displays of wealth which characterize most song-dance sequences point to a central truth about Bollywood: that it is a sensationalist and escapist art form which is driven solely by the dictates of the marketplace and is incapable of playing any progressive role whatsoever. In this chapter, I propose to argue that song-dance sequences, far from being exploitative segments of escapist fantasy, are in fact powerful acts of imagination which play a crucial role in the construction of Bollywood film as a unique and powerful popular art.

Seemingly redundant to the text, the song-dance is actually an enabling device which allows the Hindi film to express versions and visions of modernity that would otherwise be unrepresentable. Song-dance contributes to the development of a film style which is in conscious opposition to that of classic Hollywood, and represents a stance towards the world quite different from that of the West. Song-dance is therefore both a measure of Bollywood's difference from western cinema, as well as an explanation of Bollywood's immense popularity all over the global South. This chapter examines the Indian popular as it constitutes itself through the distinctive practice of the song-and-dance.

I begin by looking at the processes by which Hindi or Bombay film becomes redefined as "Bollywood." I then examine how song-dance functions within the typical Hindi or Bollywood film: it stages exterior and interior scenarios of modernity that the narrative is unable to depict, it envisions ways of acting and behaving not coded into the text, it registers the shock of the new not recordable by the prose of the film, and it affords the possibility of *jouissance* or joyous release that cannot be spoken by any character or voice. I conclude the chapter by suggesting that song-dance is a sign that helps us read the meaning of Bollywood films and of Indian popular culture as a whole.

Bollywood and the Nation

At a certain crucial point in the recent past, popular cinema in India underwent a change in nomenclature. In the first decades after Independence movies lacked a "proper name". Thus an early classic text on the subject by Erik Barnouw and S.Krishnaswamy, published in 1963, was simply titled *Indian Film*. Given India's cultural and ethnic diversity, this umbrella term actually referred to a large set of regional cinemas which had very distinctive identities. Of these many cinemas, the product of the Bombay film industry—known in popular discourse as "Hindi film"— was of special significance. The term was not a mere descriptive phrase on par with "Bengali film" or "Tamil film" but a more substantive category whose meaning was based on a number of factors: the quantitative dominance of Bombay with respect to budgetary resources, number of releases, distribution networks and box office revenues; its success in creating stars whose appeal was nationwide; the status of Hindi-Urdu as a quasi-national language; and the astonishing popularity of Hindi film music. The growth and dominance of Hindi film came at the expense of both regional cinema (excluding the south) as well as more traditional forms of entertainment like dance and theater. The immense popularity of Hindi film has always elicited a complex set of reactions amongst Indian intelligentsia. As we saw above, it was often dismissed as being simplistic and vulgar, yet commentators were forced to concede that it was the closest thing India had to a national cinema: "It is the only cultural product that has a pan-Indian market—it transcends regional, linguistic and religious identities in both its personnel and its consumers."[1] Or as Sunil Khilnani observes, "Along with cricket and voting, the cinema is among the most important collective experiences Indians have."[2] Though Hindi film is but a fraction of the totality of Indian cinema—only one fourth of all films produced in the country are in Hindi—its aesthetic dominance has compelled observers to grant it the status of national cinema. Thus Kobita Sarkar in the Preface to her book entitled *Indian Cinema Today* asserts "The *Indian* Film, as we know it, is really the Bombay-based *Hindi* film."[3] Again, noted film scholar Ashish Rajadhyaksha divides all of Indian film into two paradigms: "the Hindi movie," which includes the typical formula film made not only in Hindi but also in a dozen other regional languages, and "Satyajit Ray" which signifies the parallel tradition of art film developed through the work of Ray, Ritwik Ghatak, Mrinal Sen, Shyam Benegal, Adoor Gopalakrishnan and others. Since art film has never succeeded beyond reaching a small minority of the viewing audience, this categorization is tantamount to naming Hindi film as equivalent to Indian film as a whole. The importance of regional cinema and of art film notwithstanding, the arc of cultural production that runs from *Raja Harishchandra* to *Kal Ho Na Ho* defines the entity known as Indian cinema.

The extraordinary impact of Hindi films on Indian culture has led many observers to legitimately conclude that Hindi films are perhaps the most important chronicler of the nation's history. In her seminal study on national identity in popular Indian cinema, Sumita Chakravarty argues that "An understanding of the lived history of contemporary India may well hinge on the way we interpret (or fail to interpret) the power of Bombay popular cinema."[4] If one accepts the premise that a nation's essence is best analyzed by means of the myths it tells about itself, then Chakravarty's thesis must also be accepted as valid. But because an art form plays a crucial role in representing and constituting the nation, it does not follow that it is therefore contained within the nation. Hindi film may have articulated the formation of India as a colonial and postcolonial nation, but neither its function nor its meaning was necessarily contained within the borders of Bharatvarsha. Indeed, Hindi film had a global audience from its very inception. Many of the films made by India's first film director—Dadasaheb Phalke—were shown to Indian audiences in Burma, Singapore and East Africa.[5] Hindi films were also very popular with other segments of the Indian diaspora. By the end of the 1920s, Indian silent films began to have an overseas market in Africa, Mauritius as well as in many parts of the Caribbean. In Trinidad, for example, the popularity of Hindi films created a demand for Hindi film songs as well, thus leading to an abandonment of traditional Bhojpuri folk music brought over by the original immigrants to the island. It wasn't merely the diasporic audience that found Hindi movies irresistible, many of the films produced in the fifties proved immensely successful all over the "Third World." Thus " Raj Kapoor's *Awaara* swept through Iran, Iraq, Syria, Egypt, Turkey, and the Soviet Union like an uncontrollable bush fire, Raj Kapoor and Nargis became virtual folk heroes; the film's songs were translated into a dozen different languages and were sung on the streets of cities and small towns thousands of miles away from India."[6]

The global growth of Hindi film got a new impetus with the second Indian diaspora that came into being in the 1950s and 1960s. This NRI diaspora, as I have shown in the chapter on desi culture, was concentrated mainly in the United States, Canada, Britain and Australia, has seen great economic success and has experienced a far less tenuous relationship with the "motherland" in comparison with the earlier diaspora based on plantation labor to the various colonies of the British Empire. Not surprisingly, as Vijay Mishra points out, the original export markets (Afghanistan, Iran, the Middle East, Sri Lanka, Malaysia, Fiji, Mauritius, Trinidad etc.) which were based on the older Indian diaspora have gradually been superseded by markets in the new diasporas in the First World.[7] The United Kingdom, for example, has one of the largest and wealthiest South Asian communities in the world, the UK market grosses around 100,000 pounds sterling each month in the large screen market and close to 15,000 pounds sterling a month in the video market, amounting to almost 50 per cent of all foreign revenues earned by Indian films.[8] The opening up of new markets has made it possible for Indian film to become a global commodity. The 800-odd Indian films made each year (of which approximately 200 are from Bombay) are exported to over 100 countries and earn vast revenues. In 2001 alone, these earnings amounted to $1.3 billion, with a further $108 million coming in from sales in overseas DVDs, videos and satellite films. Though this combined figure is still very small compared to Hollywood's $51 billion for the same year, the popularity of Indian films is clearly on the rise. In 2003 for example, *Taal* became one of the highest weekly grossers in the domestic US market, earning $788,000 from 44 venues the weekend it opened, and ranking 20th on *Variety*'s box office charts. The first Indian multiplex in the United States also opened up recently in Freemont, California—it regularly shows Hindi films on eight screens, complete with *samosas* and *chai* being sold in the concession stands. Desi films are a hit not only with the diaspora but with an international audience as well—*Lagaan* and *Devdas* being the most obvious examples. More significantly, Indian films produced in the West have succeeded in creating a whole new market. Mira Nair's *Monsoon Wedding* earned $35 million worldwide, Gurinder Chaddha's *Bend it like Beckham* became a cult hit, and films like *American Desi* (2001), *The Guru* (2002) and *Hollywood/Bollywood* (2002) have added to the desi wave. Finally, the thematization of Hindi film aesthetics in Baz Luhrmann's *Moulin Rouge* (2001) and Andrew Lloyd Webber's theatrical production *Bombay Dreams* underscored the fact that Hindi film was more than a national cinema; it now functioned as a concept which denoted a particular sensibility and aesthetic of filmmaking. That concept had a name, and that was "Bollywood."

The term Bollywood was coined, according to common lore, by some unknown gossip columnist in the English-language press in the late 1970s. Given the stance most westernized Indians took towards Hindi film—"Like many others of my anglophile generation growing up in the urban India of the '60s and '70s, I had developed an early scorn for Hindi cinema" is a typical instance—the author probably intended the term to be one of ridicule and derision. Those who are opposed to the term point to its pejorative connotations. Thus, the popular actor Ajay Devgan insists that film journalists write about "the Indian film industry" and not "Bollywood." Similarly, Amitabh Bachchan has criticized the use of the word Bollywood to describe the Indian film industry, saying it was demeaning and belittled the impact the industry had made on the world. In an interview with a South African newspaper Bachchan said that the word Bollywood was a warped version of Hollywood, coined to make fun of an industry which had restored pride in Indian culture:

> Yet, Indian cinema has been making rapid progress. Whether we like it or not, it has become almost a parallel culture for people of Indian origin worldwide. There has been a lot of identification with India because of our movie industry. We go out and are identified in countries which don't speak our language, don't know anything about our culture but have seen our films.[9]

The noted film director Subhash Ghai echoed these sentiments in observing that "The BBC invented the term about 10 years ago, as if we were aping Hollywood ... It is scoffing, somehow demeaning. You've seen what India has done with IT. We'll make the same leap with Indian cinema."[10] Devgan, Bachchan and Ghai and others like them are reacting to what they see as a trivialization of a rich cultural tradition. From their perspective, Indian film—understood as a complete entity comprising the Bombay Hindi film, regional film, and parallel or art cinema—is far more than a subcontinental clone of Hollywood. The term "Bollywood" is doubly pejorative: the suffix "ollywood" signifying the crass commercialism, hyperbole, manipulation of taste, and conservative politics which we associate with Hollywood; the "B" before the suffix further connoting a litany of vices exclusive to Bombay alone—imitation, plagiarism, unoriginality, melodrama and escapism. To rename Indian film as Bollywood is, from this perspective, to reduce it to a set of lowest common denominators, diminish its import, erase its magnificent history, and ultimately to insult the nation itself.

This "nationalist" critique is somewhat misplaced relying as it does on a purely literal, or even orthographic, reading of the term. It is possible to come to a very different interpretation of the word Bollywood—one that sees it as encoding surplus rather than deficit, possibilities rather than limitations. "Bollywood" from this perspective would connote the astonishing globalization of Hindi film in the last few decades. In his perceptive essay entitled

"This thing called Bollywood," Madhava Prasad observes that the hit films of the last decade—(*Hum Aapke Hain Kaun, Dilwale Dulhaniya le Jayenge, Kuch Kuch Hota Hai, Kaho Na Pyar Hai, Lagaan*, and others)—have relocated the seismic center of Indian identity somewhere in Anglo-America, thus entrusting it in the hands of the NRI. "Could Bollywood" Prasad asks, "be a name for this new cinema, coming from Bombay but also, lately, from London and Canada, which has over the last ten years or so, produced a new self-image for the Indian middle classes?"[11] and proceeds to answer his own question with a tentative yes. Certain basic changes in the mode of filmmaking indicate the shift in accent and functionality. Thus English, rather than Urdu, is now the meta-language of Hindi films, and *love* has replaced *pyar* or *ishq* as the signifier of affect. Moreover, Prasad argues, films made by NRI directors like Mira Nair or Gurinder Chaddha as well as those made by "foreign-returned" sons of industry magnates increasingly seek to capture a timeless Indian essence which provides a diasporic population with "a way of accessing the 'home culture' for their own needs in a globalized world." For Prasad then, Bollywood is a construction born out of the desire to represent identity as difference on the world platform. This constructedness is evident in the reflexive manner in which these films foreground what they consider to be the fundamentals of Indianness and it "is this reflexivity and the demand it is responding to that can be said to constitute the very stuff of the new NRI film." Prasad's main point— that Bollywood signifies India at the global level—is very well taken, but we need to go beyond his analysis. While it is certainly true that most films made under the sign of the NRI and the global are politically reactionary (the gender politics in *Kal Ho Na Ho*, a huge international hit, is a good example), certain exceptions point the way to a more progressive global Indian cinema. Thus *Lagaan*, which is as global a text as any, recapitulates anti-colonialism at the moment of unprecedented economic adjustments with the western world, while *Bend it Like Beckham* manages to articulate the existence and validity of lesbian desire in spite of its sentimental accounts of the Indian family. In other words, Bollywood has a potential for a progressive politics which some critiques may fail to notice. In any case, when analyzed as a vehicle for diasporic identity, Bollywood can be seen as possessing a content and meaning that goes beyond the scope of descriptors like "Hindi film," "Bombay film" or "Indian film." Whereas the latter restrict the art within regional or national parameters, "Bollywood" recognizes that in a global age both art and identity are mobile categories whose meanings necessarily spill over national boundaries. The noted Hindi film screenwriter Javed Akhtar emphasizes this distinction between art and nation when he observes that "Hindi cinema's culture is quite different from Indian culture ... but it is not alien from us ... As a matter of fact Hindi film is our closest neighbor. It has its own world, its own traditions, its own symbols, and those who are familiar with it understand it."[12] This "own world" of the Hindi film belongs not just to natives, but to Indians who live abroad, and beyond them to all those who may not be Indian but who "are familiar with it." Indeed, even though the Indian diaspora may currently provide Hindi film with its energy as well as its ideology, the sense of "Bollywood" exceeds even this determination. As Mira Nair says "Our films have reached half the world, the Middle East, all of Africa, all of Russia, the Far East, and the Indian diaspora everywhere—the half of the world that Hollywood has not yet recognized."[13] Bollywood's annual audience of 3.6 billion compared to Hollywood's 2.6 billion is numerical proof of Nair's assertion—Bollywood today is a truly global phenomenon which goes beyond ethnicity. The First World has suddenly woken up to this long-standing truth, as is evident in the Bollywood "buzz" or "boom" that seems to be everywhere. Consider the following: Aamir Khan got 30 Hollywood scripts thrown at him after the success of *Lagaan*; Gurinder Chaddha has just directed *Bride and Prejudice* an adaptation of Jane Austen with Indian characters; Julia Roberts has described Rai as "the most beautiful woman in the world;" shooting started in 2003 for the *King of Bollywood* starring British supermodel Sophie Dahl as well as on *Marigold*, a story of an American B-movie actress stranded in India; the American cable channel Turner Movie Classics recently showed 50 Hindi film classics from *Awaara* to *Sholay* on television, and *Time* magazine's film critic Richard Corliss writes,

> Ask me today to name ten great international filmmakers and the list would have to include Guru Dutt—the supersensitive actor-writer-producer whose *"Pyaasa"* and *"Kagaz Ke Phool"* are rhapsodic expressions of a poet's dreamy isolation, Ask what's the best film I have seen this summer, and I might reply *"Awaara"*, Raj Kapoor's volcanic parable of righteous paternal mistrust, with one of the all-time sadistic-sexiest beach scenes and a dream sequence that revs up to delicious. Ask what actress has my heart at the moment, and I'd confess, without guilt or irony, Waheeda Rahman, the whore-muse in *"Pyaasa"* and Dev Anand's radiant, misunderstood companion in *"C:I.D."* and *"Guide."*[14]

One might be tempted to read the above as incontrovertible evidence that Bollywood is not just ubiquitous but is now a universal of world culture in the way First World art forms and aesthetic conventions are. But that is not the case. While Bollywood's appeal in "the half of the world that Hollywood has not yet recognized" is vast and secure, its hold on audiences and markets in the western hold is far more tenuous. *Lagaan* may have been nominated for the Oscars, but it failed to lift Bollywood from the margins of American culture into the mainstream. Its success remained restricted to South Asian audiences and it grossed a negligible $73,276 in the American market. During its premiere at Cannes, Miramax sought very hard to obtain US and UK rights for *Devdas* but no distributor was keen to pick it up. It was ultimately released through Eros Entertainment—the film's producer and the largest distributor of Indian films at a global level—earning $4.9 million after being exhibited at mainly Indian-specific theaters.[15] As Jaishree Mishra points out about market conditions in the UK, "Indian films are still ghettoized, playing only in a handful of cinemas in far-flung Southall or Ilford. Even when distributors pull out all the plugs to achieve a Leicester Square release for *Devdas*, the audiences are predominantly South Asian, give or take the odd White, roped into a new experience by an Indian or Pakistani friend."[16] These economic facts are mirrored by aesthetic responses to Bollywood. Richard von Busack's comments are more typical of western reception that Corliss' enthusiastic praise:

> Traces of Bollywood have spiced American movies, such as the finale of *Moulin Rouge* or the beginnings of *Ghost World*. At the art houses, we've seen releases of much-vaunted Bollywood epics, most notably *Lagaan*, which I found paralyzing, like being stuck at a real-time cricket match ("baseball on Valium" as Robin Williams once quipped). The endless contest alternated with halftime breaks of particularly obvious messages of brotherhood: touch an untouchable today.
> Who can object to joyous, colorful films for relaxation of a hard-working people? It's just that the Western celebration of the commercial qualities of Bollywood helps ensure that Indian cinema is going to remain at its most common: gaudy, tinsel, inoffensive merch.[17]

As Lalitha Gopalan has observed, this indifference extends to even those who consider themselves students of cinema: "At film conferences in America, for instance, one finds a polite interest in Indian cinema—alternative or popular—but little enthusiasm. The same small clutch of listeners migrate from one international panel to another—Russian, Chinese, Indian, Iranian—with hordes of American film scholars crowding into auditoriums for papers on the latest Hollywood blockbuster."[18]

Bollywood film, then, occupies a curious middle ground between the local and the global. Its immense popularity all over the South grants it a status larger than that of a national cinema, at the same time the obvious resistance it faces with western audiences makes it somewhat less than a global universal. Bollywood clearly lacks the reach of those processes which we commonly associate with globalization: the English language, information technology, rock and roll and rap music, American style management, free market ideology, fast food, the internet, the Oscars, even Chinese food. These phenomena can justly be called universals in that though their reach may not be planet-wide in an empirical sense, in principle we see nothing that could limit their growth. With Bollywood, there is the sense of a natural limit which restricts and curtails its universality. In spite of the Bollywood boom, even its most ardent fan probably agrees more with von Busack than with Corliss, in thinking that in its present form Bollywood can never conquer the West. For many the product is just plain inferior, and many Indians, especially westernized urban ones, would probably agree that Satyajit Ray's scathing remarks made 55 years ago still hold true today:

> What is wrong with Indian films? Starting a production without adequate planning, sometimes even without shooting a script; a penchant for convolutions of plot and counter-plot rather than the strong, simple unidirectional narrative; the practice of sandwiching musical numbers in the most unlyrical situations, the habit of shooting indoors in a country which is all landscape—all these stand in the way of the evolution of a distinctive style.[19]

Later critics have reiterated the lack that Ray had pointed to. Writing in 1975, Kobita Sarkar observes "Basically, we are still indissolubly wedded to the idea of a formula film as imperative to success. In this we are committed to the boy-meets-girl run-around. Reluctant to think for itself, the audience prefers a familiar pattern. It shows its gratitude repeatedly at the box office."[20] The sense of inadequacy implicit in these pronouncements is a function of the desire to have a cinema which replicates the aesthetic modes of western film. As Madhava Prasad has observed, it is not just western or westernized critics who are governed by the notion of "the not-yet-ness of the Indian popular cinema", it is also current with those within the industry as the instrument of a drive towards change.[21] This point is made brutally explicit by Ram Gopal Verma, one of Bollywood's leading producer-directors:

> There's going to be a massive change. A lot of filmmakers are going to go out of business. Anyone who looks at film as a formula of one song, two comedy scenes and three action scenes ... is lost now ... And anyone who doesn't follow the West is gone. For many people in the business their pride won't let them. But following the West is not surrendering. Following the West, the best of the West, is following originality. Western innovation is superior, and I think we are just beginning to understand that. With my films I am targeting the urban multiplexes, the sophisticated media-savvy young crowd. I couldn't give a f---for the villages.[22]

Though couched in contemporary language, Verma's argument is a very old one. Ever since the nineteenth century, Indians have been tormented about the inadequacies of Indian modernity. This anxiety has a lot to do with our colonial history. Macaulay's infamous and over-quoted Minutes—asking for the creation of a "class of persons, Indian in blood and color, but English in taste, in opinions, in morals, and in intellect"—have largely been read as a blatant pronouncement of racist imperialist ideology. We must also look at its positive and productive aspect, which lay in the creation of a lack which has energized the Indian mind for almost two hundred years. Macaulay's utopic vision of "brown modernity" has always acted as an unattainable limit for subsequent thought. It is almost as if a rigorous project of "debrowning" is needed before modernity can become available to us. This predicament means that modernity, which masquerades as a temporal category, is at bottom only a racial one. After all, many notions which underlie "the modern" are, by now, very old, dating back at least to the seventeenth century. The foundational thinkers of white modernity—Descartes, Locke, Rousseau, Adam Smith, Marx and Freud—have been granted an atemporal status which places them, quite undeservedly, outside of history. In other words, modernity gains its appearance by erasing whiteness and history from its ambit and thus grants white culture the authority of a universal. "Native" cultures, from this perspective, are plagued by history and specificity, carrying an immense burden of "rituals" and "traditions" which inevitably act as impediments to the attainment of modernity. What this then entails is that the concept of brown modernity demands a total erasure of history, and is doomed to be asymptotic because non-brown and white can never coincide. Anyone who doesn't follow the West is gone, says Verma, but so is the one who does—to follow the West is to set out on a chase that is condemned to be endless. The futility of such a project teaches us that modernity must be given back the temporal dimension which it superficially encodes, and be rethought as the sum of all that is at play at the given moment. Thus "if respect for elders" is crucial to most Asian cultures, it must therefore be thought of as part of modern sensibility as much as "the inalienable rights of individuals." Modernity is therefore something which all cultures possess in equal measure, an inquiry into modernity then consists not of determining whether a given culture is (adequately) modern—an additional problem being whether the ideal modernity is located, in New York, or Oslo or Tokyo—but rather in delineating what its modernity (which is unique to it) consists of. By revising our notion of modernity we move away from a model of lack and incompleteness to one based on difference. Modernity takes different values in different fields, and these values are not quantifiable into a calculus of more or less. "Different from" rather than "less than" should be the operational relation in our analysis. We must approach Bollywood films not by asking how they succeed or fail in approximating to Hollywood. Instead we must ask how Bollywood films are different and what implications this difference has for our conception of Indian modernity.

Music and the Movies

It is universally agreed upon that if there is one feature which radically distinguishes Bollywood from other cinemas, it is the ubiquitous presence of the song-and-dance sequence. This difference is most keenly felt by western observers used to the very different conventions of Hollywood filmmaking. Thus David Chute asks us to "take the one thing that almost everybody knows about Bollywood movies: that by rigid convention they all contain five or six (or more) elaborate song and dance sequences."[23] and Richard Corliss observes that "in the midst of the starkest plot twists, everyone sings and dances. Virtually all Bollywood films are musicals."[24] What Chute and Corliss point to has held true of Bollywood from its earliest days. The very first Indian talkie *Alam Ara* contained 12 songs, and in the early days of sound, some films had as many as 40 song fragments! Songs have been essential to the form; in the entire history of mainstream Bollywood only a handful of films—*Munna* (1954) by K.A. Abbas, *Kanoon* (1960) by B.R. Chopra, *Ittefaqh* (1969) by Yash Chopra, *Bhoot* (2002) by Ram Gopal Verma being notable examples—have been songless. The presence of the song-dance-sequence is the most problematic feature of Bollywood film. Even sympathetic foreign critics like Chute are forced to admit that "For many westerners, though, the songs are the real deal-breakers—which is why they are often the first element a Bollywood go-getter thinks about removing when plotting a crossover to the 'mainstream' (read 'white') audience in America and Europe."[25] But songs aren't a problem only for white audiences, many Indian commentators also believe that song-and-dance sequences extract a terrible toll from the aesthetic value of Hindi films:

> The most irritating aspect of the song in the Hindi film is its sheer irrelevance. Many of them can be deleted entirely without in any way affecting the film's content, and many of them suppressed would do much to improve the general quality of the film. In an avowed musical of the *Baiju Bawra* type, it is a different matter—for it is part of the film—but the interminable singing in films of a totally different nature is rarely justified. It merely slows up the action and confuses the major issues at stake. The

mounting tension of a drama suddenly collapses and it holds up the story. In the middle of what should be an exciting chase, it is an inanity. These sort of things account for the illogical and shapeless nature of an otherwise good Hindi film.[26]

Addressing the topic almost thirty years later, Ram Gopal Verma reiterates Sarkar's critique when he states that "I believe—and today everyone is giving me a hearing—that songs are principally responsible for 70 per cent of the bad films we make today. Songs will work ... when they are integral to a film ... but the problem arises when no matter what the nature of the subject, you *ghusao* some songs into it and start manipulating the screenplay ... I'm not going to have any songs in *Bhoot* either. My intention is to scare the hell out of people. Why should I subject them to locations in New Zealand?"[27] Some critics go even further than Verma, denying all validity to artworks that employ these devices. Questioned by an interviewer as to whether she would ever try her hand at a Hindi film extravaganza, the noted director Aparna Sen announced "No, I am not into song-and-dance movies. That's not my kind of cinema so I can't do it very well. I usually opt for meaningful cinema."[28]

There does exist a line of thinking which explains the existence of the song-and-dance sequence by arguing that it evolves both from the classical traditions of Indian civilization as well as from the tenor of daily life. As Barnouw and Krishnaswamy point out in the "Golden Age" of Sanskrit theater the idea of drama was inseparably linked with song, dance and music. In his *Natyashastra* Bharata says "Instruments are the very bed of a performance." Though drama in India went into oblivion under Muslim rule, it was revived in the nineteenth century. Even though this new drama sought to imitate and adapt European models, it simultaneously reverted back to ancient usage by including song and dance. This practice was then imported into cinema with the advent of sound, "the Indian sound film of 1931 was not only the heir of the silent film; it also inherited something more powerful and broad-based.

Into the new medium came a river of music, that had flowed through unbroken millennia of dramatic tradition."[29] This argument from tradition is not very convincing, for it begs a number of important questions. First, since so little of contemporary culture has any links to the age of Kalidasa, why was song-dance the one element which has survived till today? "Continuity" by itself is not sufficient to account for this persistence; we need to demonstrate why this one facet from classical Sanskrit culture continues to be of such importance in the modern world. Secondly, the Barnouw thesis cannot explain why song-dance sequences are so popular in cultures (like Russia, the Middle East, and East Asia) which have no Sanskritic antecedents. Are we then required to posit similar underlying features for the classical traditions of all these cultures? Thirdly, this argument makes no attempt to account for the entertainment value of the song-dance sequence. If, as the critics quoted above have held, the song-dance is detrimental to the art work as a whole, why do so many people continue to be fascinated by this device? The traditionalist explanation for the song-dance is complemented by a culturalist or anthropological account, like the one below from film director Vinay Shukla, which argues that the song-dance is a reflection of what happens at the level of the day-to-day:

> Why don't we just look at our own society, at our culture? There are songs for every occupation, for every occasion, for every season! For every occupation, whether a fisherman or postman, a farmer or a warrior, a raja or a jogi—each one has a song attached to it. Every occasion has a song attached to it with which it is celebrated, or observed. Be it birth or death, marriage or separation and various other occasions. Every festival, Holi or Diwali, Baisakhi or Raksha Bandhan and every season has a song about it. Songs are a way of life for us. If an important occasion is a meal, songs are the spices of that meal—leaving the meal incomplete without it.[30]

Shukla's point may be empirically true, but it lacks force. A culturalist account of this sort is true not only for India but for all primitive and traditional societies. In fact the only societies in human history where songs are *not* a way of life are the modern, industrial societies which we now inhabit and where music and all arts in general are detached from daily life practices and placed in a sector labeled "entertainment." The weakness of the culturalist approach is that it takes the relation between music and ritual or practice found in traditional societies (the link between music and religion or sowing and reaping for example) and illicitly transposes it onto that between two spheres of culture (music and narrative film). Nor does such an argument offer any evidence that we are more musical than other cultures. In fact, one could point to instances where we are *less* musical. Thus, while it is common for sports fans in Britain or the United States to start singing in unison, sports audiences in India are noisy but never burst into song the way they do in the terraces or stadiums in the West. Moreover, what such an argument forgets is that Bollywood is also a factory which produces art in a commodity form, it is pure artifice which need pay no fealty to the "real" conditions of life. Even if song-dance is integral to our daily lives—and this is an assumption which, as I have just suggested, is questionable—there is little reason for Bollywood to pay such an extraordinary degree of importance to it. To put it in crude quantitative terms one-fourth of real life is not song and dance, but twenty five percent of a typical Bollywood film *is* so.

Neither the traditionalist nor the culturalist accounts, then, provide adequate explanations of a phenomenon which is not only important in its own right but has also had a huge impact on other cultural forms. Early Indian television is unthinkable without *Chitrahar*, and song-dance's continuing relevance is shown not only by the success of shows like *Antakshari* but by the countless song clips that circulate both by means of television and DVDs. Though song-dance is often known by the modest name of "song picturization" it could be argued with some justification that Bollywood invented the music video forty years before MTV did. And so important was the contribution of song picturization that unlike the case in the West, "film music" emerged as a distinct category of music. Popular music in India *is* filmi music, as William O. Beeman points out "In India ... 'film music' is readily recognizable as such. Popular songs are always identified with the films in which they occurred. The songs appear to have no identity independent of the films, and it may well be that the appreciation of the song has a lot to do with the viewer's recall of the context in which it was sung on the screen."[31] Given the extraordinary significance of the song-dance, it is quite astonishing that Indian academics writing on film have largely chosen to ignore the topic. The seminal *India International Quarterly* issue of 1981 devoted to popular film had only one piece on film song, by William Beeman—which was mainly a historical piece rehashing the arguments already put forward by Barnouw and Krishnaswamy. The two most prominent anthologies of contemporary film studies— *Making Meaning in Indian Cinema* and *The Secret Politics of our Desires* don't have a single chapter on song-dance, nor do more general anthologies on Indian popular culture like *Pleasure and the Nation* and *Consuming Modernity*. Perhaps the most substantial work on contemporary Indian cinema—Madhava Prasad's *Ideology of the Hindi Film* has no index entries on "song" or "dance" or "music". Prasad refers to song-dance once in his entire book, only to describe it as an unimportant residue from a past era. Claiming that the "social" is the dominant if not the sole genre constituting Hindi film he goes on to add "With a few exceptions, these socials are usually musicals. The musical ... has become a marginal form in Hollywood, whereas in the Hindi cinema the continuing dominance of the musical-social is a symptom of the continued dependence of the cinema on the resources of other cultural forms."[32] Prasad seems to be operating here with an unnecessarily restricted notion of cinema. Why is song-dance not integral to the cinematic form? The demise of the Hollywood musical can be read as a change in the fundaments of cinematic form only at the risk of being ethnocentric. Leaving aside the merits of Prasad's summary dismissal of song-dance, it is still curious that a book-length study of Hindi film should devote only one page to the topic. Prasad's frugality in this regard as well as the silence of most other commentators on Indian cinema leads us to conclude that song-dance produces an acute theoretical discomfort amongst film scholars. Yet song-dance refuses to go away. While welcoming the changes that Bollywood is undergoing, Aamir Khan (the actor who played the hero in *Lagaan*) reiterates the crucial importance of song-dance:

> I am very happy doing Indian films and working with the musical form we have. Of course, Bollywood can be quite ghastly, but at its best it's a wonderful form ... Music and singing and dancing are also part of our culture and our aural tradition ... Bollywood is not something I look down upon. When people say, 'Indian films are Bollywood musicals' I think that's great. When it's done right, it's like opera. It can be truly great ... In *Lagaan*, when the first song happens, the clouds are coming and the villagers think it's going to rain. Imagine that without a song, it could easily be done, but with the song it completely enhances the moment, it makes you feel more, it sucks you into the story.[33]

And in a recent interview, Karan Johar remarks:

> How can we run away from songs? They make us what we are. Yes, we do stop our narratives to sing songs, but then that's us, just as the martial arts are what makes Hong Kong films what they are.[34]

Song-dance, then, remains crucial to Hindi film. Any film theory which aspires to completeness must therefore engage with the phenomenon and seek to explain it. The film scholar Lalitha Gopalan has taken a step in that direction in a recent book where she looks at three kinds of interruptions which are conventional to Indian cinema—song and dance sequences, the interval, and censorship—to argue that they help to create a national style of filmmaking which is very different from the hegemonic Hollywood form. Gopalan challenges the commonly held view that song and dance sequences are inserted into films only as entertaining spectacles with tangential links to the narrative. It is not productive to think of these sequences as purely extra-diegetic, external to the story line. Rather, she argues, we need to differentiate their relationship to the storytelling and examine how they delay the development of the plot, distract us from other scenes of the narrative, yet also bear an integral link to the plot. Moreover, song and dance sequences call our attention to other interests "For instance, the abrupt cut to exotic locations sparks the tourist interests of the viewer, and similarly the object-laden *mise en scene* endorses consumerism."[35] Gopalan's work must be commended for its attempt at a positive interpretation of song-dance. Her intervention is a welcome change from the negative and dismissive tone adopted by the majority of writers on the subject. More importantly, Gopalan brings to the foreground a notion that many others have only implicitly alluded to—that the alliteration is misleading, that Bollywood cannot be read as a kitschy version of Hollywood, and that in fact its utilization of song-dance constitutes a radically different way of filmmaking.

The specific role played by song-dance in Bollywood films can only be understood by analyzing its relation to the rest of the film text. As we have seen, most commentators have held that the song-dance does no work for the text, and is a mere distraction or diversion. My argument here is that song-dance in Bollywood films is in fact a crucial component of the text because it performs a function that the rest of the text—the "story" or the narrative—cannot perform. We shall discuss this point in the next section. However, before we identify this unique function, it may be methodologically preferable to analyze the nature of the narrative film itself. As is conceded by everyone, the "story" in a typical Bollywood film is a composite of many excesses. Kobita Sarkar typifies the westernized intellectual's patronizing attitude towards the fantastic plots in these stories, when in a chapter tellingly titled

"Anything Can Happen in the Hindi Film!" she observes, "if you are prepared to willingly suspend all your critical faculties and your sophisticated approach, there is a certain crude amusement, and genuine fun to be had from seeing the more professionally made Hindi film."[36] What Sarkar is referring to is of course the many devices that place Hindi film at a very far distance from the realist conventions that dominate mainstream western cinema. For westernized Indians like Sarkar, the resultant fiction is something of an embarrassment, to be tolerated at best. For Sarkar, and for other likeminded critics, all Hindi film can be characterized in the following manner: First, the presentation of strong pathos, that is, the elicitation of a powerful feeling of pity. Second, the depiction of overwrought emotions and heightened states of emotive urgency, tension, and tribulation. Third, an extreme moral polarization between good and evil such that "the hero and the heroine are very, very good; the villain and the adventuress are very, very bad". Fourthly, a nonclassical mode of narration which eschews classical narrative's logical cause-and-effect structure in favor of outrageous coincidence, implausibility, convoluted plotting and too much action. Fifth, a pervasive sensationalism that puts great emphasis on action, violence, thrills, awesome sights, and spectacles of physical peril. These five features do indeed describe almost every Hindi film ever produced yet the descriptors I have just outlined are taken from Ben Singer's work on early American film! In his study on melodrama and modernity Singer alerts us to the fact that throughout the nineteenth century and at least the first quarter of the twentieth, melodrama was a dominant mode of artistic expression. Melodrama flourished first in the theater; then, with the invention of cinema, it moved to the screen and thousands of films with titles like *The Perils of Pauline* (1914), *The Exploits of Elaine* (1914), *The Grip of Evil* (1916), and *The Screaming Shadow* (1920) were produced in the early years of American film. As Singer makes patently clear, these texts were not the remnants of some old-fashioned mode of representation, but absolutely contemporary:

Melodrama was quite literally a product of modernity: it emerged as a distinctive dramatic form almost exactly around the year 1800. Its appearance at that time was possible only as a result of legal changes stemming from the French Revolution, a crucial watershed event marking the disintegration of the traditional order and the advent of the modern era. A number of scholars have interpreted melodrama as a cultural response to the moral insecurity and material vulnerability people felt as they faced a world no longer moored by monarchic, feudal and religious authority. Classical melodrama filled a psychological need by offering moral certainty through utterly unambiguous designations of virtue and villainy. At the same time, melodrama's "paranoid" fixation on the relentless victimization of innocents expressed the inherent anxiety and disarray of the postfeudal, postsacred world of nascent capitalism.[37]

Singer's concise summary—which draws upon the seminal work of Peter Brooks, Thomas Elsaesser and others—alerts us to melodrama's connections to modern capitalism and also helps us understand why "in both form and content, melodrama was an appropriate genre for working-class audiences, evoking the instability and vulnerability of their lives in the unstable market culture of the early nineteenth century."[38] Melodrama in the West, then, was a popular and contemporary form which both grew out of and gave shape to the particular historical period in which it was a dominant mode of artistic expression. From most accounts it appears that early Indian cinema—whether mythologicals like *Raja Harishchandra*, musicals like *Alam Ara*, stunt films like *Hunterwali* or socials like *Devdas*—relied exclusively on melodrama for its narrative form. It would be interesting to enquire whether this was an instance of colonial imitation or whether the roots of Indian cinematic melodrama lay in nineteenth century drama, especially Parsi theater. Whatever its genealogy, a random list of some of the greatest films produced in the last 50 years—*Awaara, Mother India, Mughal-e-Azam* (1960), *Sangam* (1964), *Upkaar* (1967), *Deewar* (1975), *Sholay, Lagaan*—demonstrates the truth that melodrama became enshrined as the major mode of storytelling for Indian cinema.

How do we explain Bollywood's exclusive commitment to melodrama? Or, to approach the problem from another angle, why did realism fail to take hold in India? The factors that lay behind the emergence of melodrama in the West suggest a possible answer. If western melodrama was a consequence of the transition from feudalism and the *ancien regime* to capitalism and modern democracy, then Indian melodrama too is the outcome of a similar trajectory from tradition to modernity. While in the western case we have a simple dichotomy between the feudal classes (whether noble or serf) and the emerging bourgeoisie; the peculiarities of the colonial situation made the Indian case a more complex one. Thus "tradition" had as its objective correlate not only "backward" groups like the peasantry or women, it also included native elites (conservative Brahmins for example) for whom tradition was a bulwark against the wholesale imposition of foreign values and practices. At the same time "modernity" was represented not only by white sahibs but by a substantial number of westernized elites (many of whom contributed to the Bengal Renaissance) who believed that an adoption of modern ways was a prerequisite to the attainment of independence and nation-building. The relationship between tradition and modernity was therefore far more complicated in India. Not only were elements of the same class or group split on the question, often single individuals were conflicted between the contrary pulls exerted by the two notions. If one accepts the thesis that feelings of uncertainty, anxiety and vulnerability led to the creation of melodrama as a narrative form in nineteenth century Europe and America, then it is all the more plausible that melodrama should have become the dominant mode of storytelling in colonial and postcolonial India. In *The Ideology of Hindi Film* Madhava Prasad notes that the feudal family romance—a form that he claims dominated Hindi commercial films in the 1950s and 1960s—is itself a "melodramatic" form corresponding to the stage melodrama of early capitalism. Prasad goes on to observe that "Indian film melodrama, and its most important precursor, the Parsi theater, together compress the almost 200-year old history of European/ American melodrama into less than 100 years of discontinuous evolution."[39] An NRI film like *Kal Ho Na Ho* has "tracks" of voyeuristic realism (shot sequences of New York), of loud comedy, of global music (disco music, adaptation of Roy Orbison's "Pretty Woman"). Yet the central core of the narrative consists of a highly melodramatic triangle that seems eternal in its structure and resolution: Naina (played by Preity Zinta) is in love with the (dying) Aman (played by Shah Rukh Khan) who is also in love with her. Aman comes to know that Preity's friend Rohit (played by Saif Ali Khan) is in love with her as well. Concerned perhaps for her future happiness, Shah Rukh conceals his love for Naina causing her to marry Rohit. At the very end of the film Naina gets to know of Aman's love for her, and pledges that she will be united with him in their next lives. The momentous and breathless dynamic of the film is wonderfully caught by a contemporary preview:

> What would you do if your road in life is heading for a dead-end? What would you do if you had to fight a fatal illness when you haven't yet reached a peak moment in your life? What would you do if the love of your life is being snatched from your hands while you're drowning in the agony of your terminal ailment?
>
> Would you turn to your family for love and support? Would you change your perspective on life? Or would you just take a step back and leave the world of sorrow and spend your last moments alone in solace. These are some of the difficult decisions that Aman Mathur (Shah Rukh Khan) has to make ...[40]

For all its "modern" trappings *Kal Ho Na Ho* is constituted by a discourse that has its roots in nineteenth century French and Parsi theater, it is a direct descendant of *The Perils of Pauline* and *Kismet* (1943). The continuity in form is not surprising when we consider that KHNH is similar to these predecessors in that it negotiates, yet one more time, the polarities of tradition and modernity within the framework of a romantic tale, replacing the traditional binaries of rural/urban and feudal/bourgeois by one in which diaspora and western geography stand for modernity while ethnicity and ritual signify traditional India. The specifics of the plot aside, KHNH explores the processes by which "cultural values" can be preserved and reproduced in the alien West, an endeavor which may be said to constitute the theme for all NRI films in general.

What are the consequences of this strong presence of melodrama? In a pioneering article analyzing the specific pleasures of Indian cinema, Rosie Thomas warned us not to yield to the temptation of "impertinent criticism according to the canons of Western film-making" and dismissing Indian films as inferior works of art. The comment that "*Mother India* is a rambling tale of personal woe, narrated episodically in unsuitably pretty Technicolour" made by a British reviewer writing in the *Observer* (in 1961) is a perfect example of such a tendency.[41] Many Indian critics repeat this gesture when they complain "about the films' 'lack of realism', about the preposterous 'singing and dancing and running around trees', and that the films 'are all the same' and simply 'copy Hollywood'."[42] Thomas correctly goes on to argue that Indian films involve an indigenous set of aesthetic criteria based on different notions of spectatorship, fantasy and pleasure. In another essay dealing more specifically with the defining role of melodrama and morality in Hindi film, Thomas describes Hindi films in general as "centrally structured around contradictions, conflicts, and tensions primarily within the domains of kinship and sexuality" going on to add that "it is an expectation of Hindi film as a genre—in accordance with the conventions of melodrama—that these conflicts are resolved within the parameters of an ideal moral universe."[43] Taking our cue from Thomas, we may say that while the melodramatic mode of Hindi films deprives us of the "realistic" pleasures of western cinema, it does not leave us empty-handed. It replaces verisimilitude with the fantastic, psychology with histrionic emotionality, and cause and effect with coincidences and surprises. These substitutions may detract from a film's "reality effect" but at the same time they allow it to articulate a deeper sort of realism. Indeed, many recent commentators have held that melodrama reflects reality more effectively than a mere naturalism which only presents things just as they are. The assumption here, as Ben Singer points out, is that true reality is not to be found at the level of appearance, but rather at a deeper level, in the underlying forces which govern surface phenomena. Thus even though its characters may lack psychological depth, melodrama has the capacity to reveal truths about the psyche:

> I am arguing, up to a point, that melodrama is actually more natural than naturalism, corresponds to reality, not least to modern reality, more closely than naturalism. The melodramatic vision is in one sense simply normal. It corresponds to an important aspect of reality.[44]

Melodrama also accounts for the peculiar uses of time in Hindi film. Because the text is primarily engaged with psychic and moral structures, its relation with temporality is extremely tenuous. Thus stories are usually set in vague, timeless locales with no discernible connections to the real world and to history. Nor is time of any significance within the frame of the film. Because every story is at bottom an ethical drama unfolding over episodic encounters between good and evil—one can think of the film as a sequence of different poses that moral forces take towards each other—it does not require the naturalist progression of linear time that Hollywood realism demands. This "indifference" to time shows in the various uses of temporality. Hindi films rarely make use of flashback—a device whose basic point is that time elapsed is crucial to the constitution and understanding of present time. At the same time they make extensive use of the "flashforward"— introducing characters, often a pair of future lovers, as children and then abruptly portraying them as adults a decade or two later. While this practice may be taken to mean that a certain kind of predestination works in this life, the fact that the film rarely makes any reference to the period it skipped also signifies the low value linear time has for the evolution of story and plot. Again, the relative absence of sequels demonstrates that time plays a different role in Hindi film than it does in Hollywood. An amazing example of this difference can be found in the "Vijay" films of Amitabh Bachchan, where continuity of theme (angry young man fighting against social injustice) is established not through the temporal stages of the hero's life (as in the *Rocky* movies, starring Sylvester Stallone) but through nomenclature alone—"Vijay" signifies a type of character, but these several Vijays are all different "people."

Bollywood's melodramatic form may explain its weak commitment to realism, but there still remains the obdurate problem of why song-dance has been so crucial to it. Melodramas may have been the dominant mode in early Hollywood, but the films from that era did not include song-dance. Clearly, therefore, song-dance is not intrinsic to melodramas in general. There was of course one particular Hollywood genre that was an exception. The musical came into being almost immediately after the introduction of sound in 1927, and was immensely popular during the 1930s and the 1940s, with talented directors like Busby Berkeley (*Forty Second Street*, 1933) and Vincent Minelli (*Meet me at St. Louis*, 1944) churning out hits in conjunction with superstars like Fred Astaire, Ginger Rodgers and Gene Kelly. Musicals stayed popular until the mid-fifties (*Oklahoma*, 1955, *Singing in the Rain*, 1952) but they then lost their mass appeal. In spite of occasional hits like *My Fair Lady* (1964), *The Sound of Music* (1965), and *Fame* (1980), they were, by the late 1960s, a thing of the past. The sudden demise of the musical is comparable to that of the western except that it is far easier to come up with an explanation for the latter case. The very features that made the western attractive to earlier audiences: the fetishization of hypermasculinity as articulated by figures like John Wayne, the barely concealed racism towards native Americans and blacks, the deployment of rural accents and homespun wisdom in an effort to create "authenticity", and the foregrounding of pre-industrial materiality through the representation of signifiers like barns, wells, horses and cattle—all these became liabilities for modern audiences whose alienation from agriculture and rural America was quite absolute and whose consciousness had been shaped by the emergent politics of race and gender. It is harder to explain the demise of the musical, partly because it is not clear why they were so popular in the first place. So accustomed are we to the standard realist form of Hollywood cinema, that it becomes very difficult to conceive of western audiences enjoying a form where characters break into song at the slightest provocation. Contemporary audiences are loath to accept such devices: the TV producer Steven Bochco who became famous by producing hugely successful realistic shows like *Hill Street Blues*, *L.A. Law* and *NYPD Blue* had his biggest flop with *Cop Rock*, which tried to marry the conventions of the musical with that of police drama. Precisely why audiences in the West responded to a format of song-dance is still partly an unresolved question. Clearly, realism exerted a pressure towards verisimilitude on the musical, leading to the creation of a sub-genre—the backstage musical—which accommodated the demands of realism by creating plots in which the main characters were putting up a play or shooting a film which was a musical. By placing a song-dance inside double brackets or parenthesis—within the "play-within-the-play" that is—the backstage musical tried to have its music and its realism too. That one of the very first musicals—*The Broadway Melody* (1929)—as well as what is considered the last great musical—*Singing in the Rain*—were both of the backstage variety only reinforces the thesis that in spite of the genre's non-representational stance it could not completely ignore the imperatives of realist discourse.

The Meaning of Song and Dance

Bollywood films may involve a lot of singing and dancing but there can be no justification for equating them to Hollywood musicals. In fact, as many commentators have pointed out, most Hindi films contain elements of all the genres: comedy, slapstick, musicals, action adventure, thrillers, and drama. The proliferation of styles within the same text has led some to claim that all Bollywood films fall under the rubric of one super-genre—the "social." That may well be true, but we also ought to acknowledge the possibility that a categorization based on western notions of genre may not be very productive in the case of Indian cinema. The use of indigenous genres—like "Bachchan films" or "NRI films"—is more likely to give us a better grasp of the similarities and differences that make up the body of Bollywood. Such an inquiry must still of course account for the universality of song-dance. Since an analysis based on genre is unlikely to provide us with an answer to this question, my strategy will be to try to elucidate the meaning of the song-dance by looking at its functionalities, that is, by analyzing the work that it does within the film itself. More specifically, I want to suggest that the song-dance performs two crucial sets of tasks on behalf of the film text: first, it creates an "outside" for the text providing both a context for the film as well as linking it to other cultural practices; and second, it acts as an instrument for building interiority and subjectivity, for projecting models of the individual self. In the enactment of these tasks the song-dance enables the film to articulate a stance which it could not otherwise. In other words, I am arguing that without song-dance the Hindi film would be less, not more.

Let us first look at the song-dance in its role as an agent of externality. As every student of the medium knows, ever since the introduction of sound, film songs have enjoyed an existence outside of the films they were written for. We have seen in an earlier chapter, film music became practically synonymous with popular music, being regularly featured on state-run media like All-India Radio and Doordarshan. Though songs and song-dances were tied by nomenclature to their textual origins—thus a song like "Gaata Rahe Mera Dil" would always be identified as being a number from the film *Guide*—their circulation on Vividh Bharati and television shows like *Chitrahaar* ensured that they ultimately became autonomous objects. This detachment is best illustrated in the case of remixes: when Bally Sagoo remixes "Roop Tera Mastana" for club audiences in London and Toronto, it is the song which is the object of reference and fetishization and its film origins lose all significance. Thus the notes in Sagoo's *Best of Bally Sagoo* CD attribute the song to Anand Bakshi and RD Burman but make no mention of its film, *Aradhana*. Songs, played on radio, cassettes and CDs, and song-dance sequences played on television and on DVDs as well as in clubs and parties constitute a vast extra-textual world which extends far beyond the films where they were originally located. In other words, song-dance establishes a cultural space which is external to film and autonomous from it. The externality of the song-dance is not just material, for it also diverges from the text at the level of semantics. It has been observed by many that song-dance serves the touristic gaze as well as ties in with an ideology of consumerism. Through the frenetic display of landscape and monuments the song-dance makes the viewer mobile, while the equally flashy montage of bodies fashioned by commodities enforces an appetite for consumption. If song-dance is a sort of advertising tool for capitalism, it is also an instrument for reportage that inserts bits of reality into the filmic text. Song-dance in Hindi film has foregrounded city streets and rural landscapes, public spaces like schools, railway stations, military displays and parades, factories and bazaars. Over the years song-dance can be said to constitute a vast documentary giving us glimpses of modern India: the machinery of its progress, snapshots of its leaders, and various other constituents that added up to make its social whole. In fact song-dance has often come closest to being a social realist art form. It is quite ironic therefore that song-dance has been repeatedly castigated as "escapist" or "fantastic" or simply "unreal". Those critics who have focused exclusively on the "singing round the tree" (which itself contains the realism of advertising) have misrecognized the strongly realistic components of the format. In conclusion then, song-dance creates a fertile external space articulated through a variety of media and energized by a flow of commodities that has very little relationship to the film itself. Song-dance can therefore be described as participating in the construction of a public or national culture, where the latter terms are to be understood in a spatial and territorial way. The more the spread of a cultural form the more public or national it is. Song-dance therefore *publicizes* film by spilling beyond its boundaries. Yet song-dance is more than just a conduit between the film and its outside; it is an autonomous art form that establishes a secondary zone of culture within the public sphere.

Song-dance produces exteriority, but at the same time it also contributes to the creation of interiority and private space. It provides a space inside which the characters of the text can be more deeply individualized than what the narrative would allow. Singing, rather than dialogue, expresses the innermost aspects of heroes, heroines and even sidekicks. This individualizing function explains song-dance's overwhelming focus on romance. If by romance we understand that desire which belongs uniquely to one individual, song-dance facilitates the process of individuation and the creation of a private self through the mechanism of romantic love and yearning. Song-dance privatizes at the level of the body by depicting lovers alone in vast public spaces. In Raj Kapoor's classic film *Sangam*, the song-dance "Ye Mera Prem Patra Parkhar" shows Gopal (played by Rajendra Kumar) and Radha (played by Vyjayanthimala) confessing their love for each other via the instrument of a letter (which is later discovered by Radha's future husband Sundar, played by Raj Kapoor). The song is sung while the lovers run around in a large garden which is absolutely empty. This desolation is not "realistic" for the song-dance knows fully well that public gardens in India are always teeming with people. Indeed, in its exteriorizing mode the song-dance overpopulates space, with ensembles of dancers or just plain crowds. The garden in *Sangam* is empty not by accident but due to a theoretical necessity: because it signifies the asocial terrain where the desire of one reciprocates the desire of the other. The evacuation of the social, the emptying out of history occurs because the philosophy of romantic love demands that the self that loves can only come into being in a shared solitude with the other. Love is private, as is well known, but more importantly only the private can love. Most Hindi film stories involve a struggle about love, because it is the burden of almost every film text to carve out some sort of independent individuality for its protagonists. Insofar that the text promotes this philosophy of individualism in conjunction with older notions of self and society (feudal, religious, etc.) it is forced to make compromises in its depiction of individualized love. Thus parental approval always casts its shadow upon romantic love: lovers often meet each other as little children pushed into friendship by their parents; or they fall in love with exactly the person their parents wanted in the first place, or the nobility of the loved one convinces a reluctant parent that this love ought to be blessed. Whatever the strategy, the narrative always flows towards parental consent, because the text is always bisected into a half that projects freedom, desire and individuality and another which brings into play societal forces structured around family and convention. By masquerading as just "song and dance" the song-dance can get away with more. It is not required to pay fealty to tradition and can represent individuality in a far more radical manner than the narrative. This is evident even in those sequences which are "peopled". It is customary for lovers to speak to each other (and only to each other) whilst in the midst of the social through the device of the song. Song lyrics very often become a secret code utilized by lovers to speak desire in the midst of many.

Song-dance is a coin stamped with the measure of the social on one side, and the likeness of a self driven by longing and desire on the other, and it allows the film text to purchase a version of modernity which the narrative cannot afford. Whereas the "story" in a Bollywood film always labors as a mediator between tradition and modernity, the song-dance is at liberty to perceive and to jubilantly announce the modern in all its contemporary glory.

The suggestion that modernity is encoded in "fantastic" song-dances may seem preposterous to those who hold that only "realistic" cinema can lay claim to representing the truth about the present. From this perspective it is not Bollywood but alternative cinema—known variously as "new cinema", "parallel cinema" or "art cinema"—which can justifiably be described as providing a window to the modern. The distinction between the two cinemas is quite evident, as the film critic Chidananda Dasgupta asserts "The difference between 'art cinema' and 'commercial cinema' is simply the difference between good cinema and bad—between serious films and degenerate 'entertainment.'" For Dasgupta, the aesthetic superiority of art cinema originates in a superior epistemology "The New Cinema in India is the creation of an intellectual elite that is keenly aware of the human condition in India."[45] This privileged position enables the makers of new cinema to produce films which are not only artistic but which are based on a superior set of values that articulate a politics based on reality:

> What really distinguishes the New Indian Cinema is a definitive set of liberal-humanitarian values, embracing progressive solutions to urgent problems, a sensitivity to the plight of the poor and the oppressed, a faith in the ultimate movement of man towards change. Drawing its inspiration largely from the neo-realists, *it is a cinema of social significance and artistic sincerity, presenting a modern, humanist perspective, more durable than the fantasy world of the popular film.*[46]

Though it owes a lot to early neo-realists like Satyajit Ray and Bimal Roy, new cinema developed as a form in the late sixties and early seventies. The following list—taken from Sumita Chakravarty's book on Indian cinema—represents one version of new cinema's canon: *Sara Akash* (Basu Chatterji), *Uski Roti* (Mani Kaul), *Bhuvan Shome* (Mrinal Sen), *27 Down* (Avtar Kaul), *Maya Darpan* (Kumar Sahani), *Garm Hawa* (M.S. Sathyu), *Chakra* (Rabinda Dharamraj), *Manthan* (Shyam Benegal), *Albert Pinto Ko Gussa Kyo Ata Hai* (Saeed Mirza), *Aakrosh* (Govind Nihalini). As Chakravarty points out, these Hindi-language films were complemented by an equivalent output from regional cinema including work by G. Aravindan and Adoor

Gopalakrishnan, Ritwik Ghatak, Girish Karnad, Ketan Mehta and others. Financed largely by the government through the agency of the Film Corporation of India, New Cinema flourished till the mid-eighties when it disappeared, somewhat abruptly, from the Indian film scene.

New Cinema continues to be revered by most writers on film, partly because its commitment to realism and progressive values has been regarded as the ideal model for responsible and worthwhile filmmaking. For most writers on the subject, it is the new cinematic tradition stretching from Ray to Nihalini and beyond, rather than Bollywood "escapism", which is capable of comprehending and adequately representing Indian modernity. However, that this dominant view needs to be supplemented. Bollywood has also played a crucial role in articulating the contours of Indian modernity. In saying this I don't mean in any way to detract from the significant achievements of New Cinema: its focus on material problems, its advocacy on behalf of the oppressed, its refreshing departure from the star system in its casting, its use of a realist mode of storytelling, and its laudable mission of exposing our societal ills. What I am contesting is the view that this list of attributes adds up to an adequate representation of modernity. Modernity, at its very core, is about the new, and I want to claim that there is nothing necessarily new about New Cinema. This is true both at an aesthetic as well as a formal level. Stylistically, new cinema was modeled on neo-realism and it inherited some of the limitations of that form. By being excessively committed to the quotidian and the ordinary, it ended up as somewhat dreary and outdated even at the moment of release. Its syntax and images were that of the documentary, its semantics was that of progressivist social engineering. These commitments did not add up to a cinema of newness, of excitement and of joy, features which, I am arguing, are central to what being modern is all about. In its determined manner New Cinema was at one with the rest of statist production: governmental architecture, dams, factories and other industrial sites that bore the mark of planning, as well as with utilitarian consumer goods like Ambassador cars, Godrej almirahs, Janata stoves churned out by a protected private sector. It is hardly surprising that like all state goods, New Cinema had little appeal for either a global cosmopolitan market or for the public at home. In other words, it failed to capture the imagination of Indians at large.

Those who hold new cinema to be inherently superior to Bollywood face the burden of answering two crucial questions. First, why did new cinema fail to tantalize a foreign audience in the way Bollywood is doing today? Second, why does new cinema gather dust in the archives, while films like *Awaara*, *Mother India*, *Sangam* or *Sholay* continue to resonate in the collective memory of the film public? The fact that new cinema petered out at the very moment when India opened up to global media via television suggests that new cinema belonged to a protectionist moment. Bred by state patronage and overly committed to a mission of earnest reformism, it collapsed under the pressure of the global real. This failure of New Cinema to survive the advent of globalization ought to lead us to also question its most vaunted attribute: realism. It could be argued that the adoption of realism by new cinema was a function of its role in nation-building. As Madhava Prasad has observed "Under the FCC aegis, realism became a national political project ... It was a realism devoted to the mapping of the land, producing the nation for the state, capturing the substance of the state's boundaries."[47] And as the work of the western film theorists on mainstream Hollywood cinema has demonstrated realism can be an ideological tool serving to legitimize the given state of things and block out the possibility of radical thought. While such a critique may not apply to the more progressive, or documentary realism characteristic of new cinema, my concern here is to ask whether such a realism was ever capable of capturing and transmitting modernity to the film audience.

The limitation of a pure or extreme realism is that it is a slave to history; it passively represents what history has already performed. Realism's mode therefore is that of the afterward, it is condemned to repeat what has already transpired. In this sense all realism is already neo-realism. Such a mode of representation, I argue, is incapable of productive fantasy and of imagining the new. Why is this deficiency of any consequence? Because the revealing of the new constitutes a significant aspect of what may be called the speech of modernity. Modernity is not simply the transposition and application of a set of ideals and practices that are already in place (and it is this limited sense of modernity that motivates New Cinema), it is equally concerned with the articulation of what has yet come to be. Thus only those forms which re-present reality, and not just represent it, through a manufacturing of the new, can truly be called modern. New cinema fails as a work of imagination when it is too closely bound to the given and is therefore incapable of positing the new. It needs to be pointed out that this shortcoming is not shared by Hollywood film. Though Hollywood is often held up as "realistic" in contrast to Bollywood, even a cursory consideration of classic films—*On the Waterfront* (1954), *The Graduate* (1967), *The Godfather* (1972), *Star Wars* (1977), *Raiders of the Lost Ark* (1981), *The Matrix* (1999), *Titanic* (1997)—will show that Hollywood's realism is actually a mixture of naturalistic description and melodramatic fantasy, thus enabling it to be forever novel and captivating.

Unburdened by New Cinema's doctrines, Bollywood too can produce moments of transcendence where what is truly new can emerge. This generative power has been noticed by even those whose artistic philosophy is at some distance removed from the Bollywood aesthetic. Writing on Hindi film music, Satyajit Ray, the father of alternative Indian cinema, observes:

I have been able to watch the development of the Hindi film song over the years thanks to my son's continued interest in them. I keep being amazed at the inventiveness that is poured into them. As poetry they are no great shakes but how many songs are? But the really striking things are in the tunes and in the orchestrations. They embrace all possible musical idioms—classical, folk, Negro,

Greek, Punjabi, Cha-Cha, or anything you can think of from any part of the world. The latter shows a brashness and a verve in the combination of instruments—again as disparate as you can imagine—and a feeling for tonal colour and contrast which call for high praise.[48]

What Ray is overtly responding to is the astonishing vitality and eclecticism of film music, but what he really implies is that we are here witnessing the production of something new. From the various juxtapositions that Ray catalogues there emerges something which had not existed in the past and which presents itself to us with enormous exuberance. Ray's account of "brashness and verve" hints at the joy of creation implicit in the production of the new. Hindi film's ability to generate utterly new conceptions of the present is very well brought out in Sudipto Kaviraj's marvelous essay focusing on the song "Ay Dil hai Mushkil" from the Dev Anand film *C.I.D.* (1956). Kaviraj contrasts the image of the city produced by this hit song with more literary representations of urban spaces found in the work of several "modernist" Bengali litterateurs. The latter can only pessimistically portray the cityscape as one of decline and death, the song, on the other hand, while cataloguing the many hardships that attend city life, can simultaneously affirm *yeh hai Bombay meri jan* (this is Bombay, my love). As Kaviraj points out:

Both poetry and popular films gave rise to specific aesthetic structures with very different readings for the meaning of city life. For the high poetic discourse the image of the city is a dark one where lives are unfulfilled and people go through the subtle defilement of their everyday existence.... By contrast, the cinematic image of the city is more complex, it contains the dark image, but this is constantly relieved by an opposite image of hope and optimism ... The filmic representation might be less self-consciously artistic ... but ... its image of the city was of a space of contradictions—where different types of things took place. It was not just a scene of constant, unremitting despair. The Bombay of the films was in this respect in subtle and important ways, unlike the high artistic depiction of Calcutta, *a city of joy*.[49]

The joy that Kaviraj points to is the joy of urban life; it is the *jouissance*, or ecstasy, that arises from being in the city. This being is *new* in the sense that it cannot be derived from history, from cause and effect, from tradition and convention, or from previous expectation and anticipation. Nor is the new of modernity oriented towards the future, it is most definitely not a blueprint or a precursor. It stands resolutely in the present; its duration is only of the moment. The new is never realized, it never fully comes to be. We only glimpse the new but never grasp it. That explains its eternal allure, the song from *C.I.D.*, or the song-dances from *Awaara* or *Sholay* remain forever fresh precisely because history did not bear them out. In contrast, progressivist cinema operates with plans, programs, manifestoes—which are all realizable in the banality of the future. That explains why *Sholay* lives on, always present, while *Manthan* (1976) has long been relegated to history.

Modernity is recorded not just by historical representations of its encounter with tradition (which involves a fixed notion of what modernity is) but also by the eruption of the new and the joyous. Song-dance is the device which presents modernity in its autonomous version, unmediated by history, as that which is radically novel. The presentation is a mere glimpse, for both the new and the joyous are ephemeral and transitory. They can be fixed but cannot be developed. Song-dances are packets of bound energy, that tantalize us with the notion of possibility. Consider two examples one from the 1960s, one contemporary. The song-dance sequence "Kya Karu Raam Mujhe Buddha Mil Gaya" performed by Radha (Vyjayantimala) is a production of female sexuality which is radically new for its time: it suggests that the heroine, normally represented as "pure", can perform a "cabaret" and yet remain within the space of conjugality. Moreover, the song-dance grants Radha an agency and authority that is denied her in the narrative. The "story" marginalizes Radha's desire in favor of the homoerotic dynamic between Gopal and Sundar. Thus even though Radha loves Gopal, and he secretly loves her in return, he is unable to announce his love because Sundar has already laid claim to her. Gopal's friendship for Sundar becomes the hegemonic principle which governs the action in *Sangam* leading in the end to Gopal's sacrificial suicide. While this negation of female desire is in keeping with the patriarchal practices of Indian society of the 1960s, the song-dance "Kya Karu Ram" produces a set of new possibilities for female sexuality. It may be argued that such an empowered sexuality has not yet come to be and that desire is still under patriarchal control. Such a critique is misplaced because it assumes that the new, to be valid, must be predictive. We ought to countenance the possibility that the new may never be realized, and that the aesthetic force of the new may lie in precisely the fact that it is never witnessed in history.

To take a more contemporary example, consider the song-dance "Pretty Woman" in *Kal Ho Na Ho* (KHNH). During this sequence Aman Mathur (played by Shah Rukh Khan) stands outside the house where Naina Catherine Kapoor (played by Preity Zinta) lives, and proceeds to woo her through song. The gesture is common enough in the tradition of song-dance, what makes the difference here is the locale. By situating the song-dance sequence on a Manhattan street, the film is able, through a number of innovative artistic moves, to transform a simple love song into a stunning tableau of global India. First, there is the audacious transformation of the classic Roy Orbison song into a "Hinglish" number that melds Hindi lyrics, English phrases and electric guitar into a contemporary love song. What is different here from previous borrowings from the West is that the "theft" is openly announced, indicating India's growing global stature and increasing sense of equality with the First World—if the Beatles could put classical sitar into English pop, we can as easily place rockabilly into Hindi *gana*. Globalization at the level of music is replicated at the level of visuals. As Aman sings his romantic message, he is joined not just by New York desis, but an entire rainbow of coalition—black, white, yellow, brown. Suddenly, the entire world is singing along in Hindi, the new global lingua franca! The moment is a fecund one for it amounts to a revelation of two intertwined but independent truths: Indians are now fully global, they are here, there and everywhere, at ease and assured of their place; and secondly, our sensibility, our way of singing and dancing, which we may call "Bollywood" is now the world's mode of being as well. The "Pretty Woman" sequence in *KHNH* is extraordinary; what we witness is Bollywood using its own techniques to announce its arrival on the world stage. Song-and-dance, judged by common sense to be a peculiarity or aberration, paradoxically becomes, in this context, a passage to universality.

I had claimed, at the beginning of this chapter, that song-dance functions as a sign for Bollywood and for Indian popular culture as a whole. We have seen that song-dance is a device of *excess*, one that allows the film text to express ecstatic visions of the new. It is this very excessiveness that allows Hindi film to find international fans and thus become transformed into the cultural form known as "Bollywood." The song-dance, known and loved all over the world, is Bollywood's essence, its ultimate meaning. Bollywood, more than any other cultural form, has taken on the task of presenting the emerging shapes of modernity to our eyes. It has done so with song and with dance, and has in the process, enabled our popular culture to become truly global.

This chapter is based on a paper entitled "Engines of Desire: Song and Dance in Hindi Cinema" co-authored by Sangita Gopal and Biswarup Sen.

5

Desi World

The Uses of Tradition in the Culture of the Indian Diaspora

All of a sudden the term "desi," which once signified all that was rural, backward and hick, has come to connote what is hip and trendy. Consider this list of desi events which all took place over one weekend in 2003: bhangra by "Sexiest Boy Band" Josh in Toronto, Samsar Thursday by DJ Suhel in New York, Desi Friday with Djs Bombay Boys in New Jersey, Aaja Nache California's Biggest Bhangra Bash, and Drop Da Tumbi night at Club Zeus in Leicester, England. Desi is much more than a weekend of ethnicity, it is a cultural phenomenon that has come to stay. Folk dances like the *garba* and the *dandia* are the rage at clubs like SOS in Manhattan or the Wild in London, elite universities like UCLA field their own "Bruin Bhangra" team, films like *Monsoon Wedding* and *Bend it like Beckham* become cult hits, Madonna and Gwen Stefani start wearing bindis, Internet radio stations like Club Asia in London play desi music round the clock, cutting edge rap artists like Timbaland and Dan "The Automator" Nakamura regularly sample Hindi songs. A New York networking organization announces the launching of *Bibi Magazine*, a fashion and bridal magazine, to coincide with the national US release of the film *Where's the Party Yaar* (2003)? In the new millennium, desi is everywhere.

Till recently though, the term "desi" enjoyed very little glamour. Our pre-eminent national symbols—bullock cart, spinning wheel, khadi, Gandhi—were admittedly of the *desh*, but their prestige was superficial and largely a matter of form. The faintly ridiculous figures of the *kisan* or the *sadhu* that have featured regularly in literature and in films are a far better index of the culture's real take on the value of being desi. While readily designating "desiness" as the source of eternal but dull verities, our cultural discourses have consistently hinted that the real action—knowledge, progress, fun and pleasure—lay elsewhere. Nehru, Bhakra Nangal, the IITs, Kishore Kumar, Zeenat Aman, Sunil Gavaskar—these and similar figures have constituted the lexicon of worth and significance. Such a perspective reflected the dominant view that native ways and wisdoms, while adequate perhaps for the domains of worship and domesticity, were plainly insufficient for the purposes of realizing our national destiny, one needed what was foreign in order to come into one's own. This hierarchy of cultures conveniently mapped onto a divide in the sociology of the nation: an English-speaking middle class population located in metropoles like Bombay or Calcutta pitted against a timeless peasantry, brought to mind by unreal place-names like Bundelkhand or Belgaum. Thus "desi"—an adjective which should have literally qualified all that was of the nation—came instead to connote an object of condescension and derision, and sometimes of sentimental nostalgia. Clearly the lesser term in the binary, desi became modernity's subaltern, acquiring the uneasy status of that which is tolerated but never desired.

The sudden refashioning of "desi," its transformation from a signifier of rural backwardness to that of global cool has been made possible by the remarkable phenomenon that is the Indian diaspora. This new desi has little to do with village India or with the country's ancient past, it is rather a postmodern cultural construction which is transmitted by global currents and is located in a space which is thoroughly trans-national. This radical change in meaning is an effect of the history of the various Indian communities settled in the West, and it is to this history we must turn in order to understand how the term became a positive category that answered the diaspora's needs for self-validation. Early immigrants to the West did not have the solace of pre-existing Indian communities to which they could attach; adrift in an alien culture they tended to desperately hold on to bits of "home" which would help them negotiate the pain of assimilation. The makeshift culture that they relied on consisted of an ensemble of items sanctified by state and middle-class ideology which could be imported with relative ease: Bharat Natyam, Urdu poetry, Hindustani or Carnatic classical music, Mughal paintings, Vedic rituals. Redolent of the museum and the lecture room, these arts, periodically doled out by the many Indian Associations celebrating Diwali or Independence Day, constituted a "culture from above" that had little to do with day to day immigrant life and would often lie inert on mantelpieces and display cases. However, things changed as the diaspora evolved. Indian communities in places like Southall or Jackson Heights began to grow in size, providing a ground for the location of livelier versions of Indian culture. Equally crucial was the coming of age of the "second generation"—people whose parents had come from India but who themselves were born and brought up in the West. These two developments would be instrumental in the creation of a new culture based on the encounter between Indian sensibilities and western forms which were simultaneously local and global, traditional and contemporary, desi and pardesi.

Since the world at large increasingly accesses India through the diaspora, it is not surprising that desi has come to connote everything that is Indian. The classic symbols of Indianness—sitars, sadhus, Sanskrit and sculptures—have been replaced by the signifiers of desi culture—Bollywood and bhangra, *parothas* and *pakoras*, designer pujas and *shaadis*. Moreover, Indian popular culture itself is being reshaped by desi influences, as is evident by the great popularity of NRI films like *Dilwale Dulhaniya Le Jayenge* or *Monsoon Wedding* and of recording artists like Apache Indian or Bally Sagoo. Desi culture relays back to India an entire encounter with the West, it is a document of the vicissitudes of the Indian popular as it travels beyond the nation. Desi culture must be examined because it is Indian popular culture's global face. This chapter will analyze the evolution and implications of desi culture by examining the three key elements of its constitution: the global migration of labor made possible by the changing needs of capital; the connectivity and commoditization of immigrant subjectivity enabled by the Internet and other forms of electronic communication and by the global flow of consumer goods; and the rise of identity politics and multiculturalism due to changing demographic patterns in the first world. The flow of labor from India to the United Kingdom, the United States and other western nations led to the formation of sizeable diasporic communities and the consequent changes in cultural practices alluded to above. Secondly, the considerable economic success enjoyed by diasporic Indians made them especially receptive to the technologies of the digital age. The new modes of information exchange and flow made possible by the electronic media diminished the distance between home and abroad, and led to fundamental changes in the nature of immigrant subjectivity. Finally, the advent of multicultural politics in the countries of the West caused minority communities to develop an ethnic consciousness that would search for its roots and for indigenous ways of cultural expression. It is the burden of this chapter to trace out the processes by which these three factors succeeded in creating what we now designate as desi culture. We end our analysis by focusing briefly on a specific instance of desi cultural politics—the use made of Hinduism by Indian communities in North America in developing what the writer and activist Vijay Prashad has aptly termed Yankee Hindutva. The essay, which is, in part, a celebration of the desi phenomenon, will end on a precautionary note by pointing to the dangers inherent in any project of cultural essentialism.

The Indian Diaspora

The years after Independence saw a huge migration of Indians to the English-speaking nations of the West. This phenomenon was made possible by the changes in the economies of countries like Australia, Canada, Great Britain and the United States. A combination of factors—loss of life in the war, the need for post-war reconstruction and falling birth rates—led to a demand for labor that could only be met by the importation of human capital from the Third World. Consequently, restrictive immigration laws which had till then discriminated against non-whites were repealed, thus reversing a situation that had been in place for decades and even for centuries. Prior to the 1950s Indians had very rarely been allowed to settle in the West. The entire colonial period, for instance, saw only a trickle of emigrants from colony to the seat of the Empire. The nature of this immigration was a function of the peculiarities of British rule. By the eighteenth century, the custom of employing Indians as servants and ayahs was well entrenched, and sahibs and memsahibs returning "home" were often accompanied by their Indian servants. When Warren Hastings left India his entourage included four maids and two "boys." By 1850, there were as many as 140 ayahs reputed to be living in London lodging houses. Most of these domestics have left no record whatsoever, one exception being Deen Mohammed. Brought to England by Captain Baker of the East India Regiment, Mohammed was to gain fame as one of the earliest marketers of an exotic India, as proprietor first of the Hindoostanee Coffee House in London, and then of the Indian Vapour Baths and Shampooing Establishment in the resort town of Brighton! A second, more unfortunate, group of migrants consisted of seamen who had been recruited to provide cheap labor for British shipping. Due to the vagaries of maritime practices, these ship hands, known popularly as *lascars*, would arrive in England as part of a ship's crew and often find no means to return home. Knowing no English and completely unacquainted with the culture, they often ended up as destitute beggars. As one contemporary witness described in 1757:

> The public has seen here some of them miserable objects about
> the streets of London, begging charity, and exposed to all the
> distress incident to persons so remote from their native country,
> friendless and abandoned, for want of knowing the laws and
> customs here ... rendered them a prey to all the little low designing
> people, amongst whom their station in life and misfortune has
> cast them away.[1]

Aside from servants and abandoned *lascars* the only other Indians
in Britain were a few students and expatriate politicians. Thus, in
spite of the colony's "crown jewel" status, the Indian presence in
imperial Britain was extremely negligible—a survey conducted
in 1932 by the Indian National Congress estimated that of
Britain's total population of 44 million only 7,128 were Indians.[2]

There were even fewer Indians in the United States at this
time, in 1940, for example, the US census counted only 2,405.
Quite astonishingly this number had not changed in forty years,
the 1900 Census having recorded as many as 2,050 Indians! What
this demographic inertia points to is the complicated history of
racism and exclusion that characterized American immigration
policy over this entire period. By the latter half of the nineteenth
century, America was in the grip of an anti-immigration fever,
this movement culminated in the Immigration Act of 1882 which
made it unlawful for Chinese laborers to enter the United States.
Indians were not subject to this Act and between 1904 and 1910
more than five thousand of them, mainly peasants from the
Punjab, had settled in the lumber towns of Washington state and
the agricultural fields of California. It wasn't long however before
these new immigrants, a majority of whom were Sikhs, came to
be seen as a threat to white labor. Anti "Hindu" riots broke out
all along the West Coast—in Bellingham, Washington in 1907
and in Live Oak, California in 1908 for instance—while the Asiatic
Exclusion League issued warnings about a new "menace" from
India and observed that "from every part of the Coast complaints
are made of the undesirability of the Hindoos, their lack of
cleanliness, disregard of sanitary laws, petty pilfering, especially

of chickens, and insolence to women."[3] The US Congress reacted quickly, and in 1917 passed a law placing India, along with other Asian countries, in a "barred zone. " This law prohibited the entry of Indian laborers into the United States, but still left undecided the status of those Indians already residing in the country. The matter lay under the jurisdiction of an old law passed in 1790 which declared that only "white persons" could be considered eligible for citizenship. Indians, in the judgment of contemporary historians and anthropologists were thought of as "Caucasian." Did this mean that they were also "white" and therefore eligible for citizenship? Public opinion did not think so. The Asiatic Exclusion League, in a document published in 1910, held that the Caucasian "forefathers of the Hindu went east and became enslaved, effeminate, caste-ridden and degraded" and that Americans should not be asked to receive this "horde of fanatics" into their midst. The issue then went to the courts. Two decisions—the 1910 *US v. Balsara* and the 1913 *US vs. Ajoy Kumar Mazumdar*—held that Asian Indians were Caucasian and therefore eligible for citizenship. This victory was however short-lived, for in the deciding 1923 decision in *US v. Bhagat Singh Thind* the Supreme Court ruled that Asian Indians could not be naturalized because "white" and "Caucasian" were not synonymous. "It may be true" the Court declared "that the blond Scandinavian and the brown Hindu have a common ancestor in the dim reaches of antiquity, but the average man knows perfectly well that there are unmistakable and profound differences between them today."[4] The Thind decision shut the door on any future immigration from India, and was the reason why there was no net gain in the Indian population between 1900 and 1940. The small Punjabi community that had stayed on was unable to reproduce itself. Most of them were males and were unable to bring back brides for fear of being denied reentry. Many ended up marrying immigrant Mexican women, and merged into the larger Hispanic population. Today, little trace of them remains. The saga of the first Indians in America was doomed to end in utter anonymity.

Thus, around the middle of the twentieth century, Indians were barred from settling in both the United Kingdom and the United States. Australia and Canada had similar restrictions, the infamous White Australia policy instituted in 1901 and the Canadian Immigration Act of 1910 effectively excluded all non-white immigrants. There was a dramatic change in all these policies after the end of the Second World War. In the British case, the demand for labor generated by post-war reconstruction efforts could no longer be met by traditional sources like Ireland and Eastern Europe. Responding to the crisis, the British government passed the 1948 British Nationality Act conferring the right to enter, work and settle on all citizens of the British Commonwealth. This led to a large influx both from the West Indies—commemorated by the landing of the SS Windrush in 1948 carrying 492 Caribbean immigrants—as well as the Indian subcontinent. This open-door policy was short-lived; rising racial tensions (resulting in the famous race riots in Notting Hill in 1958) as well as a fall in the demand for labor soon led to a reversal with the passage of the Immigration Acts of 1962 and 1971 which effectively stopped any further flow from within the Commonwealth.[5] Yet, the seeds of change had been sown. Today, Britain has sizeable South Asian and Caribbean communities—numbering two and one million respectively out of a total population of fifty million—and has become a thoroughly multicultural society. Even as Britain was shutting the doors on immigrants from its former colonies, opportunities were opening up elsewhere, especially in North America. The reform laws passed in Canada in 1962 virtually eliminated racial discrimination as a major feature of Canada's immigration rules. Australia did the same when it quietly abolished the White Australia policy in 1973. But the greatest impact on contemporary Indian immigration came with the changes in American laws in 1965. While the old 1790 law restricting immigration only to whites had been repealed in 1952, immigration policy continued to be discriminatory—countries in South and East Asia were allowed only 100 immigrants per year, while those from Europe were permitted much larger numbers. Under the new Act, Asians and Africans gained equal status with Europeans. Indians took full advantage of this latitude, and starting from the early 1970s, the average number of Indian entrants was over twenty thousand each year. According to INS figures, a total of 469,000 Indians were admitted into the United States between 1961 and 1990.[6] Predominantly Gujarati (60 per cent) and Punjabi (30 per cent), this group was composed largely of professionals, skilled white-collar workers and small business owners—thus 83 per cent of Indians who entered the US between 1966 and 1977 came under the category of "professional and technical" workers, and included 20,000 scientists, 25,000 doctors and 40,000 engineers.[7] Given this background, it is not surprising that as of the 2000 US Census, 57 per cent of Indians held a Bachelors or a higher degree, compared to 20 per cent nationally; 30 per cent were employed in professional specialty occupations compared to a national average of 13 per cent, and the median household income was $60,000 compared to $41,000 nationally.[8]

The Indian diaspora of the past fifty years is, by any set of measures, an unqualified success story. Not only are these immigrants well settled in their adopted lands, their children now constitute a second-generation which is western in upbringing but Indian in identity. In other words, there is now a substantial population of people who permanently reside in the countries of the West who still consider themselves to be essentially "Indian." A formal recognition of this phenomenon came with the creation of the category of the non-resident Indian. Coined in the 1970s, the term designated those Indian citizens who resided abroad for work or study (it later included foreign citizens of Indian origin as well) and was introduced partly to encourage investment from overseas Indians. Whether such a move was a success is a matter of debate amongst economists, what is undoubtedly true is that the nomination granted legitimacy to those who had left the country since under the new definition one could live permanently in a foreign country and still be considered desi. The referential scope of "Indian" was further increased in the late nineties with the invention of another category—the PIO (People of Indian Origin). More catholic than NRI, PIO included anyone who had one great-grandparent of Indian origin. The purpose of the new category was to include immigrants of an earlier generation—who had settled in places like South Africa, Fiji, and the West Indies—under the purview of "Indian." PIOs were no longer required to get a visa in order to visit India, a striking example of how the nation's boundaries were getting fuzzier. This process of creating a transnational, pan-Indian community found symbolic expression at the Pravasi Bharatiya Divas organized by the Indian government in January 2003. Attended by a massive gathering of diasporic Indians from 110 countries, this meet formalized the links between the nation and its diaspora, and held out promises of dual citizenship as proof of the nation's embrace of its departed.

Many factors have contributed to the success of the diaspora but perhaps none more so than the achievements of Indians in the information technology sector. So outstanding has this contribution been that "Indian" is almost a brand name for IT in many quarters. Proficiency at IT has enabled Indians to migrate in large numbers, to develop a strong indigenous industry which outsources for the entire world, and to be fully receptive to the new modes of communication which have emerged in the past few years. The diasporic community's enthusiastic participation in the information revolution has been a crucial factor behind the creation of the global subjectivity which we have named desi. The influence that the new technology would have on the diaspora was due to the astounding level of success enjoyed by Indian software professionals working in Silicon Valley. This story is by now well-known but bears repeating: at the height of the boom over one third of all engineers working in the Valley were of Indian origin as were ten per cent of all Microsoft employees, as well as 30 per cent of all software workers worldwide. There were more than 100 Indian-owned or Indian-backed companies with a combined market cap of over $40 million. This widespread success was matched by outstanding individual achievements as well. Sabeer Bhatia created Hotmail, then sold it to Bill Gates for $390 million. Kanwal Rekhi became one of the richest investors in Silicon Valley and could afford to give a $2 million grant to his alma mater, IIT Mumbai. Vinod Dham is known as one of the fathers of the Pentium chip, and Vinod Khosla was recently described as being "by common consent, the most important money guy in the entire fibre-optic world." K.B. Chandaresekhar's company Exodus is responsible for carrying 30 per cent of all traffic on the Internet. Lata Krishnan was, at one point, the highest-paid woman executive in Silicon Valley. This phenomenal success was made possible by the excellence of the Indian education system, especially that of the IITs which came to be recognized as the source of some of the world's best technical talent. The commerce in information technology was reflected at the level of bureaucracy and government policy. The high demand for software professionals led the US government to increase the quota for the H-1 B visa to 195,000 in 2001. The strategy allowed US companies to remain competitive since those "bodyshopped" through these means were willing to work at far lower salaries than their American counterparts. Though bodyshopping, like outsourcing, has been denounced from both ends of the political spectrum—as taking away jobs from American professionals and as a contemporary version of coolie labor—it has had a significant cultural impact by enabling thousands of young Indians to travel and work abroad. Not only have these new immigrants assimilated the mores of the global economy but working and living in large groups, they have through the sheer force of their numbers (44 per cent of all H-1 B visa holders at one time were from India,)[9] created a culture of Indianness in many American companies.

This software revolution impacted India as well, as the rise of Bangalore testifies. The phenomenon of outsourcing has enabled Indian companies like Wipro and Infosys to become players on a global scale. So competitive are the services provided by these companies that thousands of white-collar jobs are now being exported from the United States to India. The case of West Palm Beach-based Ocwen Financial Corp. is instructive in illustrating how companies are profiting on Indian soil. Ocwen, which once had nearly 1,000 employees at its Palm Beach Lakes Boulevard headquarters, now employs more workers in Bangalore than in West Palm Beach. At the end of 2002, Ocwen had 843 employees in two locations in India, compared with 474 in West Palm Beach and 534 in Orlando. None of these jobs are of the sweatshop variety, most of Ocwen's Indian employees are college graduates; they include 80 software developers, along with workers in residential loan servicing, human resources, accounting and risk management. "We established operations in India to take advantage of a highly skilled but relatively inexpensive labor force," said Mark Zeidman, Ocwen's chief financial officer. Ocwen is responding to brute economic logic, it can hire microchip designers or financial analysts who make $7,000 a month in the United States for only $1,000. As a result of this move, Ocwen's salary expense fell to $17.7 million in the first quarter of 2003, down from $21.1 million a year ago. Ocwen is not the only company transferring jobs out of the US, dozens of blue chip companies including IBM, Microsoft, Oracle, Bank of America, JP Morgan Chase and General Electric have set up shop in India. So great is the exodus that the consulting firm Forrester Research predicts that 3.3 million service-sector jobs will move from the United States to India and other nations by 2015. The call center sector has been especially prominent in outsourcing, young urban Indians now answer customer calls for companies like Delta Airlines or Dell Computers. Such ventures are not without their lighter side—Sierra Atlantic, a California-based software company has hired an ex-colonel from the Indian army to instruct its Indian employees on the complexities of sipping wine and wearing neckties.[10]

Immigration and the Self

The happy conjunction between Indians and IT has not only been an economic boon for Indians both at home and abroad, it has also created a computer-savvy culture which relishes using all forms of electronic communication. A search on Yahoo generated the following data concerning the number of sites for each country: Pakistan (2,007), Russia (3,755), Germany (10,490), China (13,185), Italy (15,547), France (21,771). India has 31,712 sites, a figure topped only by Australia and Britain. An appetite for the Internet and other forms of electronic communication is especially true of the diasporic population. In the United States, for example, 69% of all Indians are online compared to only 43% nationally. Connectivity enables a specific kind of lifestyle:

> Kirtidev Bhatt, an engineer in Columbia, Md., is a self-professed news junkie. Years ago he waited for the weekend to listen to a local radio program to find out what was happening in Indian politics. These days Bhatt has found a more satisfying method to feed his appetite for news from back home. Each morning, as he sips his cup of tea, he turns on his computer, logs on to the Internet, and visits Samachar.com—a website owned by Chennai-based Satyam Infoway, India's second-largest Internet services provider. Bhatt starts by browsing through the day's editions of the *Times of India*, the *Indian Express*, *Hindustan Times*, the *Hindu* and *Deccan Herald*. He then goes on to read *Sandesh*, a regional newspaper that covers Gujarat, and *Akila*, which reports on news from Rajkot, his native town. "I spend at least 30 to 45 minutes each morning reading about India," he says.[11]

Though it links users to every kind of Indian newspaper both national and regional, Samachar.com is more than a mere portal for news. Its home page bills itself as the "Bookmark of the Global Indian;" its true significance lies in the way it projects a template of desi globality. This becomes evident if we disregard the site's content which is a predictable mix of South Asian news, business, film, sports, technology and religion and focus instead on more extraneous aspects. What the site does through the formal features and the advertisements which frame its pages is to decompose the immigrant subject into a set of flows, each of which is transnational and consumerist.[12] Thus every advertisement on the site's home page initiates a movement which bridges the gap between the immigrant and home. We have flows of voice by means of telephony: "Free 10 min. calling card to India;" flows of earnings: "Send money home now Citbank rupee checking account;" flows of bodies: "Medical insurance for visitors to USA;" and flows of emotion: "Send Diwali gift certificates today." These streaming banners and flashing advertisements convert the site into a series of pulsations, an object with no fixed shape, continuously on the move. This assemblage can be seen as a metaphor for the site's conception of the immigrant self; by incessantly inserting this self into the loops of a planetary flow, Samachar.com refuses to allow it to congeal into a fixed essence. Thus the global Indian that is "bookmarked" into existence is a self which is never self-contained and complete, but always in lack, needing to be plugged in. While abstract in principle, this flow materializes itself through a sequence of commodities. Things are offered to facilitate flow— "Get 10 photo prints couriered to India for FREE, open a NRE Family Savings Account with us"—and flow in turn makes possible the circulation of commodities. Samachar has an entire page titled IndiaPlaza offering goods from *desh*—*diyas*, *garbas* and *dandiyas* for Navratri, Nirlep non-stick cookware, Akshaya pressure cookers, Revel roti makers, crystal Ganeshas and the obligatory Bollywood DVDs. The "Send Gifts" page regulates an outward flow to India: LG Microwave ovens and Electrolux washing machines for Mom (the spelling reinforcing the buyer's Americanized status), Nokia phones and Kodak digital cameras for Dad, Tin Tin comics and Harry Potter books for kids. And to emphasize the congruence between the flow of commodities and of emotion the page allows its readers the chance to send fresh flowers to recipients in India "For any reason, any season." The intertwining of immigrant psyche and affect with commodities is even better exemplified by Saranam.com which describes itself as 'the world's first puja service" and claims that "thousands of Hindus trust and come back to Saranam for their needs." Saranam instructs its readers on the doctrines of Hinduism, offers Vedic astrology services, and sells "Spiritual Products" like Rudraksha beads, Puja thalis and Surya yantras (graphic representations of mantras). Most interestingly, Saranam also enables its patrons to have pujas conducted on their behalf at a temple of their choice. For a mere $9.99 one can get a personalised puja performed at the Kasi Viswanath Temple, and then have the prasad delivered to the United States. One could also go for a package deal—$23.60 buys you the Kali package which includes three pujas, at Kanaka Durga in Vijayawada, Kalighat in Kolkata and Kaligambal in Chennai. What is of analytical interest here is not the crass commercialization of spirituality, nor the obvious manifestations of Hindutva, but the inner logic of an operation that transports spirituality across space. By permitting a most personal and intimate act—a puja—to be conducted long distance, Saranam enables the immigrant subject to insert itself into the daily practice of life in India. By virtually entering and oblating at the Viswanath temple such a subject is "dealienated," it becomes desi in India. Simultaneously the very act of transporting *prasad* across the skies exorcises the effects of crossing the *kalapani,*• one is now permitted to be a good Hindu abroad. Dollar-generated puja generates polysemy: desi now means New Jersey as well as Kasi. Connective flows and commoditization lead to the doubling, or multiplying of identity, the flashing ad on the home page of Samachar.com which reads "Gift a mobile/Stay in touch" tells the whole story: buy, relate, find your global desi self.

New technology and globalization create a new metaphysic of immigration. In its traditional mode, immigration entailed a permanent loss of home and identity. The fate of the many indentured laborers who migrated to the Caribbean, to Fiji, to Malaya with hopes of coming back rich but never made it back can serve as a trope for all immigration: there is never any return passage. This rupture was seen by some as inevitable and even desirable. Thus Nehru thought that "expatriate Indians had forfeited their Indian citizenship and identity by moving abroad and did not need the support of their mother country." Nehru's opinions became the Government of India's official policy towards persons of Indian origin:

> It is the consistent policy of the government that persons of Indian origin who have taken foreign nationality should identify themselves with and integrate in the mainstream of social and political life of the country of their domicile. The government naturally remains alive to their interests and general welfare and encourages cultural contacts with them. As far as Indian citizens residing abroad are concerned, they are the responsibility of the government of India.[13]

The Indian government's attitude towards expatriates reflected a universal theory about immigration. In this model, immigration was viewed as a difficult process of adjustment and negotiation whose eventual goal was complete assimilation into the receiving culture. Derived from the experiences of European immigration to America, this "melting pot" theory proved untenable for immigrants whose skin was of a different color. Indians were quick to adapt to western modes of work and business, the desi work ethic turned out to be as motivating and productive as the Protestant one. But success at work was not enough; there remained a terrible anxiety about acceptance by white society. Most responded to this predicament by attempting to erase all signs of ethnicity and race: eating hot dogs instead of "smelly" *pakoras*, wearing jeans in place of saris, abbreviating Sameer to Sam. The immigrant Ganguly family in Jhumpa Lahiri's novel *The Namesake* move from Calcutta to Boston and "learn to roast turkeys ... at Thanksgiving, to nail a wreath to their door in December, to wrap woolen scarves around snowmen, to color boiled eggs violet and pink at Easter and hide them around the house."[14] Imitation, however, induces only superficial change. Immigrants compartmentalize their lives, they adopt western manners when at work or in the public space, but they seek out their own kind with whom they can revert to true "Indian" ways:

The Manis met other Indians, invited them over for meals, and, if the invitation was reciprocated, a relationship was established. In this way, the network expanded ... Social life for the Manis is very intense; their weekends are booked months in advance. Ashok is a successful engineer, but other than having his American boss over for dinner, and business obligations, his true friends are among the Indian community, where he feels most at ease.

Among their own the immigrants have different behavioral characteristics. They are free to shout or sing, laugh or cry. Even their English accent is different. Among Westerners, they are superb imitators and behave properly, tell the right jokes, laugh at the correct time, and assume the correct posture, but the smiles are not as wide, the laughter not as loud, and the hug not as hard as when they are among Indians.[15]

The drive for assimilation ends up as mimicry and a disavowal of one's authenticity. But to remain unchanged is to cause a "ghettoization" of one's entire existence. The immigrant therefore forever oscillates between alternatives which both entail loss and deprivation: assimilate and compromise your true self, stay as you are and be a misfit and a reject. This to and fro motion makes the immigrant incomplete, lacking foundation. It falls on the mother in Lahiri's story to articulate this lack:

For Ashima, migrating to the suburbs feels more drastic, more distressing than the move from Calcutta to Cambridge. She wishes Ashoke had accepted the position at Northeastern so that they could have stayed in the city. She is stunned that in this town there are no sidewalks to speak of, no streetlights, no transportation, no stores for miles at a time ... For being a foreigner, Ashima is beginning to realize, is a sort of lifelong pregnancy—a perpetual wait, a constant burden, a continuous feeling out of sorts. It is an ongoing responsibility, a parenthesis in what had once been ordinary life, only to discover that the previous life has vanished, replaced by something more complicated and demanding.[16]

Lack demands substance, what fills the void for the immigrant is a nativist nostalgia which fixates on what is lost—culture, language, rituals—and then initiates an endless cycle of replenishment. Living rooms fill up with formulaic icons of Indian culture: Kashmiri rugs, Rajasthani jewelry, dancing Shivas and Mughal miniatures. Children learn classical music and classical dance. Temples built in suburbia reenact ancient mantras and rituals. Nostalgia is also institutionalized through voluntary associations, in various cities and towns of the west—Tamil Sangams celebrate *Pongal*, Kerala Associations observe *Onam*, Gujaratis organize *Garba Raas*, and Bengalis perform *Durga Puja*.

This nostalgic psyche belongs to an earlier paradigm of immigration, one characterized by small incipient communities who maintained a tenuous relationship with their origins by telephone, letters and the occasional trip "home." That way of being, associated with the "first generation" has been replaced by a new immigrant subjectivity made possible by global processes of communication and commoditization. The new modes of information flow bring about a radical change: chat rooms and e-mail introduce simultaneity, digital photography, by being infinite and incorruptible, restores visuality to what was once blankness. Blogs enable a continuous writing and reading of autobiography. The net result of circuitry is a deferral of departure and loss, the immigrant leaves but not quite, he loses his origins but not fully. The merging of home and abroad is further facilitated by the cascade of "native" goods and flavors that are available in today's international postmodern bazaar. The tiniest morsels of Indian daily life are available for consumption in Birmingham, England or Birmingham, Alabama: Lipton tea, Glaxo biscuits, MTR pickles, Lijjat *papad*. You can have all the pop culture you want—watch Zee TV on satellite, rent every Hindi movie from *Awaara* to *Bhoot*, download Bollywood, bhangra and indipop. You can eat dhaba-style Indian food at the Jackson Diner in Queens or in Curry Lane in London, or go haute desi cuisine at Tabla in New York, or at the Cinnamon Club in London. You can watch

Asha Bhosle or Amitabh Bachchan in concert, send your kid to a Hindu summer camp, get married at a Hindu temple. You can live as if you almost never left the *matribhumi*. The first model of immigration was based on loss, nostalgia and sameness. The current paradigm is constituted around retention, desire and difference. What was lost can now be retained: family, locality and nation are all recoverable by means of the circulation of information and goods. Nostalgia is replaced by desire: instead of reaching for a frozen past, the immigrant subject contemplates a future made possible by connectivity and consumption. And difference supplants sameness: the self no longer needs to return to its likeness for the sake of identity, it composes itself by picking and choosing from a set of cultural signifiers. The immigrant *then* felt bereft of his origins, yearned for the artifacts of his past and sought identity by fusing with those of his kind. The immigrant *now* has access to all his social and cultural antecedents, can dream of a range of possible futures and construct a self distinctive in style from others around him. This new immigrant subject—global, mobile, confident and totally at home while living abroad—facilitates the birth of the desi. What is distinctive about the new immigrant is that he is both more local and global simultaneously: enabled by communication technology to be intimate with family or friends, yet fully cosmopolitan in situation and in his manner of interface. What this amounts to is the local articulated through the global, which is the essence of what it is to be desi.

The emergence of a second generation of diasporic Indians has also proved to be of absolute importance for the development of desi culture. This second generation is now numerically significant—in Britain, for example, locally born Indians equal the number of Indians born elsewhere.[17] Similarly, children of those settled in the United States—popularly known as ABIs (American Born Indians) or ABCDs (American Born Confused Desis)—have come to constitute a distinct and visible social group. British or American by citizenship and schooled in the dominant white culture, Indian at home and intimate with the culture of their parents, these hyphenated children of immigration found themselves at a conundrum which was rife with political implications. Should they adopt Shakespeare and the Beatles and grow up as perfect brown sahibs? Or should they persevere with Indian culture even if it was barely relevant to their lives? The answer was not a matter of individual volition or choice. The path that second generation Indians would eventually follow would be determined by a new logic of cultural politics that began to take shape in the western world from the 1960s onwards. Traditional politics in liberal democracies had been organized around the two-party system, where parties were essentially ideological umbrellas containing disparate interest-groups. Political identity was taken to be a function of socio-economic attributes like family, class, income and religion. To take the paradigmatic American case, the Democratic party was traditionally based on union labor, blacks, Jews and Catholics, and (until recently) Southern whites. The Republican party was seen as the party of millionaires, small businessmen, social and fiscal conservatives, libertarians of every stripe. This however was not a truly representative system—ostensibly standing for all the people of the nation, these parties were, in actuality, controlled and run by a group of privileged white males. So ingrained was this tendency that even today, in spite of sustained efforts at inclusiveness, almost all 100 members of the US Senate are white, and only a handful are women.

This invisible hegemony began to be challenged in the late 1960s and 1970s with the rise of movements which expressed the aspirations of groups which had hitherto been marginalized from the centers of power. The Civil Rights movement led by Martin Luther King struggled to win basic rights for a disenfranchised black community, the growth of feminism and the Women's Rights movement sought a similar outcome for women. Based on the premise that the present predicament of blacks or women was largely if not wholly to be explained by the factor of race or gender, these movements created a very different conception of the meaning of politics. From this perspective, politics had little to do with political parties, but was seen as growing from the life-experiences of particular ethnic communities (blacks, Hispanics, Asians) or social groups (women, gays and lesbians, environmentalists). In other words, culture was posited as the fundamental ground for all politics, and cultural identity (more than class or religious identity) became the crucial version of a person's political self. This prioritizing of identity politics reconfigured society as *multicultural*, it became an aggregate of distinct cultural groups struggling for hegemony against each other. The advent of multiculturalism affected the nature of immigration and minority consciousness. Previously, as we have seen in the instance of the first Indian immigrants, the imperative was to assimilate into the new culture through a systematic erasure of "nativeness" and a wholesale adoption of mainstream values. The arbitrary changing of names at Ellis Island for immigrants coming to America was a metaphor for this cultural violence. A multicultural polity on the other hand encouraged immigrant groups to retain and promote the culture they brought with them. More importantly, multiculturalism enabled a process of revivalism initiated by the desire on the part of second and third generation immigrants to discover their "roots." The end result was the establishment of localized cultures whose sole basis was ethnicity.

Second-generation Indians answered the question about cultural identity by choosing brown over sahib, with this proviso: brownness as constituted within a field of multiculturalism was not a return to some imaginary nativism, but a category robustly rooted in the West:

Indobrits are British nationals who possess an Indian heritage. Until recently, we were faced with the option of dissociating from our own culture by assimilating or being marginalized by maintaining our rich cultural and linguistic traditions. We live in a world in which the post modern era of globalisation interfaces with popular culture—Bollywood goes mainstream and pluralism is the only viable option. Indobrits possess fluid identities and this is our strength, we can adapt to both cultural environments with ease. We are the fortunate ones who can be bilingual and bicultural ... There is a renewed sense of belonging and shared commitment to both our ethnic roots and our place of birth or adopted home, Britain. Finally we have achieved 'reciprocal assimilation' in which there is a two-way flow between the ethnic majority group and us. The financial, academic and political presence of Indo-brits is becoming obvious as we stride towards a higher profile in multi-ethnic Britain. One thing is certain, no matter how much we acculturate ... *phir bhi dil hai Hindustani.*[18]

Desi is the outcome of being British or American and *phir bhi Hindustani*, the fruit of transplanting Indian culture onto western soil. But what Indian culture is being talked about? In her book *Doing the Desi Thing* Sunita Mekhi introduces a useful distinction between "official" and "vernacular" Indian culture. Official Indianness, she argues, derives from a brahmanical Great Tradition and is promoted by governmental and other elite agencies. Striving to project Indian culture in a pure, traditional, non-Western light, this approach ends up being classical, touristic and folkloric. There is another more living culture which belongs to the domain of the popular: "This emerging vernacular Indianness or Desiness includes song and dance sequences taken from Hindi popular films, folk dances specific to particular regions of India, fashion shows, Indian and contemporary disco music played by bands, and comedy skits."[19] It is this vernacular culture which is the inspiration for the creators of desi culture filmmakers like Deepa Mehta (*Hollywood/Bollywood*) or Srinivas Krishna (*Masala*, 1991), musicians like Apache Indian or Bally Sagoo, or deejays like DJ Rekha or DJ X. Growing up in a predominantly white culture, yet desiring a voice of their own, second generation Indians had to find the artefacts from which to assemble their identity. What was precious to them, what they could call their own, were those cultural texts and practices which were part of their daily lives as immigrants: Hindi films and filmi music, bhangra and quawaali, saris and curries. The second generation developed a passionate attachment towards these cultural objects, a fixation succinctly expressed in Cornershop's (the band's name being a play on the stereotype of the Asian-owned grocery stores in Britain) international hit song about Asha Bhosle:

> There's dancing behind movie scenes,
> Behind those movie screens—saddi rani.
> She's the one that keeps the dream alive,
>
> From the morning, past the evening, till the end of the light.
> Brimful of Asha on the forty-five.
> Well, it's a brimful of Asha on the forty-five. (x2)
>
> And singing
> Illuminate the main streets and the cinema aisles.
> We don't care about no government warning,
> About the promotion of the simple life and the dams they are building.
> Everybody needs a bosom for a pillow, everybody needs a bosom, (x3)
>
> Everybody needs a bosom for a pillow, mine's on the forty-five.
> Mohammed Rafi—forty-five. Lata Mangeshkar—forty-five.
> Solid state radio—forty-five. Ferguson Mono—forty-five.
> Bonn publeek—forty-five.
> Jacques Dutronc and the Bolan Boogies ...
> The Heavy Hitters and the chi-chi music ...
> All Indian radio—forty-five. Two in ones—forty-five.
> Ovvo records—forty-five. Trojan records—forty-five.
> 77,000 piece orchestra set,
> Everybody needs a bosom for a pillow; mine's on the RPM ...
> (fadeout)

The last line of this evocative song emphasizes the psychic importance of this distant voice. For those who grow up in the multicultural jungle, Asha Bhosle's songs become "a bosom," a place to regress into and get succor from. Asha Bhosle *is* Mother India, she and other singers from the "golden era" of Hindi filmi music like Lata and Rafi serve as talismanic figures for those attempting to compose their own sense of self. The immense popularity of bhangra and other folk dances is part of the same syndrome. Why, one may ask, did desi culture turn necessarily to the lowbrow and the *dehati*? As we have seen, most immigrants to Britain—unquestionably the birthplace of desi—came from rural or working class backgrounds. The only culture they possessed which would serve as raw material for the construction of desi, was a culture of the masses. The desi beat thus got made up from the rhythms of common life. But we need to go beyond the sociological to fully grasp the meaning of the concept. The logic of its use entailed that desi be exclusively based on the popular. It must be remembered that desi mobilizes ethnic identity within the context of the First World, and in order to do so it is called upon to freeze the meaning of being Indian. Thus while romantic love may make the western world go around, in India, according to Apache Indian, there is just "Arranged Marriage." The fluidity of multicultural identity in the West is thus obtained at a price—India itself is reduced to a set of unchanging essences. Desi, a global category of modernization, needs an eternal version of *desh* which only the popular can provide. A corollary of this argument would be that desi has little to do with westernized middle-class Indian culture. That is borne out by the lack, till very recently, of desi cultural production in the United States. Unlike in the British case, the Indians who came to America in the 1960s and 1970s were middle-class, professional and westernized. Their children lacked the resources to build a desi culture. American-born Indians have performed outstandingly as a group: winning spelling bees, emerging as school valedictorians, attending Ivy League universities in large numbers, and being more than well-represented in the professions. But they have failed to produce a vibrant culture which is distinctively Indian. The few who have succeeded in the arts—Jhumpa Lahiri being the most prominent—have focused on "higher" forms like literature, classical music or jazz. There is as yet no American equivalent of Bally Sagoo or Gurinder Chaddha.

Music and Identity

In what follows I want to explore two forms of music—one belonging to the global North and the other to the South—that helped crystallize immigrant identity in the manner just described and are notable exemplars of desi art. Bhangra, a rural music from the Punjab, is now a worldwide phenomenon that reflects the exuberant success of the Indian diaspora. The development of chutney amongst the Indians of Trinidad is, on the other hand, an example of how music can dignify the lives of those who are less fortunate but still strive to create a desi identity of which they can be proud of. The exact origins of bhangra cannot be pinpointed, but there are reports as early as the 14th century of Punjabi farmers dancing and singing songs about village life as they worked the fields.[20] Over time these became more ritualized as part of the harvest festival held at *Baisakhi* (New Year). In the modern era the dance was detached from its agricultural context and became part of weddings, New Year parties and other celebratory occasions. By the late 1960s and 1970s bhangra had become more than a rural art form. Artists like Kuldip Manak, Amar Singh Chamlika (who died a violent death at the age of twenty-seven) and A.S. Kang (Big Daddy) transformed bhangra into a mass art. They in turn were followed by singers like Malkit Singh "The golden voice of the Punjab," whose song "Gurh Naloo Ishq Mitha" has become a bhangra classic, and Gurudas Mann. The most outstanding features of bhangra—actually a portmanteau term referring to different dances and arts like the Jhumar, Luddi, Giddha, Dhamal, Gatka and others—are the vigor and spectacle of its movements and the energy of its singing. Participants sometimes use swords and daggers and perform many stunts—in the popular *moor* (peacock) for example, a dancer sits on someone's shoulders, while another person hangs from his torso by his legs. The singing, accompanied by the classic *dhol*, a large high-bass drum played with two sticks, as well as stringed instruments like the tumbi and the sarangi, is fast and high-pitched and interspersed with lusty shouts of "*Balle balle*" or "*Hey aripa*." Unlike most Indian folk music, bhangra contains an accelerative element which is particularly suited for the enunciation of modernity. This attribute no doubt explains in part why it would become the paradigmatic form of desi music.

The migration of Indian, and specifically Punjabi, labor to Britain in the years after Independence led to the rise of "western bhangra." The initial settlers, mainly farmers and rural artisans, kept to themselves and avoided a display of ethnicity for fear of drawing censure from white neighbors. What little music existed was largely derivative—word by word covers of popular Hindi film songs as well as Hindi and Punjabi versions of pop songs by bands like Abba and Boney M. As Sabita Banerji points out in a piece on the early years of British bhangra, this imitative music did not meet the needs of young British Indians who had no memory of an India left behind and could not relate directly to Hindi music.[21] Moreover, having suffered the effects of racism from an early age, they felt radically alienated from white society and white culture and so desperately sought an art form which would express their unique identity and predicament. Steve Kapur, better known as Apache Indian, says

> I was from a new generation of Asian kids who were brought up alongside black kids, but we had no street culture or heroes to relate to—all we had were videos from India. We were discouraged from talking about things like sex or contraception or arranged marriages. The new generation of Asian kids wanted to talk about these things and we wanted a street culture of our own.[22]

The culture that Apache Indian was looking for would emerge not from the classical Indian tradition, or the intellectualized experiments in Indi-pop fusion typified by the music of Sheila Chandra and her band Monsoon, or even from the "bosom" which was Hindi film music, but rather from a simple and rustic music carried to Britain by farmers from north India. This music was kept alive by local Punjabi bands who performed lively sets of bhangra at weddings and birthday parties. Traditional devotional music was the other genre to find root in expatriate culture, being played regularly at the many Hindu and Sikh temples that had been built in immigrant neighborhoods. Both of Bally Sagoo's parents, who were among the first Asians to settle in Birmingham, were local performers in the early 1960s. As Sagoo recalls

> My father was in one of the first ever Indian bands in this country way back in the early sixties. What they used to do was film tunes, and they were like the Shadows, there were four guys with these black suits and black ties. Obviously that was the era they were in ... There's a record sleeve that's worth seeing, they looked like the Beatles—they were called the Musafirs ... they'd do famous film tunes on the accordion and things ...
>
> My mother is a priest in the temple, she's doing shabads and gurbani all the time. She's very religious. She plays the harmonium all day long ... when I was a kid I used to play the harmonium and copy people ... In our house there was always Hindi and Punjabi music, all this was the background that has influenced me today.[23]

The originary moment in British bhangra came when one of these groups, Alaap, approached the producer Deepak Khazanchi with a proposal to make a bhangra record. Khazanchi had worked with a number of musical styles and decided to infuse Alaap's traditional bhangra with the sounds of electronic disco. The album that resulted from this experiment, "Teri Chunni De Sitare," had an incredible impact on the South Asian music scene. As one contemporary recalls "In some ways there was a vacuum when you were listening to Soul, Funk, Reggae and those kinds of tunes. Asian Bhangra groups were doing the wedding circuits, and then along came a massive young Asian population looking for something to relate to, so this Bhangra scene exploded."[24] Alaap and the groups that followed them like Heera, Pardesis and Holle Holle proved so popular that their acts were booked two years in advance. Concerts by bhangra bands regularly drew thousands of fans. Many of these concerts happened during the day—since young women with traditional parents found it difficult to go out late at night, inventive promoters came up with the idea of "daytime discos" where college kids of both sexes could congregate.

The music world began to take notice of this new phenomenon, BBC gave it air time, the papers wrote pieces on it, Alaap was invited to perform at prestigious Arts festivals, and recording companies like Avera Multitone and Arishma began to make Bhangra available at mainstream record shops. The music was contemporary enough to appeal to outsiders. As Ranjit Kaur, one of Britain's most successful Asian female DJ recalls:

> I remember the best buzz was when I was playing Bhangra music to two hundred white kids in Liverpool, they loved it, they listened to it for about two and half hours. One of the women came in and said "Ay, ay, this is brilliant, what is it?" I said, "It's bhangra." She said, "It's wicked." and walked off.[25]

Bhangra's infectious beats turned it into an international pheno-menon; its sounds are now heard in nightclubs, discotheques, radio stations and music stores all over the world. Following in the footsteps of Alaap, Heera and others, a whole new generation of Bhangra artists have sprung up in those western countries where the Indian diaspora is numerous and successful: Jazzy B in Canada, Bhinda Jatt "the Folk Warrior of California" in the United States, and Balwinder Safri and Panjabi MC in the UK. The music too has developed in many directions: Bhangramuffin (Bhangra with Reggae as in the work of Apache Indian), Acid Bhangra, Bollywood Remixes (Bally Sagoo) and Asian Rap and Jungle. The United Kingdom continues to be the center of bhangra in the western world. Indian Lion, a British bhangra artist explains this dominance by pointing out that it is much easier for bhangra bands to earn a living in Britain because of the tradition of having bhangra bands play at weddings (where they earn up to 1800 pounds an engagement). Moreover, because of England's small size it is possible for bands to tour the country constantly. On the other hand "In Canada it takes 3 days to get to the other side of the country, so there's no circuit there. And it isn't a tradition [in North America] to have live music at weddings."[26] What needs to be added to Indian Lion's analysis is the fact that as yet there is no significant Indian street culture in the United States. The suburban, middle-class nature of the Indian diaspora has not encouraged such a development; however with the growth of high-density Indian immigrant pockets like Edison, New Jersey, it will not be long before an indigenous Indian-American culture begins to evolve. Bhangra is already very big with college students. A recent Bhangra Blowout held at the campus of George Washington University drew a crowd of 4000 people, with scalpers reportedly charging $80 at the door. The transformation of bhangra from a rural folk music into "hip" desi music for affluent teenagers in the First World is an example of the constitutive powers of diasporic culture. Forced by circumstances to migrate to a foreign land, Indian immigrants not only obtained the economic benefits they had sought, but they succeeded in articulating their native identity through acts of cultural creativity. The music of small wedding bands has, by dint of a productive engagement with a variety of global beats, become one of the cutting-edge sounds of the new millennium. This new bhangra was made by the diaspora, of the diaspora, and for the diaspora. As Gurinder Chaddha, the British Indian maker of *Bend it like Beckham* observed

> Bhangra ... music was important in that it gave us something we could be nationalistic about—because I never had this as a teenager ... [It] gave back something for ourselves, it had nothing to do with English people or white society. It consolidated the debate about whether we are Black, British or Asian.[27]

Chutney, a form of diasporic music not so well known as bhangra, represents a second and very different instance of the intimate relationship between music and desi identity. Created by the descendants of the Indian "coolies," chutney records the story of a marginalized and dispossessed people who have struggled to preserve their dignity and culture in the face of tremendous odds. These Indians had migrated in large numbers to Trinidad and other destinations in the western hemisphere in response to fundamental changes in the nature of the global economy. Following the abolition of slavery in 1834, British sugar plantation owners in the Caribbean and elsewhere were faced with a severe labor shortage. Freed blacks were no longer willing to work on the estates, while experiments with Chinese and European immigrants proved unsuccessful. As a last resort, plantation owners turned to the vast labor pool available in colonial India. An elaborate system of indentured labor was devised to utilize this resource: a class of native agents known as *arkatis* and *duffadars* recruited 'hands' from the hinterland and brought them to ports like Calcutta or Bombay, while companies like Gillanders, Arbuthnot and Sandbach Tinne arranged the long voyages that transported these recruits to various destinations in the Caribbean—Jamaica, Guyana, Trinidad, Surinam and many of the smaller islands—as well as to Ceylon, Malaya, Mauritus, Fiji, Natal and Burma. The first such "coolie"ship reached Mauritus in 1834, followed by the *Whitley* and the *Hesperus* in 1838 to British Guyana, and the *Truro* to Durban in 1860. Thus was instituted one of the greatest immigration sagas of modern times—by one estimate, over one million Indians went overseas to tropical plantations in the four decades upto 1870.[28]

Indian immigration to Trinidad began on May 30, 1845 when the *Fatel Rozack* arrived with a load of 225 men, women and children. That day, known as Indian Arrival Day, is now a national holiday in Trinidad. The flow of immigration continued until 1917 when the system of indenture was abolished. In all about 143,000 Indians came to Trinidad in these seven decades, mainly to work as indentured laborers in the sugar plantations. Immigrant life in the Caribbean was brutal and demanding. Before leaving India each recruit had to sign a contract of indenture to a particular plantation for a period of three years with no freedom to change jobs or bargain for better wages. Two further years of work were required before an indentured worker was declared free. Even then, he had to wait another five years to qualify for a free return passage to India. This provision proved a deterrent against eventual return, most freed Indians ended up staying in Trinidad. Once out of indenture, most Indians took to farming of some sort: they worked in cocoa plantations, started growing rice using methods brought over from India, and used their background in sugar to develop the cane farming industry. After the abolition of indenture, Indians continued to live on the land as free wage laborers who worked in the white-owned plantations, or subsisting as small peasants. Most were illiterate, partly because parents were reluctant to send their children to Christian schools for fear of conversion. In 1868 a Canadian missionary reported that 'there was scarcely an Indian child to be found in school in the whole island.' Though missionary schools would start educating Indian children by the end of the 19th century, levels of education remained low until the establishment of Hindu and Muslim schools in the late 1940s. As a consequence, though some Indians succeeded in gaining middle class status, the population as a whole remained rural, poor and uneducated. The following statistics tell a grim story: In 1960, Indians had an annual per capita income of sterling pound 195, compared to £260 for blacks and £1,250 for whites. In 1964, 83 per cent of Indo-Trinidadians lived in rural areas in comparison with 51 per cent of Afro-Trinidadians. In 1970, Indo-Trinidadians also had the lowest level of education, only 7.5 per cent had post-primary education and 26.1 per cent had no education at all.[29] Not only were Indians economically disadvantaged, they were also seen as social outcastes. The low status of Indians went back to the days of indenture when they were the only group who were subject to restrictions on free movement. "Slave, where is your free paper?" was a common taunt used by Africans who had by then been emancipated and free to go as they pleased. Indians continued to occupy the lowest strata even after the abolition of indenture, and were commonly referred to as "coolies" and "heathens" by both whites and blacks. They were excluded from urban occupations—punitive measures like the Habitual Idlers Ordinance, which imprisoned persons who could not prove that they were employed, were designed to stop the flow of migration by Indians from rural areas—as well as into government jobs which gave access to power and money. Economic and social marginalization added up to a systematic political disenfranchisement. Though Indians would eventually come to constitute the largest single ethnic group in Trinidad— the 1990 Census figures showed that 40.03 per cent of the total population (approximately 1,100,000) were of East Indian descent, compared to 39.6 per cent of African descent—Trinidad was ruled continuously by the black-dominated People's National Movement (PNM) from 1962 (the year of independence) till 1995.

That run was broken with the election of Basdeo Pandey, leader of the United National Congress, as Prime Minister of Trinidad. Pandey's election reflected not just the demographic but also the growing economic clout of the Indo-Trinidadian community. In her study of race relations in Trinidad, anthropologist Viranjini Munasinghe notes that the oil boom of the 1970s was largely responsible for the change of affairs. The oil revenues enabled Indians to achieve more prosperity and social mobility in the single decade of the 1970s than they had during the previous 130 years on the island. As Indians started to penetrate into sectors like the civil services, armed forces and other government offices, Afro-Trinidadians feared an Indian takeover of society. On the occasion of the 1976 elections the black chairman of the broadcasting corporation observed:

> The East Indians have increasingly acquired education and have been increasingly invading the fields of the Civil Service, the professions and the Government ... Should this time come when the East Indian section owns most of the property, business and wealth of the country as well as control of the Government, an imbalance could develop in our society that would cause undesirable stresses and strains that would not be good for the nation.[30]

This fear led to the destabilization of the Pandey government and a set of questionable maneuvers by the black President A. Robinson which resulted in reinstalling the PNM back in office.

This reversal was a setback, but the remarkable rise of the Indo-Trinidadian community from its beginnings as indentured labor to a position of parity and strength within Trinidadian society is now an established fact. This achievement has led to the creation of one of the most exciting Indian musical forms to be found on the globe today—chutney music. In its early years the Indian community tended to be very traditional in its musical practices, holding on tenaciously to the music brought over by its forefathers. This musical repertoire included classical genres like hori, dhrupad, thumri and ghazals, devotional singing of bhajans, and a variety of folk songs accompanied by the *dholak* (a double-headed barrel drum) and the *tassa* (a clay kettledrum). As in Birmingham and Southall, there were many Trinidadian artists who also produced covers of popular film songs from India. As long as the Indian community remained isolated in its rural context, it clung on to a pure, nativist version of its cultural heritage. And because Indians had little purchasing power, the music stayed uncommodified—even as late as 1940 there were no recorded East Indian artists. A turning point came, in 1958, with the release of "King of Surinam" by Ramdeo Chaitoe. This album of religious songs sung to a strong *dholak* beat was a huge hit all over the Caribbean as was "Let's Sing and Dance" released in 1968 by another Surinamese singer called Dropati. Chaitoe's and Dropati's music brought together all the East Indians in the Caribbean whether they were Guyanese, Jamaican, Surinamese or Trinidadian, and paved the way for the birth of chutney. Chutney proper came into being when an unknown artist from Barrackpore, Trinidad—Sundar Popo—released a song called "Nana & Nani." Sung in Hindi and Trinidadian creole, backed up by the *dholak* as well as guitar and synthesizer, the song's ebullient lyrics—"Nana drinkin rum and Nani drinkin wine"—made it an anthem for the new music which was as spicy as its name.

However, chutney did not stay confined within the Indian community. The rapid changes in Trinidadian society meant that Indians and blacks had far more contact with each other even if such engagements were not free of tension. Black Trinidadian music was at that time undergoing a major transformation. The traditional calypso form was being fused with American rhythm and blues to create a new form of music called soca (soul plus calypso). Black musicians began to sing chutney songs in the soca style thus giving birth to the genre called Indian Soca. While the songs included Indian instruments like the *tassa* and the *dholak* they also incorporated a calypso flavour with the use of the steel pan and guitars. The lyrics of the songs provided the chutney even though the singers were black: Baron's "Raja Rani", Mighti Trini's "Curry Tabanca," Sugar Aloe's "Roti & Dhalpourie." This appropriation of chutney by black singers inspired Indian artists: in 1987 Dropati Ramgoonai shook up the chutney world with songs like "Pepper Pepper" and the mega hit "Mr. Bissessar". The conservative elements in the Indian community were aghast that an Indian girl would "throw her high upbringing and culture to mix with vulgar music, sex and alcohol," but Ramgoonai's popularity was unharmed by such condemnations. Other successful Indian soca artists included Babla & Kanchan, a husband and wife team from India, the Dutch singer Atiya, and Terry Gajraj of Guyana, whose album "Guyana Baboo" (1994) became one of the best-selling Caribbean records of all time.

Indian soca had absorbed black and western influences to open up chutney's range of expression. In the mid nineties an opposite trend, which emphasized roots rather than fusion, came into play. Known as chutney soca this involved singing almost entirely in Hindi and relying on traditional instruments like the *dholak* and the *dhantal*. Anand Yankarran of Trinidad brought out the first major chutney soca album ("Zindabad") but it was another Trinidadian—Sonny Mann—who would emerge as the genre's biggest star. Mann's "Lootala" became the most successful Indo-Caribbean single ever, and the album which contained the song—"Soca Chutney"—sold even more copies than Gajraj's "Guana Baboo". With the advent of chutney soca, the music became internationally recognized, it now began to be sampled by DJs in America and elsewhere, another form of desi music came to fruition. Chutney, like bhangra, emerged as the interface between the native Indian culture that the diaspora had brought with itself and the alien contexts in which it was forced to create a new life. Bhangra and chutney articulate the struggles and the joys of two very different Indian communities settled in two very different parts of the globe. They are actually nativity songs; they sing the birth of the desi.

This analysis of diasporic culture has taken into account a set of social processes which have been at play for the past five decades. Immigration out of the country in the years after Independence planted the seeds which would mushroom into the large Indian communities that exist today in the various countries of the West. The development of new modes of electronic technology and communication which have made "home" readily available with the click of a mouse has altered the nature of immigrant subjectivity. No longer consigned to the unproductive dialectic between assimilation and nostalgia, the immigrant subject became able to construct a version of being Indian which was based on continuous flows of information and commodities. Finally, the coming of age of the second generation and its search for its own identity within the framework of multiculturalism provided a ground for the cross-fertilization of Indian popular culture with western forms and sensibilities. Desi is the culmination of these processes: it is "India" processed through the first world, it is a political and cultural badge for all immigrants, it is Bharat in its globalized form and shape. If "desi" as used before connoted what was traditional and essential, desi, in its new usage, points to something which is resolutely contemporary and transnational. Located at the metropoles, desi represents the cutting edge of native culture even as it exceeds the bounds of the nation. Desi is the celebration of an Indianness which is larger than India, a signifier of diasporic achievement and empowerment.

Desi and the Hindu Religion

The logic which constitutes desi as a category is not without its problematic consequences. In appropriating India for its purposes, desi totalizes and essentializes aspects of Indian society in ways that are politically ambiguous. The India that desi desires is unfortunately often the version of the nation imagined by the most reactionary of forces. This coincidence is best brought out in the case of religion—desi use of Hinduism often propels it into the most virulent forms of Hindutva. The processes behind the formation of desi make immigrant subjects of both generations especially susceptible to the call of religion. For the first generation, religion helps allay fears about the dilution of family values and the estrangement of their children from them. Religion is seen as a protection against and a remedy for the "spiritual crisis" of the West and the proper inculcation of religious values is considered a means of holding the family and the culture in place. Mahesh Gupta, chairman of the Overseas Friends of the BJP, observes "American children visit their in-laws only for Thanksgiving, but in Indian arranged marriages the young couples spend months with the parents and parents-in-law."[31] As is evident from this statement, there is a need for a kind of reassurance that, in spite of all the compromises and accommodations the immigrant has to make, his value system is ultimately the superior one. This belief is itself of some vintage, as early as 1894, Swami Vivekananda, speaking to an audience in New York declared "When the Occident wants to learn about the spirit, about God, about the soul, about the meaning and mystery of this universe, he must sit at the feet of the Orient to learn."[32]

For the second generation, religion serves as an ideal tool for the construction of ethnic identity within a framework of multiculturalism. Sucheta Mazumdar discusses the case of Mallika Rao, a teenager in Texas who said that "when she was small, she dreamed of painting herself white and having white children."[33] Mallika wanted "to fit in," and what eventually enabled her to negotiate this crisis was "a Hindu renaissance." And Shyam Mudgal, a second generation Hindu activist remarks "I think deep inside I believe I am strongly Hindu ... Hinduism is very consistent with science, so there's less of a dichotomy ... You can find reasons in Hinduism to get involved in social work. We are just using Hinduism as a driver force to get involved in daily life. Not in a fundamentalist way. But just to be proud of being Hindu."[34] Mudgal's comment points to the different ways in which Hinduism may be articulated. While the first generation doctrine is characterized by a strident militancy in tune with the growth of dogmatic Hindutva in India, that of the second generation, fostered within the context of American liberalism, is far more ecumenical in character. Arvind Rajagopal's work on the rise of Hindu nationalism compares VHP promotional literature in India and the US to highlight this crucial difference. The Indian version is full of aggressive posturing and war-like rhetoric:

All castes and all classes of Hindus throughout the world unite in it [VHP] with one desire, one hope, and one aspiration: that Hindu society, Hindu religion and Hindu culture, the drums of whose victory used to resound throughout the world ... will once again reach the heights it occupied. In other words, our country Bharat once again should lift its head up in front of the whole world and, offering the message "I am Brahman" ... teach the lesson of universal fraternity.

VHP publications in America, which are addressed to a more multicultural audience, speak in a softer tone. Here the concern is to "promote time tested Hindu values so we can enrich the American society" and to "preserving rich spiritual, cultural Hindu heritage and creating positive identity and confidence in the children."[35] The distance between these two positions is the gap between two versions of Hinduism: *deshi* and desi.

The dissemination of Hinduism in America and other parts of the West is enabled by a variety of institutions and practices. At the most tangible level, religion is organized around the many Hindu temples—estimates range from a total of 80 to 125 for the whole

United States—to be found wherever sufficient concentrations of Indians exist. The Chicago area alone features the Hindu Temple of Greater Chicago (built according to architectural plans designed by experts at Tirupathi), the Sri Venkateswara Swami Temple of Greater Aurora built primarily by the Telegu community, and the Swaminarayan Temple in Wheeling, Illinois catering mainly to the area's numerous Gujaratis, the Manav Seva Mandir and the Hari Om Mandir in Medinah. The area is also host to a number of sects, including the International Society for Krishna Consciousness (ISKCON), Brahma Kumaris and the Sathya Sai Baba organization. The temples serve as facilitators of a total Hindu way of life: apart from being sites of puja and darshan they also serve as venues for celebrating major Hindu festivals like *Janmashtami, Ganesh Chaturthi, Dussehra* and *Divali*; provide ritualistic services like *Grihapravesam* (housewarming), *Ypanayanam* (sacred thread initiation), *Satyanarayana Puja* and *Shradham* (memorial rites), and hold "Sunday school" where second generation children take classes in languages and in the scriptures. While the proliferation of temples reflects the tendencies traditional to Hinduism, a countervailing syncretism, induced largely by the necessities of the American context, is also at play. Thus, the Shiva-Vishnu temple near San Francisco utilizes architectural concepts from all parts of India, incorporating both the *shikhara*, a dome in the North Indian style as well as the South Indian *gopuram*. Again, the Hindu Temple of Greater Chicago houses most of the gods in the Hindu pantheon under one roof enabling it to be patronized by different sects and ethnic groups.

While temples cater to the day-to-day religious needs of the Indian community, other organizations hawk a more strident and proselytizing version of Hinduism. The Vishwa Hindu Parishad, which was established in 1964, opened its American counterpart in 1970. The VHP of America, its student wing the Hindu Student Council and the quasi-political Overseas Friends of the BJP constitute a nexus responsible for an aggressive parlaying of latter day Hindutva. As part of its campaign to educate second generation children the VHPA promotes the *Amar Chitra Katha* comic series which recount the epics and Indian history from a blatantly pro-Hindu perspective. Sucheta Mazumdar provides a list of VHPA's sectarian activities, "essay competitions on the life of Dayananda and Vivekananda; weekend educational events, heritage language classes, summer youth camps with sessions of 'Hindu history'; hikes set up on trails with miniature replicas of famous temples and children reciting the saga of each temple; and entertainment programs of dance and film shows."[36] As Vijay Prashad has pointed out, the VHPA participates in fundraising for the Hindu Rights, raising millions of dollars in the United States and channeling it to India through innocuous-looking programs like the Vanvasi Sena and Support a Child.[37] Desi's use of religion is clearly a double-edged sword, it enables diasporic Indians to be proud of their culture and to develop a unique sense of identity, at the same time however, it promotes an aggrandizing brand of Hindu politics which is divisive and replete with disturbing implications. In this regard, desi, the category par excellence for transnational Indian globality, accurately reflects the state of the nation: a sign of achievement and promise, yet forever full of foreboding.

End Notes

Introduction: The Study of Culture

1. Richard Dyer and Ginette Vincendeau, *Popular European Cinema* (New York: Routledge, 1992), p. 5.
2. Arjun Appadurai and Carol A. Breckenridge, "Why Public Culture?" in *Public Culture* 1:1, p. 6.
3. Christopher Pinney, "Introduction," in *Pleasure and the Nation*, Rachel Dwyer and Christopher Pinney eds. (New Delhi: Oxford University Press, 2001), pp. 6–7.
4. Quoted in Pinney, p. 7.
5. Quoted in Ashish Rajadhyaksha, "The 'Bollywoodization' of the Indian Cinema: Cultural Nationalism in a Global Arena," in *City Flicks*, Preben Kaarsholm ed. (Calcutta and New Delhi: Seagull Books, 2004), p. 121.
6. Ashraf Aziz, *Light of the Universe* (New Delhi: Three Essays Collective, 2003), pp. xxiii–xxiv.

Chapter 1: A Whole Nation Padded Up: the Roots of Cricket Mania in Contemporary India

1. Sunaad Raghuran, "Cricket is Life," www.rediff.com, Feb. 8, 2003.
2. Rowland Bowen, *Cricket: a History of its Growth and Development: Throughout the World* (London: Eyre & Spottiswoode, 1970), p. 69.

3. Keith Sandiford, "England," in *The Imperial Game: Cricket, Culture and Society*, Brian Stoddart and Keith A.P. Sandiford eds. (Manchester and New York: Manchester University Press, 1998), pp. 9–33.

4. Sandiford, p. 29.

5. Tony Mason, *Sport in Britain: A Social History* (Cambridge: Cambridge University Press, 1989), p. 70.

6. Richard Holt, *Sport and the British* (Oxford: Oxford University Press, 1990), p. 175.

7. Ibid. p. 205.

8. Ibid. p. 206.

9. Richard Cashman, "The Subcontinent," in *The Imperial Game: Cricket, Culture and Society*, Brian Stoddart and Keith A.P. Sandiford eds. (Manchester and New York: Manchester University Press, 1998), p. 118.

10. Holt, p. 213.

11. Ian Copeland, *The Princes of India in the Endgame of Empire, 1917–1947* (Cambridge: Cambridge University Press, 1997), p. 23.

12. Mihir Bose, *A History of Indian Cricket*, (London: Andre Deutsch, 1990), pp. 44–62.

13. Ashis Nandy, *The Tao of Cricket*, (New Delhi: Oxford University Press, 2000), p. 56.

14. Bose, p. 40.

15. Ramachandra Guha, *A Corner of A Foreign Field: The Indian History of a British Sport*, (London: Picador, 2002), pp. 29–30.

16. Guha, pp. 35–36.

17. Boria Majumdar, "The Vernacular in Sports History," *Economic and Political Weekly*, 37(29), 2002.

18. Tony Mason, "Football on the Maidan: Cultural Imperialism in Calcutta" in *The Cultural Bond: Sport, Empire, Society*, J.A. Mangan ed. (London: Frank Cass, 1992), p. 150.

19. Bose, pp. 16–17.

20. Bose, p. 17.

21. Ramachandra Guha, "Cricket and Politics in Colonial India," *Past and Present*, No. 161, pp. 155–190 (184).

22. Guha, p. 178.

23. Bose, p. 47.

24. Cashman, "The Subcontinent," p. 130.

25. www.rediff.com, April 4, 2000.

26. Sheela Reddy, "Hooked," www.outlookindia.com, March 24, 2003.

27. Subhash K. Jha, "Will Stumped Give Cricket Another Chance?" www.rediff.com, February 19, 2003.

28. Sandipan Deb, "I Am Not Daft, It's the Game," www.outlookindia.com, February 10, 2003.

29. *The Telegraph*, March 30, 2003.

30. Richard Cashman, "Australia," in *The Imperial Game: Cricket, Culture and Society*, Brian Stoddart and Keith A.P. Sandiford eds. (Manchester and New York: Manchester University Press, 1998), p. 40.

31. Cashman, p. 39.

32. Cashman, p. 45.

33. Cashman, p. 49.

34. www.immi.gov.au/facts/08abolition.html

35. Cashman, 52.

36. Hilary Beckles, "The Making of the First 'West Indian' Teams, 1886–1906," in *Liberation Cricket: West Indies Cricket Culture*, Hilary Beckles and Brian Stoddart eds. (Manchester and New York: Manchester University Press, 1995), pp. 192–204.

37. Hilary Beckles and Harclyde Walcott, "Redemption Sounds: Music, Literature and the Popular Ideology of the West Indian Cricket Crowds," in *Liberation Cricket: West Indies Cricket Culture*, Hilary Beckles and Brian Stoddart eds. (Manchester and New York: Manchester University Press, 1995), pp. 370–383.

38. Richard Burton, "Cricket, Carnival and Street Culture in the Caribbean," in *Liberation Cricket: West Indies Cricket Culture*, Hilary Beckles and Brian Stoddart eds. (Manchester and New York: Manchester University Press, 1995), p. 90.

39. C.L.R. James, *Beyond a Boundary* (Durham: Duke University Press, 1993), p. 233.

40. Boria Majumdar, "End of White Hegemony?" www.sjc.ox.ac.uk.

41. *The Telegraph*, February 18, 2003.

42. Mike Marquesee, *Anyone But England: Cricket and the National Malaise* (London and New York: Verso,1994), p. 143.

43. Malcolm Knox, "Wake up Australia, Racism is a Problem," www.sport.guardian.co.uk, January 20, 2003.

44. Marquesee, p. 138.

45. Knox, www.sport.guardian.co.uk, January 20, 2003.

46. Mike Marquesee, "Cricket, Politics and Peace in South Asia," www.thewicket.com, May 24, 2001.

47. *The Telegraph*, March 4, 2003.

48. www.mrdowling.com

49. Nissim Mannathukkaren, "Subalterns, Cricket and the 'Nation'," *Economic and Political Weekly*, December 8, 2001.

50. Sudhavana Deshpande, "Subaltern Fantasies," *Economic and Political Weekly*, June 7, 2003.

51. Boria Majumdar, "Politics of Leisure in Colonial India," *Economic and Political Weekly*, September 1, 2001 and also Chandrima Chakraborty, "Subaltern Studies, Bollywood and *Lagaan*," *Economic and Political Weekly*, May 10, 2003.

52. Quoted in Ian McDonald, "Between Saleem and Shiva: The Politics of Cricket Nationalism in 'Globalising' India," in *Sport in Divided Societies*, John Sugden and Alan Bairner eds. (Aachen: Meyer & Meyer Sport, 1999), p. 221.

53. Arjun Appadurai, *Modernity at Large: Cultural Dimensions of Globalization* (Minneapolis: University of Minnesota Press, 1996), p. 110.

54. Cashman, "The Subcontinent," pp. 116–117.

55. Bose, p. 16.

56. Ashis Nandy, *The Tao of Cricket* (New Delhi: Oxford University Press, 2000), pp. 2, 124.

57. Nandy, p. 7.

58. Nandy, pp. 21–22.

59. Nandy, p. 26.

60. Nandy, p. 121.

61. Quadri Ismail, "Batting against the Break: On Cricket, Nationalism, and the Swashbuckling Sri Lankans", in *Sport Cult*, Randy Martin and Toby Miller eds. (Minneapolis: University of Minnesota Press, 1999), p. 109.

62. Guha, *A Corner of a Foreign Field*, p. 335.

63. Guha, pp. 337–340.

64. Guha, p. 340.

65. Appadurai, p. 90.

66. Appadurai, pp. 104–105.

67. Appadurai, p. 112.

68. Appadurai, p. 113.

69. Ismail, p. 89.

70. Ismail, p. 99.

71. McDonald, p. 215.
72. McDonald, p. 233.
73. S. Anand, "The Retreat of the Brahmin," www.outlookindia.com, February 10, 2003.
74. Deb, "I'm not Daft, It's the Game."
75. Manu Joseph, "Fine Strokes, Copybook Style," www.outlookindia.com, April 7, 2003.
76. Amrit Mathur, *Sportstar*, Nov. 23–29, 2003.
77. Mario Rodrigues, "The Corporates and the Game: Football in India and the Conflicts of the 1990s," in *Soccer in South Asia: Empire, Nation, Diaspora*, Paul Dimeo and James Mills eds. (London and Portland, Oregon: Frank Cass, 2001), p. 124.
78. Quoted in Deb, "I'm not Daft, It's the Game."

Chapter 2: Tragedy in Two Acts: The Sudden Death of Hockey and Football

1. www.news.bbc.co.uk Aug. 9, 2000.
2. *Indian Express*, Sep 7, 2002.
3. www.fieldhockey.com, July 7, 2003.
4. www.bharatiyahockey.com\5.
5. Richard Holt, *Sport and the British* (Oxford: Oxford University Press, 1990), p. 129.
6. http://www.indiadaily.com/editorial/12-20f-04.asp
7. www.hockeyonline.co.uk
8. www.walthamforestha.co.uk
9. www.usfieldhockey.com
10. Holt, 218.
11. www.bharatiyahockey.com\5.
12. Ibid.
13. http://news.bbc.co.uk.sports/hi/english/olympics2000
14. Ibid.
15. www.bharatiyahockey.com
16. Ibid.
17. http://news.bbc.co.uk.sports/hi/english/olympics2000
18. *The Week*, July 27, 2003.
19. *Indian Express*, September 7, 2002.

20. J.A. Mangan, "Soccer as Moral Training: Missionary Intentions and Imperial Legacies," in *Soccer in South Asia: Empire, Nation,* Diaspora, Paul Dimeo and James Mills eds. (London and Portland, Oregon: Frank Cass, 2001), p. 52.

21. *Indian Express,* September 7, 2002.

22. S. Thyagarajan, "Enchanting Vista of History," *The Hindu,* May 30, 2002.

23. Siriyavan, "Eating with Our Fingers, Watching Hindi Cinema and Consuming Cricket," www.himalmag.com, March 2002.

24. www.fieldhockey.com, July 7, 2003.

25. Novy Kapadia, "What Ails Indian Football," *Frontline.* 19(14) (2002).

26. Bill Murray, *Football: A History of the World Game* (London: Scolar Press, 1994), p. 11.

27. Tony Mason, *Sport in Britain: A Social History,* (Cambridge: Cambridge University Press, 1989), pp. 1–2.

28. Mason, p. 227.

29. Paul Dimeo, "Football and Politics in Bengal: Colonialism, Nationalism, Communalism," in *Soccer in South Asia: Empire, Nation, Diaspora,* Paul Dimeo and James Mills eds. (London and Portland, Oregon: Frank Cass, 2001), p. 60.

30. Tony Mason, "Football on the Maidan: Cultural Imperialism in Calcutta," in *The Cultural Bond: Sports, Empire and Society,* J.A. Mangan ed. (London: Frank Cass, 1992), p. 143.

31. Dimeo, p. 62.

32. Mason, p. 144.

33. Dimeo, p. 68.

34. Ibid.

35. Quoted in Dimeo, p. 69.

36. Novy Kapadia, "The Story of Indian Football: 1889–2000," in Dimeo and Mills, p. 22.

37. Dimeo, p. 70.

38. James Mills, "Football in Goa," in Dimeo and Mills, p. 87.

39. Kapadia, "The Story of Indian Football", p. 20.

40. Mario Rodrigues, "The Corporates and the Game: Football in India and the Conflicts of the 1990s," in Dimeo and Mills, p. 116.

41. Rodrigues, pp. 116–120.

Chapter 3: Hindi-Pop: The Quest for Modernity in Film Music

1. "Bappi Drags Addictive to US courts," *The Times of India*, November 1, 2002.
2. Ibid.
3. www.musicindiaonline.com/MIO-Artists/MusicDirectors/Pages/BappiLahiri.html
4. Ibid.
5. Ibid.
6. "Straight Answers," *The Economic Times*, Feb. 16, 2003.
7. www.angelfire.com/music4/sangeet/copiedsongs.html
8. Daniel M. Neuman, *The Life of Music in North India: the Organization of an Artistic Tradition* (Detroit: Wayne State University Press, 1990), p. 22.
9. Gerry Farrell, "The Early Days Of The Gramophone Industry in India: Historical, Social and Musical Perspectives," in *The Place of Music*, Andrew Leyshon, David Matless, and George Revill eds. (New York and London: The Guilford Press, 1998), pp. 59–61.
10. Theodor Adorno, *Introduction to the Sociology of Music*, E.B. Ashton trans. (New York: The Seabury Press, 1976), p. 29.
11. Ibid, p. 106.
12. Theodor Adorno, "On the Fetish-Character in Music and the Regression of Listening," in *The Culture Industry*, J.M. Bernstein ed. (London: Routledge, 1991), pp. 29–60.
13. www.meadvic.nic.in/media/ari.html
14. Erik Barnouw and S. Krishnaswamy, *Indian Film*, Second Edition (New York: Oxford University Press, 1980), p. 210.
15. Barnouw, pp. 208–212.
16. Peter Burke, *Popular Culture in Early Modern Europe* (New York: New York University Press, 1978), p. 25.
17. Lawrence Levine, *Highbrow/Lowbrow: The Emergence of Cultural Hierarchy in America* (Boston: Harvard University Press, 1988).
18. Simon Frith, *Sound Effects* (New York: Pantheon Books, 1981), pp. 16–19.
19. Robert Palmer, *Deep Blues* (London: Penguin Books, 1981), p. 45.
20. Burke, p. 3.
21. Charles Capwell, *The Music of the Bauls of Bengal* (Kent, Ohio: The Kent State University Press, 1986), p. 30.

22. Capwell, p. 25.

23. Edward O. Henry, *Chant The Names of Gods: Music and Culture in Bhojpuri-Speaking India* (San Diego: San Diego State University Press, 1988), p. 118.

24. Richard Dyer, "In Defence of Disco," in *On Record*, Simon Frith and Andrew Goodwin eds. (New York: Pantheon Books, 1990), p. 411, italics mine.

25. Henry, p. 20, italics mine.

26. David B. Reck, "India/South India," in *Worlds of Music*, Second Edition, Jeff Tood Tilton et al eds. (New York: Schirmer Books, 1992), p. 213.

27. Reginald & Jamila Massey, *The Music of India* (New York: Crescendo Publishing, 1976), p. 78.

28. Ashok D. Ranade, *On Music and Musicians of Hindoostan* (New Delhi: Promilla & Co. Publishers, 1984), p. 69.

29. Quoted in Arnold E. Alison, "Hindi Film Git: On the History of Commercial Indian Popular Music," unpublished Ph.D. dissertation, University of Illinois at Urbana-Champaign, 1991, p. 265. I am greatly indebted to Alison's outstanding analysis of the development of Hindi film music.

30. Arnold, p. 232.

31. Siddarth Dey, "The 24-Carat Magical Voice," www.screenindia.com, October 17, 2003.

32. Ibid.

33. www.Panchamonline.com

34. Bipan Chandra, Mridula Mukerjee and Aditya Mukherjee, *India After Independence 1947–2000* (New Delhi: Penguin Books, 2000), p. 215.

35. Ibid, p. 178.

36. Ibid, p. 177.

37. Ibid, p. 353.

38. Fred Bronson, *The Billboard Book of Number One Hits* (New York: Billboard Publications, 1988), p. 385.

Chapter 4: A Boy, a Girl and a Tree: Song and Dance in Bollywood Cinema

1. Mukul Kesavan, "Cine Qua Non!" *Outlook*, August 18, 1997.

2. Sunil Khilnani, "A New Cultural Lexicon," *The Hindu*, September 1, 2002.

3. Kobita Sarkar, *Indian Cinema Today* (New Delhi: Sterling Publishers, 1975), Preface.
4. Sumita Chakravarty, *National Identity in Indian Popular Cinema 1947–1987* (Austin: University of Texas Press, 1993), p. 17.
5. Erik Barnouw and S. Krishnaswamy, *Indian Film*, Second Edition (New York: Oxford University Press, 1980), p. 16.
6. Chakravarty, p. 134.
7. Vijay Mishra, *Bollywood Cinema: Temples of Desire* (New York and London: Routledge, 2002), pp. 240–241.
8. Manjunath Pendarkur and Radha Subramanyam, "Indian Cinema Beyond National Borders," in *New Patterns in Global Television*, John Sinclair, Elizabeth Jack and Stuart Cunningham eds. (Oxford: Oxford University Press, 1996), p. 78.
9. *Sunday Times*, Oct. 13, 2002.
10. *CIO Magazine*, December 2003.
11. Madhava Prasad, "This Thing called Bollywood," *Seminar*, 2003.
12. David Chute, "The Road to Bollywood," *Film Comment Magazine*, June-July 2002.
13. David Chute, "Planet Bollywood?" *LA Weekly*, March 7–13, 2003.
14. Richard Corliss, "That Old Feeling," *Time Online Edition*, July 30, 2003.
15. Supriya Kurane, "Across the Oceans," *Business World*, March 24, 2003.
16. Jaishree Mishra, "Bombay Meri Jaan," *Outlook*, March 10, 2003.
17. Richard von Busack, "Two 'Woods' Don't Make a Right," www.metroactive.com, Oct. 2, 2003.
18. Lalitha Gopalan, *Cinema of Interruptions: Action Genres in Contemporary Indian Cinema* (London: British Film Institute, 2002), p. 15.
19. Sunil Khilnani, *Hindu*, January 9, 2002.
20. Sarkar, p. 1.
21. Madhava Prasad, *Ideology of the Hindi Film: A Historical Construction* (New Delhi: Oxford University Press, 1998), pp. 5–6.
22. Ram Gopal Verma, "The Trailblazer," Interview, *Timeasia Magazine*, October 20, 2003.
23. Chute, "Planet Bollywood?"
24. Corliss, "That Old Feeling."
25. Chute, "Planet Bollywood?"
26. Sarkar, p. 1.
27. Ram Gopal Verma, *Filmfare* interview, March 2003, pp. 64–65.
28. Aparna Sen, *Filmfare* interview, March 2003, p. 104.

29. Barnouw, p. 72.
30. *Screen*, Jan. 30, 2004.
31. William O. Beeman, "The Use of Music in Popular Film: East and West," in *Indian Popular Cinema: Myth, Meaning and Metaphor, India International Centre Quarterly*, Special Issue, Pradip Kishen ed. {8 (1) (1980)}, p. 86.
32. Prasad, p. 136.
33. www.timeasia.com
34. *Moviemag International*, December 2004, p. 69.
35. Gopalan, p. 19.
36. Sarkar, p. 18.
37. Ben Singer, *Melodrama and Modernity: Early Sensational Cinema and its Contexts* (New York: Columbia University Press, 2001), p. 37.
38. Judith Walkowitz, quoted in Singer, p. 133.
39. Prasad, p. 64.
40. www.theindian.com
41. Quoted in Rosie Thomas, "Indian Cinema: Pleasures and Popularity," *Screen* 26 {3(4), 1985}, pp. 116–117.
42. Thomas, p. 119.
43. Rosie Thomas, "Melodrama and the Negotiation of Morality in Mainstream Hindi Film," in *Consuming Modernity: Public Culture in a South Asian World*, Carol A. Breckenridge ed. (Minneapolis: University of Minnesota Press, 1995), p. 159.
44. Singer, p. 51.
45. Quoted in Chakravarty, p. 242.
46. Raghunath Raina, quoted in Chakravarty, p. 241, italics mine.
47. Prasad, p. 190.
48. Quoted in Barnouw, p. 279.
49. Sudipta Kaviraj, "Reading a Song of a City—Images of the City in Literature and Films," in *City Flicks: Cinema, Urban Worlds and Modernities in India and Beyond, Occasional Paper No. 22*, Preben Kaarsholm ed. (Roskilde University, 2002), p. 70, italics mine.

Chapter 5: Desi World: The Uses of Tradition in the Culture of the Indian Diaspora

1. Rozina Visram, *Asians in Britain: 400 Years of History* (London: Pluto Press, 2002), p. 18.
2. Visram, p. 254.

3. Ronald Takaki, *Strangers from a Different Shore: A History of Asian Americans* (New York: Penguin Books, 1989), p. 297.
4. Takaki, pp. 298–299.
5. David Mason, *Race and Ethnicity in Modern Britain,* Second Edition (Oxford: Oxford University Press, 2000), p. 28.
6. Padma Rangaswamy, *Namaste America* (University Park, Pennsylvania: Pennsylvania State University Press, 2000), p. 3.
7. Vijay Prashad, *The Karma of Brown Folk* (Minneapolis: University of Minnesota, 2000), p. 75.
8. www.iexpressusa.com
9. Prashad, p. 81.
10. *The New York Times,* August 19, 2003.
11. www.littleindia.com, May 2002.
12. Sangita Gopal, "Home Pages: Immigrant Subjectivity on the World Wide Web" in *Globalization and the Humanities,* David Li ed. (Hongkong: Hongkong University Press, 2003).
13. Bipan Chandra, Mridula Mukerjee and Aditya Mukherjee, *India after Independence 1947–2000* (New Delhi: Penguin Books, 2000), p. 45.
14. Jhumpa Lahiri, *The Namesake* (Boston: Houghton Mifflin, 2003), p. 64.
15. Arthur M. Helweg and Usha M. Helweg, *An Immigrant Success Story: East Indians in America* (Philadelphia: University of Pennsylvania Press, 1991), pp. 121–127.
16. Lahiri, pp. 49–50.
17. www.indiamonitor.com
18. www.indobrit.com
19. Sunita Mukhi, *Doing the Desi Thing: Performing Indianess in New York City* (New York: Garland Publishing, 2000), p. 7.
20. www.pujaonline.com
21. Sabita Banerji and Gerd Baumann, "Bhangra 1984–8: Fusion and Professionalization in a Genre of South Asian Dance Music" in *Black Music in Britain: Essays on the Afro-Asian Contribution to Popular Music,* Paul Oliver ed. (Milton Keynes: Open University Press, 1990), p. 141.
22. Timothy Taylor, *World Music, World Markets* (New York and London: Routledge, 1997), p. 157.
23. Shirin Housee and Mukhtar Dar, "Remixing Identities: 'Off' the Turntable," in *Dis-Orienting Rhythms: The Politics of the New Asian*

Dance Music, Sanjay Sharma, John Hutnyk & Ashwani Sharma eds. (London and New Jersey: Zed Books, 1996), pp. 81–82.

24. Housee, p. 84.

25. Housee, p. 86.

26. www.punjabonline.com

27. Sanjay Sharma, "Noisy Asians or 'Asian Noise'?" in Sharma et al, p. 32.

28. Hugh Tinker, *A New System of Slavery; the Export of Indian Labour Overseas, 1830–1920* (London and New York: Oxford University Press, 1974), p. 115.

29. Viranjini Munasinghe, *Callaloo or Tossed Salad?: East Indians and the Cultural Politics of Identity in Trinidad* (New York: Cornell University Press, 2001), p. 148.

30. Munasinghe, p. 232.

31. Prashad, p. 147.

32. Stephen Hay, *Sources of Indian Tradition, Volume Two: Modern India and Pakistan* (New York: Columbia University Press, 1988), p. 115.

33. Sucheta Mazumdar, "The Politics of Religion and National Origin: Rediscovering Hindu Indian Identity in the United States" in *Antinomies of Modernity*, Vasant Kaiwar and Sucheta Mazumdar eds., (Durham, North Carolina: Duke University Press, 2003), p. 244.

34. Arvind Rajagopal, *Politics After Television: Hindu Nationalism and the Reshaping of the Public in India* (Cambridge: Cambridge University Press, 2001), p. 256.

35. Rajagopal, pp. 265–266.

36. Mazumdar, p. 250.

37. Prashad, p. 146.

Selected Index